Postcolonial Astrology

Many people do astrology, and some of them know from where the tradition emerged. But very few rigorously consider how and why the language of astrology has developed in relation to power. With a critical eye and expansive research, Alice Sparkly Kat examines the historical significance of astrology's symbols to trace an alternative genealogy of modern Western astrology. This important work is crucial to a discipline as steeped in tradition as astrology is; without a deep consideration of history, how can we create space for new astrologies to root and take hold?

BANU GULER, Founder & CEO of Co – Star

Alice Sparkly Kat's *Postcolonial Astrology* does something immensely paramount: its sweeping analyses rip off the togas worn by Western astrology's planetary gods that Rome appropriated from the Greeks. Sparkly Kat shows how their loosely woven fabric drapes nothing but White privilege created at the expense of stolen land and the labor of people of color for millennia. In their book, there is no lapsing into trying to track astrology's depths through the jungles of Jung's putative collective unconscious. No awestruck adoration of Western astrology's masquerade of itself as a path toward transcendence, a map for the evolution of consciousness, or a gateway for freedom from the tortures of our supposed ids, egos, or superegos. Instead, Sparkly Kat stays rooted in a body of critical theory and postmodern analysis to expose Western astrology, as an "anachronistic archive" and a myth-making machine more for racism and maintaining Whiteness at the expense of the poor and people of color. Yet, Sparkly Kat doesn't commission the reader to discard all Western astrology's borrowed and tattered notions. They instead direct us to look at the shredded heap of its motley meanings as just one important story that can indeed be told differently. We can learn to connect the dots of astrology's fabled constellations of motley meanings, assembled with blood and burglary, in ways that create a canopy of heaven that includes all peoples of Earth and leaves us whole and restored.

SAMUEL F. REYNOLDS, MA, CAP ISAR, NCGR-III

"[Alice Sparkly Kat's] analysis strikes that rare balance of being richly contextualized and accessibly written, making this 'history and toolkit' an essential addition to any queer astrology lover's library."

LOGO, *NewNowNext*

Postcolonial Astrology

Reading the Planets through Capital, Power, and Labor

ALICE SPARKLY KAT

North Atlantic Books
Huichin, unceded Ohlone land
aka Berkeley, California

Published by
North Atlantic Books
Huichin, unceded Ohlone land
aka Berkeley, California

Cover art © gettyimages.com/CSA Images
Cover design by Jess Morphew
Book design by Happenstance Type-O-Rama

Printed in the United States of America

Postcolonial Astrology: Reading the Planets through Capital, Power, and Labor is sponsored and published by North Atlantic Books, an educational nonprofit based in the unceded Ohlone land Huichin (aka Berkeley, CA) that collaborates with partners to develop cross-cultural perspectives; nurture holistic views of art, science, the humanities, and healing; and seed personal and global transformation by publishing work on the relationship of body, spirit, and nature.

North Atlantic Books' publications are distributed to the US trade and internationally by Penguin Random House Publishers Services. For further information, visit our website at www.northatlanticbooks.com.

Library of Congress Cataloging-in-Publication Data
Names: Kat, Alice Sparkly, 1992- author.
Title: Postcolonial astrology : reading the planets through capital, power, and labor / Alice Sparkly Kat.
Description: Berkeley, California : North Atlantic Books, [2021] | Includes bibliographical references and index. | Summary: "Tapping into the political power of magic and astrology for social, community, and personal transformation-in a cross-cultural approach to understanding astrology as a magical language, Alice Sparkly Kat unmasks the political power of astrology, showing how it can be channeled as a force for collective healing and liberation"— Provided by publisher.
Identifiers: LCCN 2020042293 (print) | LCCN 2020042294 (ebook) | ISBN 9781623175306 (paperback) | ISBN 9781623175313 (epub)
Subjects: LCSH: Astrology.
Classification: LCC BF1708.1 .K38 2021 (print) | LCC BF1708.1 (ebook) | DDC 133.5—dc23
LC record available at https://lccn.loc.gov/2020042293
LC ebook record available at https://lccn.loc.gov/2020042294

4 5 6 7 8 9 KPC 26 25 24 23 22

North Atlantic Books is committed to the protection of our environment. We print on recycled paper whenever possible and partner with printers who strive to use environmentally responsible practices.

Contents

Acknowledgments

THANKS EVERYONE who talked with me and held me together when I was writing this book. Thanks to my roommates for being with me during the pandemic while a lot of this writing was happening. Thanks Ziyi Li, Ebony Martin, NB Zhong, Charmaine Bee, Yarrow, Ricky Zoker, Christian Cisneros, Emily Wang, Meng, Maya Tanaka, Maya Yu Zhang, Jerie Choi Ortiz, Ayqa, Tingying, Som, Coco Layne, Nandi Loaf, Yao, Mikala, D, Manual, Anthony Hawkins, Adder, Sakile, and more for showing me what transforming community and love look like every day. Thanks to all the amazing astrologers who laugh and scream about astrology with me, including but not limited to Sam Reynolds, Charm Torres, Oscar Moises Diaz, Shakirah Tabourn, Demetrius Bagley, Bear Ryver, Giselle Castano, Naike Swai, Naimonu James, Alejandra Alexander, Lizhen, Banu Guler, and more. Thanks everyone at Asian American Writers' Workshop for giving me a chance to create community through CreateNow, and thank you for the teens and seniors who play with me, including Auntie Li, Auntie Zhao, Auntie Huang, Auntie Qing, and more. Thanks Yellow Jackets Collective organizers Mich, Grace, Parissah, and Esther, and BUFU organizers Kat, Jazz, Tsige, and Sonia, for bringing people together so that people like me don't feel alone. Thanks to everyone who has ever gotten a reading from me. Thanks Eugene Li and Porgy for letting me pet them. Thank you to ARMY for being a collective closet global rhizome network of sapphic desire and healing, and thank you Min

Yoongi for being my emotional support K-pop boy. Thanks my therapist Joan Choi. Thanks my mom and dad, *laoye, laolao, nainai, yeye, dayi, jiujiu, gugu,* Lan Tianyi, Yang Xin, Zheng Zhi, and Cai Luhua. Thank you to North Atlantic Books and especially to Gillian Hamel. Love y'all.

Introduction

ASTROLOGY IS OFTEN compared to race. Both are exercises in imagination, pattern making, and the making of types. Both astrology and race are types of magical thinking and are not rational. Both astrology and race are social constructs and are rooted in the circulations of culture.

As Tabitha Prado-Richardson writes in their essay "Who Needs Astrology?," titled after the Stuart Hall essay "Who Needs Identity?," "Sun sign astrology is an essentialism, certainly," but "as of yet, astrology has not manifested power structures along the lines of its signs. . . . Skeptics such as Benjamin Radford have compared astrology to racism due to this stereotypical, deterministic thinking, but these critics are usually unwilling to go beyond the realm of thought, and define racism as a purely interpersonal phenomenon, rather than composite matrices of domination that limit access and freedom." If astrology can be compared to other sociopolitical markings of identity such as race, then astrology must also be a political project "bound to cultural meanings, formed by the interplay between political and historical context."

Identities, which can include astrological signs along with race and gender, are an orientation. We use intersecting orientations to look outward from within or to look inward from without. Astrology, because it is an ideology that creates identity, can be just as hierarchical, naïve, superficial, authentic, scientific, and spiritual as race.

In her book *Fatal Invention,* Dorothy Roberts writes: "Most Americans do not deduce that biological races exist from scientific evidence and reasoning. They are inculcated with this belief in the same way a child is raised in a religion ... Anthropologists describe the common meaning of race that defies scientific facts as a 'folk concept.' This is why Ashley Montagu called race 'the witchcraft of our time.' In the 1940s, he wrote, 'It is the contemporary myth. Man's most dangerous myth.'"

Later, Roberts writes, "Believing in race can be compared to believing in astrology."

In a clinical trial done in the 1990s involving 17,000 subjects, physician researchers found that patients responded differently to oral aspirin and a placebo according to astrological sign. The researchers found that those with Gemini or Libra as their Sun sign were more sensitive to the aspirin. According to Roberts, physicians often sort subjects into categories of race when conducting clinical trials, but they rarely do so for astrological signs. However, sorting subjects into any classification can force patterns to show up, and when these patterns are reinforced by political realities, they become institutionalized. Although scientists dismiss differences in sensitivity between zodiac signs as insignificant coincidences, they do not dismiss differences between groups when they sort their patients into the five or so racial categories, even when these five or so racial categories are based on histories of social and political difference rather than on biology.

Testing for race confirms racial biases. Neither race nor astrology have a biological basis, but racial biases are upheld by institutions, while astrological ones are not. Both race and astrology are methods of organization that are cultural and not genetic, but only one has been used to deny and force real medical consequences on people inhabiting these categories. Race is experienced as a political reality, while astrology is not. Race, then, is not experienced as fictional, which astrology often is. Stories around race are not usually seen to be stories that are supported by magical thinking and fictional encounters.

Before the Enlightenment, race was religious and spiritual. In the second book of the *Tetrabiblios,* Ptolemy writes that when casting a nativity, while general universal astrological concerns such as the *thema mundi* or the exaltations of the planets should be considered first, particular astrological concerns must also be investigated. Of these particular concerns, Ptolemy begins with the "peculiarities observable in whole nations; in regards to their manners and customs, as well as to their bodily formation and temperament." For Ptolemy, particular, or relative, astrological concerns began with race, or a precursor to race.

In the next section, Ptolemy writes that his climate is situated in the northern quadrants and that the people living in nations that lie below the southern parallels, whom he calls Ethiopians, are "black in complexion," "have thick and curled hair," and are "hot in disposition, and fierce in manners" on account of these nations having "the Sun in their zenith." In contrast, the natives of countries situated in northern climates are "cold in disposition, and wild in manners, owing to the constant cold." While the differences between northern and southern climates may seem to stem from differences in temperature and climate, Ptolemy's descriptions of the differences between Eastern and Western nations are even more esoteric. Ptolemy claims that "the natives of those countries which lie towards the east excel in courage, acting boldly and openly under all circumstances" since the Sun rises in the east. In contrast, the inhabitants of the west are "wilder, more effeminate and reserved" since the Moon is always seen in the west after the new moon and gives her "feminine and sinister" characteristics to the nations situated west of Alexandria.

These passages show that Ptolemy oriented cultural differences around Alexandria, which he does not describe as having as remarkable or peculiar astrological characteristics. Rather, Alexandria and the Greek empire are seen as culturally unremarkable and neutral because the *thema mundi* centers on the Greek cultural capital. Ptolemy's descriptions are not observational but speculative. He placed cultural and ethnic differences into a wider cosmology—race developed from magical or analogical thinking.

Post-Enlightenment, religion and cosmology continued to relay cultural and ethnic differences. Modern race science began as a type of magic or cosmology. Whites continued to describe race in religious and magical terms. Loren Goldner calls the cosmological interpretation of "bodies in space" through Greco-Roman classicism or Judeo-Christian messianism an "epistemological grid." Race is part of this epistemological grid. Sir William Petty, writing in his book *The Scale of Creatures* in 1676, speculates that Black people should be categorized somewhere between humans and animals, and he compared them with fantastical creatures such giants and dwarves. Isaac La Preyrere finds evidence in the Bible that there were people who predated Adam, and he speculates that people of color are the descendants of these pre-Adamites. For Roy Harvey Pearce, Indigenous Americans could only be understood through Christianity's epistemological grid as a malevolent force, because "Satan had possessed the Indian until he became virtually a beast."

Though race is often contextualized as a modern invention, making it synonymous with science, it has lived a far longer life within cosmology and religion. While race is frequently thought of as a classification system, it begins as a magical system that relies on analogy and not classification. In fact, all political life began as cosmology. Sylvia Wynter writes that:

> *Greek astronomy was to remain an ethno-astronomy. One, that is, in which the moral/political laws of the Greek polis had been projected upon the physical cosmos, enabling them to serve as 'objective truth' in Feyerabend's (1987) sense of the term, and therefore as, in my own terms, adaptive truth-for the Greeks. With the consequence that their projected premise of a value distinction and principle of ontological distinction between heaven and earth had functioned to analogically replicate and absolutize the central order-organizing principle and*

genre-of-the-human distinction at the level of the sociopolitical order, between the non-dependent masters who were Greek-born citizens and their totally dependent slaves classified as barbarian Others. With this value distinction (sociogenic principle of master code of symbolic life/ death) then being replicated at the level of the intra-Greek society, in gendered terms (correlatedly), as between males, who were citizens, and women, who were their dependents.

My motive in writing this book is to ask the question: if astrology is just as speculative as race, can we make it more responsible? Can we use Western astrology to respond to the West? The word "responsibility" has the word "response" in it. Responsibility is possible when response is possible. Race and how we construct it have not been responsive to the needs of communities around the world. Rather, race has mainly existed as a paradigm propagated by the West and used to describe the rest of the world. While race science has been central to the establishment of the modern institution, astrology has been regarded by most as a pseudoscience. As a pseudoscience, astrology is a communal practice and a silly one. It follows not only the old adage of "as above, so below," but also "as below, so above." The latter adage means that not only do the wider cultural contexts that we project onto virtual images, such as the stars, dictate what meanings we are able to construct from the world, but also that by changing our collective behavior, we are able to change what we see in the stars by changing ourselves.

In order to make astrology a more responsible cultural practice, we must understand how astrological meaning has been constructed within political economic history. We must understand what astrology has to do with courts, militaries, rule, and power— with capital, power, and labor. We must do this so we understand how it exists within neoliberalism, so we are able to make it our own again. A lot of people are surprised when I tell them astrology has lived longer as a right-wing practice than anything left-leaning. I don't understand why. Adolf Hitler, J. P. Morgan, and Ronald

Reagan all used astrology. This didn't happen because of the funny quirks of a few otherwise rather despicable men, nor is it a funny coincidence. It happens because, due to the nature of astrology's lineage, like whiteness, it makes itself visible when certain sociopolitical relations are under threat.

The thing is, far from being politically and aesthetically neutral, astrology, like race magic, has been aesthetically connected with classicalism and the manufactured memory of Roman idealism. The West attempts to revive itself again and again through the image of Rome. Modernity, because it is a Western cultural ideal, is also an anachronistic ideal because modern movements and neoclassical movements have so often coincided. The fear of Western cultural and racial decay led to a Roman revival in 1800s Austria. Scientists, philosophers, architects, and artists such as Freud, Nietzsche, Wagner, and Klimt all looked to antiquity to revive their contemporary culture, which they saw as in a state of decay. In Roman myths and forms, they saw antiquity as the key to the instinctual impulses of life that had been degraded in their contemporary conditions. For Freud, Oedipus provided the blueprint of the universal man; for Nietzsche, between Apollo and Dionysus lay a primordial tension; for Wagner, classical forms had to be resurrected by the modern style; and for Klimt, the goddess symbolized the principles of eros.

In the American South immediately after the Civil War, former slave owners/human traffickers reasserted America's cultural lineage through the Roman imagery offered by astrology. Astrologers such as Mark Broughton and schools such as The Order of the Magi emerged out of Confederate anxiety. Astrology tends to revive when whiteness is heightened and threatened, because it is said that the images used within astrology—Jupiter the Benevolent, Venus the Victorious, and the Sun the Enlightened—are Roman. The Nazis loved astrology because it gave them the romantic images they needed to dress up in Roman costumes and Roman phrases. Ideas from ancient Rome about citizenship, land, prosperity, and military might were reinterpreted by the Germans and reconstructed into the modern fascist state. The aesthetic of modern astrology is neo-classical, styled after white marble cut into *übermenschen* or Aphrodite with wide hips and a high brow. Modern associations of Saturn with citizenship or of the Sun with empire come from romanticism.

Romanticism and classicism are not unique to national socialist Germany. As Marx once said, the French Revolution was conducted "in Roman costumes and with Roman phrases." The republicanism of the new American state in the sixteenth century was inspired more by Roman ideals than by Continental or British philosophy. As William B. Warner argues, "Boston leaders like Rev. Johnson Mayhew, James Otis, Jr., Samuel Adams, and his second cousin John Adams developed a Roman republican rather than a French Enlightenment understanding of the character of society."

The attachment to and idealizing of Roman democracy and republicanism are not contained to the West; they also extend from the West to the rest of the world. Stephen Bronner believes that "Enlightenment thinking remains the best foundation for any genuinely progressive politics not simply in the West but in those states that suffered most at its hands." In other words, for any postcolonial struggle to be considered "genuine," it must support the West's fantasy of itself as the most republican, the most progressive, and the most liberated place in the world. If a political struggle wants to describe its own sense of liberation, it must argue its case in Roman phrases and in Roman costumes, in Roman law and with Roman psychoanalytic theory.

But the Roman costumes and phrases that revolutionaries in France, republicans in the United States, and National Socialists in Germany dressed themselves in are only that—costumes. The attachment of Europe and the United States to Rome is convoluted. While *Germania* by the Roman Tacticus was very popular in Germany before World War II, *Germania* was not written from the point of view of a German extolling Germania for its virtues but by a Roman describing German barbarians for his Roman peers. The National Socialists remade Rome in their own image, comparing Hitler to Plato's philosopher kings. Roman astrology and Greek astrology are not Western, because the West is a modern invention. Rather, Romans and Greeks did not see their astrology as separate from astrologies in Persia, Egypt, and India. The Western geographies most closely associated with Roman genealogy come, in fact, not from Rome, while the geographies that *were* in the Roman Empire are commonly not considered to be part of the West.

Rather than being based in historical fact, the ability to claim Roman cultural or biological genealogy is an integral part of the *storytelling* that reinforces the West as a political reality. However, the lines that connect contemporary races to Rome disappear at certain moments, splinter at others, and become one with their parallel reflections at still others. Rome is a speculative story; as Freud wrote, it is a dream within a dream. So is whiteness and so is the West. If whiteness is a dream, then astrology—with all of its anachronistic and weird neoclassicalism—is one of the languages through which that dream speaks itself into being.

An example of how Rome (and with it whiteness) is relayed through astrology: each sign derives meaning from the condition of the planets in those signs. In some signs, planets are considered to be in rulership. In others, the signs opposite to the places of rulership, planets are considered to be in exile, adversity, or antithesis. Planets that are in rulership or are dignified are thought to have the resources they need to express themselves. Planets that are in exile are thought to not have the resources they need to do their jobs. This system of essential dignities comes from Roman citizenship. Roman citizens were represented within the state, while foreigners were always slaves. In a contemporary context, this system makes sense and has modern application precisely because the West has adopted Roman ideals of citizenship in order to ascribe comfort toward some bodies while excluding others, in the words of Sara Ahmed.

Astrological ideas about where planets are allowed to be at home are also sociopolitical ideas about who is allowed to be at home.

Whiteness has not disappeared. Whiteness did not die with national socialist Germany and the totalitarianism of the 1900s. It is still a political reality, and as a living political reality, it has learned to adapt and change with the ages. Whiteness is a cosmological reality. Within neoliberalism, neoclassical aesthetics, which continue to influence contemporary astrology through the retelling and revision of myths, also continue to influence how we conduct our courts, our bureaucracies, our militaries, and our prisons.

A lot of people, whether they're millennials or boomers, white or other, queer or cisnormal, have told me they were first attracted to astrology because it seems to offer a way to talk among ourselves about ourselves without having to address the trappings of identity. Rather than talking about ourselves within the typical categories of race, gender, and class, people want to build community around identities that feel authentic and close. Astrology fans want identity to be as complex as humanity.

And I've seen astrology bring people together. I've seen queers relax and smile when their friends tease them for their Moon sign, laughing along with them about being a Leo rising because it makes them feel so seen. I've seen sarcastic New York seniors who do not otherwise want to share their stories come together and ask whether we can all talk sincerely with one another about our natal charts. I've seen teens who are otherwise self-conscious and guarded about where they are, shielding themselves with fashion or learned academic language, admit that they have a lot of deep feelings as a Scorpio. I've seen kids talk about the burdens and joys of being a Capricorn with big dreams, of being an Aquarius who is just the right amount of cynical but with a huge helping of healthy smart-assedness. I've seen the request for someone's Sun, Moon, or rising sign become a tender shorthand for "I'd like to know you better" and the invitation to talking about astrology be shorthand for "I'd like to hear you imagine yourself beyond how I was taught to perceive you." Through astrology, we are funny, sincere, and vulnerable. We use astrology to see each other.

Astrology occupies a healing role in our communities. Folks come to astrologers when they feel stunted in their careers by their lack of wealth, when they feel stuck in relationships where they are not acknowledged, when they seek to process sexual violence, when they are grieving, and so on. Those seeking astrological counseling trust that their astrologer will not diagnose their problems with the individualized and biological framework offered by the modern psychiatric industry. They understand that the lack of standardization within astrology means that no two astrology readings from different astrologers will be the same. People choose astrologers for their subjectivities. Not all astrologers know what it's like to experience racism. Not all astrologers understand what it's like to encounter sexual violence or to realize how normalized this violence is. Not all astrologers want or choose to counsel clients through trauma. If astrology is a mental health profession, then it is an imperfect one, because astrologers ourselves are imperfect. Astrology is a tool through which imperfect people try our best to talk to each other.

There are problems within astrology: where does one's gender identity fit into the gendered binaries of Venus and Mars? How can we define our abundance away from cultural capitals when the Sun collapses power and wealth into the solitary figure of the sovereign? What kind of Saturn, or government, should we be creating when we feel disillusioned by the prospect of government? Why is the concern of citizenship so related to genealogy? And the most crucial question: *why do we keep taking these Greco-Roman ideas and archetypes and applying them to everyone as if they're really universal and overarching?*

But astrology is not alone in its attempts to create universality out of classical aesthetics and a dash of scientific modernity. We don't understand Greco-Roman emotions to be universal because of astrology; rather, astrology understands Greco-Roman emotions to be universal because so many institutions also do. When we say we are depressed, are we referring to the Latin word *deprimere,* which not only means "to press down" but is also associated with a lowering of economic value? Or are we saying we are melancholic, which is associated with black humor, as if blackness is intrinsically sad or stagnant? When we say we are paranoid, are we really describing ourselves with the Latin terms *para,* which means "contrary to," and *noos,* which means "mind"? Do these Roman concepts of what it means to exist as contrary to one's own mind infiltrate those of us who do not claim Roman genealogy? When we find that the roots of the words "anxious" and "anger" connect in the Latin word *angere,* which means "to choke," do those of us who do not descend from Rome experience anger and anxiety differently, or are these emotions a part of a modernity that has already recreated the world in a pseudo-Roman image? When we use Roman ideas to describe our intimate mental conditions, aren't we accepting the promise of universality within Western hegemony? Why is it that mental illness can only be seen as a scientific and biological reality instead of a cultural imagining when it is described through Roman words?

Romanization doesn't just influence how we talk about emotions; it also influences how we classify relatedness and genealogy and kin. We call our nonhuman ancestors by their Latin names, finding that they are tetrapods or bipedal, that they are of the *Colosteus* genus (*Colosteus* refers to the Latin word *colosseus,* meaning "gigantic," and *genus* means "race, birth, or stock"), and that they are of the *Animalia* family (*Animalia* comes from the Latin root *ane-,* which means "to breathe," and family refers to the Latin concept of household). We talk about paleolithic times (*paleo* meaning "stone") without meaning to refer to either Hesiod's or Virgil's ages of the metals, in which race is either seen as slowly eroding or revitalizing itself through rebirth. Our intimate connections with family, land, and time—genealogical and historical—have a distinctly Roman flavor. This Roman flavor tastes like marble, stripped of color, because only the primitive would ever paint their statues (even though the Romans did paint their statues). It feels like reality.

It appears that the problem of Romanization is not astrology's problem but the West's problem. Science and astrology are not diametrically opposed. Both of these ideological and spiritual practices attempt to implement Roman symbols into modernity. Both of these practices understand the real as the Roman. I am not against Hellenistic astrology, but to understand the astrological techniques of essential dignity, *Caput* and *Cauda Draconis,* planetary detriment or antithesis, Fate and Fortune, and to give these concepts to a client pretending that they are universal truths made real by history is to perpetuate a certain genealogy and, by way of perpetuating a certain genealogy, a certain storytelling. To speak ourselves through these genealogies in order to feel some relief from always, *always,* having to understand ourselves as sexualized, gendered, raced subjects of someone else's imagination and to redeem ourselves as human through the archetypes within astrology is not a general or universal or natural move. It's a specific move, and it must be considered strategically.

The truth is, the thing that is astrology is not what offers healing to astrology fans. The history of astrology developed out of white supremacy and capitalism and patriarchy. The ways that we see Venus and Mars and gender, the ways that Jupiter and Sun and rulership have been defined, have served power rather than working against it. Astrology, as we have inherited it, does not offer us authentic identity. Astrology offers us Roman identity, Roman belonging, and Roman humanity.

This is why we must continually work to destroy astrology as we practice it: because we look for identity from it. The reason why astrology, as a subculture, creates beautiful community and spiritual validation is not because there is anything special about such an occult language or because it has the ability to glimpse into one's being in a way that's different from other identity languages; it's because astrology's practitioners and fans have *made it our own.* It works not because there is anything magical about the language itself but because the act of not believing readily, of believing where belief has been earned, of listening waywardly, and of owning the magic of illusion making collectively *is* magic. Astrology is not magic. The community that recreates it in the contemporary era is.

As a writer, I come from the fandom world, which is a controversial storytelling world because the writers tend to be voices who neither get published nor work to learn the tropes that can earn a writer institutional validation. Fanfiction writers are often naïve writers because we're untrained writers. It's not really an industry, because there is no money in writing fanfiction and because the work itself exists within a legal grey zone. *We write with characters who will never belong to us.* However, fanfiction continues to stick around despite all those who say it's too embarrassing and young femmes need to grow out of it. People like fanfiction because it is a space where they can be heard—because it is a community that contests the authority of authorship.

The mass media that the fandom world digests, like the Roman one that the astrological community digests, is not a neutral one. It is a world overpopulated by white men, where women never see or speak to one another, where the binary between homosexuality and heterosexuality makes it seem as though gay people are an entirely separate natural species, where people of color do not exist at all unless they are characterized in supporting or stereotypical ways. This world of images is genealogically related to white supremacist ideologies. Cartoons were originally based on white men satirizing Blackness, and early American cinema developed from the minstrel tradition.

Like astrologers—who are often not genealogically related to the Romans but seek to transcend cultural frameworks that are called too naïve and too specific to be studied outside of anthropology—fanfiction writers are often not white men, but they often reproduce images of white men in order to tell stories about themselves. Like astrologers do with their archetypes, fanfiction writers often gender-bend or racebend their characters and sometimes make them into inhuman creations or animal hybrids. Like astrologers, fanfiction writers often find their source material less than satisfactory and the available tools used to speculate new realities away from colonized imaginations disappointing. However, fanfiction writers stay in fandom for the same reasons that astrologers stay in astrology: because it feels good to speak to one another, to make inside jokes, because fellow fans and astrologers work to see *us* when we write stories or horoscope interpretations—because we *belong* in subculture even when we don't belong in culture.

What saves astrology from itself today is that it works like the fandom world. It is a community-created subculture that takes what has been mass-produced and digests it. Rather than a consumer-oriented cultural movement, which tends to spike in interest when there are big blockbuster releases from a centralized creative power and ebb after the hype has died down, fandoms that are community-created tend to stay stagnant in terms of capturing interest. After a certain magical point, fandoms are no longer dependent on the canon and function quite well on their own, neither growing nor diminishing in size (the Sailor Moon fandom is a good example of this, if you want to look up the numbers on this topic on tumblr user destinationtoast's blog). This means we are not out to evangelize or to grow as the capitalists tell us we should be if we are to stay viable. We are out here sharing ideas, healing each other, and inspiring each other on a daily, nonaccumulative, nonaccelerationist scale. There is no central corporation that pumps out astrology books that all of us then follow. Doing astrology simply means we are listening to one another. It means we are being listened to.

A Note on My Own Positionality and the Title

I am a first-generation immigrant to the United States of America from Henan province, China. I grew up in small-town USA and relocated to New York City when I was eighteen. I moved to New York because I needed to be around more people of color, and I currently rent a room in Brooklyn as a non-Black gentrifier. I am an Asian settler in occupied Lenapehoking territory. I used to fantasize about going back to China, and I imagined I could cease to be a settler if I went back. Then I learned that gentrification as a continuation of colonization has not stopped happening in China. My settlerism in the West continues to enact violence on Indigenous people, and it alienates me from the histories of my own ancestors. There is no ethical existence under capitalism. Chinese politics is a politics that eludes me because I grew up in the United States and was culturally produced by the West. My politics exist in the West, which is a place where I am racialized and complicit.

When my editor, Gillian—who has supported the journey of this book by helping me look into states of exception and complicating my arguments—and I bounced around names for this book, we decided on *Postcolonial Astrology*. Postcolonialism is a complicated area of theory because, while it strives to deconstruct some of modernity's metanarratives around race, gender, and capitalism, the word mostly exists today in academic spaces. Also, the word itself implies that there has been an end to colonialism. There has not been an end to colonialism. Settlers continue to occupy Indigenous land, and I am complicit in this ongoing occupation. While postcolonial writers often come from satellite colonies of the West, decolonization movements come from settler states.

I chose the name *Postcolonial Astrology* for the book because it is a title that recognizes my own limitations as an immigrant settler. In astrology, we talk about traditional astrology and modern astrology, and we reference Roman men or white men. *Postcolonial Astrology* is my contribution to the dialogue of astrology. It is a limited contribution because my perspective is limited. By naming this book *Postcolonial Astrology*, I only hope to contribute to what Jodi Byrd calls a cacophony, which she finds in both "the desire and fear of the colonizer who needs to continually and repeatedly articulate 'true' and 'real' representations of the colonized" and "the ways historical oppressions created by liberal multicultural settler colonies exist relationally and in collusion with the processes of racial, gendered, and sexual otherings that seek to make contesting histories and experiences resonate autochthonously through the lingering touch of the real."

For example, in this book I often compare astrology, as a system of classification, to race. Race is a language that was invented by white people, reappropriated by postcolonial thinkers, and still continues to cut into Indigenous sovereignty. Byrd writes, "Racialization and colonization should thus be understood as concomitant global systems that secure white dominance through time, property, and notions of self." As a person of color, I talk about race. Many postcolonial writers talk about race. I hope that, when I talk about race, I do so in solidarity with Indigenous decolonization, which Byrd defines as "a process that restores life and allows settler, arrivant, and native to apprehend and grieve together the violences of U.S. empire."

I hope that everyone who reads this book critiques it and uses those critiques to assert their own healing practices. I'm happy you picked it up, and I hope there is something in here that provokes you to take cosmology into your own hands.

Trigger warning for the book:

This book's goal is to make astrology more accountable to the histories in which its meaning was accumulated. This means that this book must, and does, discuss the violent processes that construct modernity which include racism, anti-Blackness, gender violence, colonization, climate violence, and other forms of social violence. People who experience these oppressions firsthand do not need explicit descriptions of violence in order to learn and this book tries its best to avoid triggering material as an effort to prioritize people of color and femmes who are reading the book. I also believe that racism, at its core, is a description of whiteness and focus my critiques by reframing whiteness in order to critique racism. However, contextualizing astrology into colonialism means that there are sections where social violence and recent events that may be triggering are either mentioned or described in what I hope to be a compassionate way and trigger warnings will be placed throughout the book to prepare readers accordingly.

1

ETYMOLOGY OF THE SUN

That Great Big Circle in the Sky

The Sun is the most visibly obvious object in the sky. It lights up the world of the day and is the source of energy for the living world. Everything comes back to the Sun. As Robert Hand writes in his book *Horoscope Symbols,* "the Sun represents the energy that enables everything to exist."

The Sun is a disc—a great big circle in the sky. The god Aten, whose name means "disc," was the god of one of Egypt's most hated pharaohs. Akhenaton broke with Egypt's polytheistic tradition and forbade his subjects to worship any god except Aten, whom he called the "sole god" and a god "like whom there is no other." Unlike other Egyptian gods who were represented through images of the living world, with dog heads and human bodies, Aten had no image—only a name. Aten's name was marked the way a pharaoh's name would be marked, and Akhenaton changed his own name to reflect his association with his god of his new world order.

Eventually, because an imageless god was hard for Egyptian subjects to worship, Akhenaton compromised on his insistence that his supreme deity be completely imageless. He allowed Aten to be portrayed by an abstract circle, a faceless face, with rays that shined down upon the earth. The abstract quality of the circle, perfect and ideal, was a representation that superseded all other representations of the imperfect world. Because Aten had no image, Egypt did not worship the god directly. Instead, Egypt worshipped images of the royal family worshipping Aten. Thus, Aten's power was completely synonymous with Pharaoh Akhenaton's royal power. As John Baines writes, this religion "was a religion of god and king, or even of king first and then god." After Akhenaton's death, his new religion was abandoned, his monuments destroyed, and his name erased from the lists of kings.

The great big circle in the sky, however, was not merely a flat disc in the two-dimensional universe or even a sphere in the three-dimensional universe. The sun is a chariot. It is circular time.

Virgil represented the golden age optimistically. In Hesiod's *Works and Days,* the world spirals from an elevated and golden position down into a horrible physical and moral deterioration. Hesiod was a pessimist. Saturn's golden age was long lost, the silver race had encouraged inertia, the bronze race had glorified violence, and the iron age had increased the amount of evil in the world. Still, Hesiod warned that there were worse days to come, when hubris would completely replace divine justice and children would be born old with gray hair.

In response to Hesiod's pessimism, Virgil proposes in his *Eclogues* that time doesn't slope downward but moves circularly. Virgil prophesies that a child will be born "under whom the iron brood shall at last cease and a golden race spring up throughout the world!" Under this new golden race, Saturn's reign returns, the Virgin returns, the snakes and their poison hide away, and the goats become swollen with milk. He compares the child whose birth will bring forth the new golden age to Apollo, and he announces that this child will be king in the new world. Whereas Hesiod wrote that new life would soon become so scarce that even children will look like the old, Virgil uses the symbol of a child to suggest a regeneration of life itself.

In contrast to Hesiod's pessimistic view of the golden age, seeing it as something lost forever, Virgil had an optimistic view and encouraged Romans to anticipate the golden age's return in the future. This contrast arose because, while Hesiod satirized the past, Virgil prophesied the future. Hesiod's main purpose was to warn Romans that hubris supplants justice. He represented the golden age as an unachievable ideal with which to compare and contrast his contemporary world order. Hesiod's poetic accounting of time also showed a racial hierarchy. On the other hand, as Charles Fantazzi writes in *Golden Age in Arcadia,* Virgil projects "the myth into the future in correlation with grandiose cosmic processes." Fantazzi goes on to describe Virgil's child "as personification of the new age," "an un-warlike hero," and "a symbol of Roman virtue."

Furthermore, Fantazzi pinpoints the moment where Virgil transitions "from the mythical to the realistic realm of the Roman political order and its propagandistic slogans." Specifically, in *Eclogue IV,* 11, Virgil abruptly links his mythic child to his contemporary Rome by bringing up Asinius Pollio, who was a friend to both Augustus and Marc Anthony. When Virgil writes that the child "shall rule the world to which his father's prowess brought peace" and that "this glorious age [will] begin" under Pollio's consulship, he keeps the identity of the child vague but uses the reference to Pollio to produce the poem's political and secular dimensions. In this context, Virgil's optimistic rebranding of the golden age, which was for Hesiod a satirical and Saturnian instrument used to critique power, foreshadows the fall of the Roman Republic and the beginning of the Roman Empire through a grandiose vision of imperialism. The child who brings in Apollo's reign and invites into the world a new golden age of the sun is a Roman hero, though later interpretations of this child would associate him with Jesus Christ.

The third aspect of the Sun within Greco-Roman astrology—or Hellenistic astrology, as it is popularly called—that we will consider is the Sun's association with Fate over Fortune. While the Moon, the nighttime luminary, is associated with *Fortuna,* the Sun is associated with Fate or Spirit. Fate referred to an abstract and metaphysical reality, while Fortune referred to the physical body or environment of a person. Greek and Roman astrologers calculated incidents happening to the physical body by calculating Fortune, while issues of Fate were more associated with the will of the gods or the will of the individual. Thus, the astrological Sun rules over life itself, whereas the Moon rules over the containers necessary to maintain and reproduce life. The Sun, as the ruler of Fate, measures those things that are abstract and unrepresentable. Like Aten the faceless god, the Sun is without image because it represents not the beings that live in the world but the abstract and permanent state of life itself. As pure spirit, the Sun cannot be captured in an image. The most one could do, if one had to represent it through images, is to draw rays of light beaming either from the sky or from some enlightened demigod or spirit.

The abstraction of the Sun was often represented as sight. The type of sight associated with the astrological Sun has both physical and metaphysical dimensions; it represents the literal surveillance of an empire by its rulers as well as the omnipotence of an all-seeing god or eye. Often, the metaphysical dimensions of sight were associated with truth and reason. The Roman Plotinus writes in his *Enneads* of sunlight: "The simple beauty of a color is derived from a form that dominates the obscurity of matter and from the presence of an incorporeal light that is reason and idea." For Plotinus, light connects "reason and idea" because it "dominates the obscurity of matter." This "obscurity of matter," for the Romans, is also a metaphysical relationship between the Moon, Fortune, and form. What Plotinus describes as the dominion of the Sun was not only physical lighting but also a power relation.

The metaphysical light of the symbolic Sun represents surveillance. Plotinus conceptualized surveillance through a figure he called the One. Plotinus's One is a supreme being that transcends all worldly objects and is able to see the world in its entirety at once. Like Aten, the One is unrepresentable, though the Gnostics represented the One as an all-seeing eye. The Gnostic book *The Secret Book of John* puts it this way: "The Monad is a monarchy with nothing above it. It is he who exists as God and Father of everything, the invisible One who is above everything, who exists as incorruption, which is in the pure light into which no eye can look." As a solar god, the One is never *seen* but always one who *sees*. This is why the Sun can never have an image of its own, because it represents the power to see but to never be seen.

As a political symbol, the Sun emerges through its associations with the utopian future and with monarchy. The type of political power that the Sun represents is always described through concentration and elevation. It is associated with surveillance because its power always emerges through a top-down approach. These top-down approaches to managing power disrupted history by inventing new religious institutions and breaking traditions. Heroes of the new world, which include both mythical beings like Apollo and the real children of Roman emperors, are celebrated for their solar attributes when they seek to liberate the empire away from historical decay by implementing liberation from the top down to the subjects. If the Sun stands for the future, then it also stands for a specific type of future that is carefully engineered, omnipotently surveilled, and designed to break society away from its own histories and traditions.

Elysium

Under the Weimar Republic, classists coined two utopias out of the circular nature of time, just as Virgil had done: Arcadia, which was described in the pastoral tradition, and Elysium, which was described in the humanistic tradition. While Arcadia was the lost age of Saturn, Elysium was the hope for a future golden age that could be achieved through moral cultivation, attained via enlightened classical aesthetics and study. While Arcadia, Saturn's paradise, was wild, Elysium was a cultivated paradise. As Friedrich Schiller declares:

> *Man was to learn to find again through reason that state of innocence which he had lost, and to return again—this time as a free, rational intellect—to that state which he left as a plant and as a mere creature of instinct. From a paradise of ignorance and servitude he was to work his way up—even if it took many long millennia—to a paradise of knowledge and freedom; that is, to a paradise where he would obey the moral law within his own breast just as unflinchingly as he had obeyed instinct in the beginning.*

Elysium, for the modern Weimar classicists, was a poetic device that combined the circular optimism for utopia with newer ideas about progress and evolution. The idea was that, through progress and moral cultivation, Europe was not attempting to return to a wild prehistorical past that they associated with the brutish lives of the colonized; they were instead creating a humanistic utopia on a "higher plane of perfection," as John R. Fowles writes. Fowles goes on to say that, while Arcadia was "naïve and innocent," Elysium would be "morally conscious." The distinction between Arcadia and Elysium was also a distinction between the uncivilized and the civilized, between nature and culture.

In ancient Greece, Elysium, or the Fortunate Isles, was referenced in myth and allegory as a section of the Underworld where mortals related to the gods or heroes went after death. Hesiod describes Elysium as "untouched by sorrow" and full of "happy heroes for whom the grain-giving earth bears honey-sweet fruit flourishing thrice a year," while Pindar writes that the good people who go to Elysium after death are given a life "free from toil."

Elysium—unlike Arcadia, from which all the races of mankind emerge—is a place for the select few, those who have achieved god-like status due to familial relation or heroic deeds. If Arcadia represents a naïve Eden all were banished from, Elysium is a heaven reserved for the few who merit it.

In the same way that the yearning *(Sehnsucht)* for Arcadia was a nostalgia and a nationalistic pining for an imagined homeland, the anticipation of Elysium was also a movement toward nationalism. Arcadia and Elysium were descriptions of the same physical location. Whereas Arcadia described the mass consciousness of a time before political history, Elysium described individual ascension. The inhabitants of Arcadia are always described in the plural, while those who are elevated into Elysium's higher moral realms enter through individual accomplishment. The lack of consciousness and individualization of the prehistoric Arcadia are solved by an Elysium that prioritizes individual moral achievement.

If Saturn is represented by a lost golden wilderness opposed to the human fabricating arts, then the Sun is represented by a cultivated utopia that embraces arts, culture, and human creations. The Sun's utopia admitted its inhabitants solely on the basis of moral elevation through European culture. If Saturn's realm describes those noble savages that seem to predate modern struggles around power, then the Sun's realm is a brightly lit and white paradise that only those en*light*ened by German *Bildung* could ever hope to enter. If Arcadia is darkened by malefic forces, then the heavenly aisles of Elysium became only whiter and whiter.

Gold

The Sun rules gold. As a visual symbol, gold often represents ultimate luxury and abundance. Representations of royalty seem off brand when these images forget to include gold. It is almost impossible to think of wealth without thinking of gold. Gold is not only a symbol of royal power but also the color of religious and divine power. Sacred places were originally temples where gold was hoarded and buried. In the Middle Ages, the Catholic Church controlled gold and solidified the representational link between gold and God.

In her essay "Why Is Gold Valuable? Nature, Social Power and the Value of Things," Erica Schoenberger writes that the earliest gold artifacts appear at the necropolis in Varna and that the society of Varna became hierarchal and stratified through the fashioning of gold. Schoenberger writes that, although gold was naturally scarce and its value is often attributed to this natural scarcity, it was also often hoarded, given as gifts in order to gain power, and deliberately pulled out of circulation and buried in the ground it was originally mined from.

"A remarkably stringent artificial scarcity is superimposed on natural scarcity from the start of organized class society," she writes. "A substantial part of the gold brought out of the ground is re-inserted, subtracting it from the available supply. The rest circulates in socially restricting channels that have the paradoxical effect of creating something like abundance within those authorized circuits and genuine dearth outside of them." If, as Schoenberger writes, "the history of the economic and cultural value of gold is a history of social power," then the history of gold is also the history of engineered scarcity and hierarchy. As Lawrence Freedman writes, Plato likened natural social harmony to differences in metallics: "The class structure was therefore the result of the different metals the gods had put into individual souls—gold for rulers, silver for auxiliaries, and iron and bronze for farmers and artisans."

Gold is social power. Gold did not begin as a commercial thing, nor did it absorb value through circulation. Originally, powerful families used gold to buy favors from each other. Extravagant and performative gift exchanges in the form of gold bound factions together. After the gold was given, it would be buried in the ground

or regifted to buy more favors and allies. The value of gold originates in the competitive system of royal gift exchange, not commodity exchange or the market, as gold was never circulated and
rarely used. As Peter Spufford writes, "the kings used their treasure-
hoards, if at all, for prestigious gifts to their subjects, or for political
payments to one another. . . . The subjects who received gifts of gold
were frequently royal relations, great noblemen, bishops or favored
monasteries. All of these hoarded rather than spent the gold."
Schoenberger contrasts the political power of gold with commercialism: "The history of gold coinage in Antiquity is rooted in the
contest for political power: it runs not from barter to coin but from
personal seal to coin." This means that gold is not valuable because
it is spent. It is valuable because it is accumulated.

Later, the issuance of gold as coin displayed the power of the
city-state. Contrary to capitalist fables about gold and commodity
exchange, the coinage of gold in Athens was a political statement
about where the cultural center of power could be found and did
not arise out of market activity, which hovered over the boundaries and shores. Even when the merchant classes amassed huge
amounts of wealth, gold was used to differentiate political powers
from commercial powers. Merchants were not allowed to display
their gold in a public way or to dress themselves with gold clothing
the way the nobility often did. The power of gold and the power
of money were seen to be distinct forms of power, sometimes in
opposition and sometimes in collaboration, just as the merchants
often collaborated with the aristocrats against the peasant class but
opposed them on other issues.

For a relatively brief period of history—between the 1500s,
when Spain began to mine the Americas for gold, and the 1900s,
when the Mineral Revolution occurred in Africa—gold was a
money commodity. The city of Johannesburg was founded in 1886,
only two years after gold was discovered in the Witwatersrand reef.
In South Africa, apartheid was built on the mining of gold. As white

labor was replaced by cheaper Black African labor, segregation laws were passed to protect the ruling class. As Salome Thema put it, the mining industry would remake the continent of Africa: "The period between the discovery of gold on the Witwatersrand and the establishment of the city of Johannesburg was a turning point in the history of not only Southern Africa but of the whole continent." England was the biggest benefactor of this operation.

In the period immediately after mining began in South Africa and the consequent racial segregation, gold was circulated throughout the West on an unprecedented level. This gold was primarily sourced from South Africa. However, by 1950, 94 percent of the gold that had been mined in Africa was pulled out of circulation and buried in underground vaults located mostly in New York and London. These centers of power became global financial capitals, controlling most of the world's gold, and with it, credit. As Schoenberger writes, the reburial of South African gold in New York and London "was to significantly constrain the amount of gold that was freely available, thus helping to sustain both its price and its social aura of exclusiveness and powerfulness."

Gold, the Sun's metal, is a symbol of exclusive power. Exclusivity is generated by engineered artificial scarcity. Exclusivity, existing within cultural centers of capital, is only possible in a hierarchical society where gifts are given performatively among a ruling elite. The exclusivity of gold did not arise spontaneously but was engineered when gold was taken out of Africa and hoarded by Western banks within financial capitals. Gold pulled from Africa and reburied in New York and London sustained white exclusivity and white power.

Illumination (Capital/Crown/Center)

The enlightenment or Enlightenment had both physical and metaphysical dimensions. Enlightenment is a process of becoming illuminated relative to the religious, dark, and superstitious past through secularism, humanism, and republicanism, while the Enlightenment is a specific historical period that occurred in the eighteenth century after the French Revolution. Interpreted through the politics of sight, the enlightenment or Enlightenment of Europe was also a cultural movement that decided what would become visible and what would remain invisible.

Akhenaton's reign in Egypt was controversial not just because it worshipped a new, abstract god instead of traditional, polytheistic gods; it was also because Akhenaton centralized his rule around a newly built capital that he named Akhetaten. The rest of Egypt was reoriented around this new city, which became its heart and center. Under the rule of Louis XIV, otherwise known as the Sun King, French power became centralized under an absolute monarch. Like Akhenaton, Louis XIV broke with tradition, limited papal powers within France, and made his court at Versailles the center of the state.

In contrast to older interpretations, William Beik finds in his essay "The Absolutism of Louis XIV as Social Collaboration" that absolute monarchy should not be thought of as a top-down domination of most of the population by one figurehead or even as a war between king and province. Rather, "the king ruled by collaborating with socially powerful elites," Beik says. These social elites organized themselves in court life and played games according to rivalries, royalties, ideologies, and romances, changing their allegiances over time in order and intensity. The court of Versailles was where various factions of the elite class bargained for favors, honors, and promotion. Rather than resisting the absolutism of Louis XIV, noblemen and other aristocrats oriented themselves around Louis and thus around the power of the state. The king achieved control over the aristocrats by selectively giving out the honors and promotions they craved. In fact, France's military class consisted mostly of aspirational captains or lieutenants who sank their personal inheritances into paying soldiers, with the understanding that they would be promoted to a higher office after one or two tours.

Glory, in the court of Louis XIV, was a commodity not unlike gold. It was given to elite classes in exchange for services and loyalty, and it was hoarded mercilessly by those who received it, in order to not diminish its value. As Beik writes, "A mammoth army was organized around favors doled out by a pompous king in a dazzling court, supported by bureaux that were becoming more efficient, but at the same time were dominated by personal interest and favoritism." Peter Campbell calls this state the "baroque state" and describes its operations in contrast to modern bureaucracy: "This was a socio-political entity, whose structures were interwoven with society, which it tried to rise above but with which it inevitably had to compromise." Absolute monarchy was not a top-down authoritarian use of power; rather, it was a social compromise between different factions of power that all oriented themselves around the king as center.

While the Enlightenment is commonly associated with secularism, modernity, and progress, Dan Edelstein argues in his book *The Enlightenment: A Genealogy* that the most active voices working during the period of the Enlightenment were actually classicists who may have acknowledged modern science but who spent their time translating and reinterpreting Greek and Roman literature. Thus, like the Renaissance era, the Enlightenment is a neoclassical movement. Even though the Enlightenment is often seen as republican, the philosophes active during the Enlightenment aligned themselves with monarchists, supporting the "Grand Siècle" of Louis XIV, which was associated with newness and spectacle. As Edelstein writes, "the primary purpose of the academies, after all, was not to disseminate knowledge—deliberations in the Académie des sciences remained secret until the 1690s—but rather to augment the glory of the French nation. . . . There was a basic convergence of interests between the French Crown and the philosophes: both sought, in the words of the person who came closest to uniting them, to 'overturn the sterile monuments' of feudalism and tradition."

Because the monarchy of Louis XIV was so closely associated with the French capital of Paris, the Enlightenment could also be interpreted as a cultural movement that refocused Western power at the centers of its empires. These cultural centers of power used new forms of technology to establish an elite, artistic culture that set itself apart from the provinces and the provincial. As Diderot would write, "it would not be wasteful to establish correspondences between the principal centers of the educated world. . . . We would exchange information about our practices, customs, publications, works, machines, etc." To be enlightened, or to be illuminated from the inside out, was to closely associate oneself with the powers and spectacle of the monarch and to create cultural works that sought to illuminate the nation as empire, asserting the European nation to be a center that the margins orient themselves toward.

Edelstein writes that the Enlightenment is distinct from other historical periods, such as the Middle Ages or the Renaissance, because, while other periods of history were labeled after they occurred, the Enlightenment was a self-conscious designation by those participating in fabricating the theories and institutions they labeled as enlightened. Warner calls this "a self-conscious act of historical narrative" and writes that the Enlightenment, in this context, is "a shared performative and finally a literary invention." If the Enlightenment is a performance space, then the central tension of its play is orchestrated between the "Moderns" and the "Ancients." This enlightened play created what later scholars would name the "public sphere." Jean-Baptiste Dubos declared that the public consists precisely of "those people who have been enlightened." Jean DeJean writes that it is through the mediums of a monarch-funded theater space and the newly emerging literary world that the "public sphere" and "public opinion" first began to self-consciously define itself. While the Enlightenment was about the creation of a secular and republican public, this public emerged from a spectacle and theater space that was closely associated with monarchy.

If the Enlightenment is really a play, then, like all plays, it needed lighting. During the seventeenth and eighteenth centuries, "enlightenment despots" such as Louis XIV provided "lavish, baroque displays of fireworks and illuminated theatricalized events . . . dazzled subjects, displayed magnificence and challenged religious power," according to Tim Edensor. The Enlightenment was the era of the first modern city, illuminated not by wavering candlelight but by static artificial light that seemed to extend the daylight into the night. Before the mass production of artificial lighting, the illuminated and known world of the day seemed to coexist side by side with another shadowy world, lit by an inconsistent moon. This shadow world was populated by entities such as ghosts, imps, elves, boggarts, ghouls, and poltergeists, which were always analogies with or interpretations of the landscape. Fairies were connected with swamps; ghosts were tied to the places where their original physical form had died; and imps, goblins, and ghouls were all associated with caves.

In the artificially lit world of the twenty-four-hour city, the landscape receded, and with it, the shadow world of the night. As Edensor writes, "the literal and metaphorical meanings of the term 'enlightenment' have been consistently aligned with a belief in the progressive function and moral desirability of banishing darkness." As Thomas Edison writes, "put an undeveloped human being into an environment where there is artificial light, and he will improve." The futurist Marinetti simply said, "kill the moonlight." Electric light was likened to sunlight due to what were believed to be its sanitizing properties. Scientists in a newly electrified Europe commented that "as far as mere colour is concerned . . . the electric light approaches nearer to the sun than does the gas-flame," and they put babies under electric lighting in order to cure them of disease, believing that electric rays were as disinfecting as the sun's rays. Artificial lighting also created nightlife, and with it, modern spectacle. Freed from the world

of shadows, city dwellers visited theaters, which were often provided by the king, and amusement. If the Enlightenment is the
era of disenchantment, then such disenchantment occurred not
only through the endless proliferation of academic essays by scientists but also through theater. Stage magicians mimicked the
ways Europeans preferred to see ethnic shamanism, and in doing
so, ritualistically seemed to overcome European superstitions
through performance.

After the French Revolution, the city of Paris was redesigned.
In preparation for the Revolution, those who wished to erect
barricades in the city roads gathered in dark alleyways and unlit
street corners. After the Revolution—after the Revolutionary Tri-
bunal beheaded not only the royal family but all of their political
rivals—Napoleon Bonaparte opened up the streets, constructed
open plazas, and illuminated everything with electric lights. Under
modern, static lighting, the city was easily surveilled.

In his book *The Victorian Eye,* Chris Otter writes that the invention of electric light was less of a technological change than a political adjustment of perception. As Europe became more and more
a visual society in which a public sphere was constructed mostly
based on visual forms of media, the social Darwinist Henry Spen-
cer considered the non-European people that he called "savage
tribes" to be "previsual." As technologies and state policies lit up
the streets, cities began to become imagined in what Otter calls an
"essentially macrovisual" way, containing "basic, large-scale information about location and color" and "devoid of nuance." This
teleological way of seeing the world reinforced Victorian ideas
around attention to detail. This attention to detail, Otter writes, was
part of an emerging liberalism that imagined society as a collection of self-governing and self-inspecting individuals. The public
sphere invented during this time period, which Habermas writes
is "always already oriented to an audience," even in its moments
of reading and private media consumption, is not observed by an

eye that watches from above. Rather, it is inspected and scrutinized by other self-governing actors within the public sphere, creating the feeling of having to perform for invisible eyes while in public spaces all of the time.

Electric light, as a political technology, reinforced the liberal idea that government is not an overarching big brother in the sky but the gaze of a self-governed public that polices and surveils itself. The regulatory issues associated with lighting (who turns it on, who turns it off, and where it goes) were entangled with political issues around class and race. While bourgeois actors had the power to turn their own lights on and off, those living in the slums often lived in darkness and along the sewers. Those in prisons were unable to control their own light or visibility conditions. Light was visibility and visibility was power, which was not accessible for so-called "previsual" societies, those living in slums, and those shut in asylums. Rather, visibility as power was the burden of bourgeois actors considered to be capable of self-regulation and self-government.

The term "enlightenment" contains the verb "lighten," which Merriam-Webster defines as "to make (something, such as a color) lighter." The lightness of light is not a technological but a political reality. It normalized certain perceptions and pathologized others. As the nineteenth-century engineer William Aryton writes, "White light is what you see most of. Simply that." This term "white light" is a flexible term used to describe "what people have become accustomed to seeing." If the Sun's job is to illuminate the world, then it also creates an order of visibility and representation. The visual culture promoted by the Enlightenment encouraged some ways of seeing—inspecting, sanitizing, and seeing in way that is oriented toward the capital—while discouraging others. In a liberal world lit up by electric lights, visibility and representation were centered in cultural capitals that were mostly urban, created a public sphere that emerged from spectacle, built public spaces in which self-regulating individuals policed themselves, and created the unenlightened subject who did not control light, visibility, or representation.

The Hyperreal

In almost all paintings before liberalism, which were also almost always religious paintings, holy figures were depicted with an aura. These halos, which were depicted as rays of light streaming out of the heads of gods such as Helios and emperors such as Caesar, lit the worlds within the paintings. Rather than lighting images with one light source, religious icons from the Roman Empire and medieval Europe showed light emanating from the religious figures themselves. Often, figures were flattened by their auras.

In contrast, religious paintings in the period of Caravaggio began to use a chiaroscuro technique in which contrasts between light and shadow were heightened, and the source of light moved off the canvas. In these high-contrast paintings, forms were exaggerated by illumination. If God is the source of light, then these paintings, which sought to propagate the gospel and the institution of the Catholic Church to a mostly illiterate population, moved God outside of the frame and focused on the theater between light and dark. In the Western canon, heroic images are often spectacularly lit. Soviet art and American graphic art also have high contrast. These heroes move through worlds that are unambiguously light and dark. Comics from the World War II era, such as *Captain America*, show shadows that curve away from the viewer, as if the light source of the images emanates from the viewer's eye. If the sun is light and light is aura, then auras have moved off the page and into the gaze of the viewer.

Light, both natural and artificial, was also a metaphor for truth and artifice. While the Roman Plotinus saw visibility as truth, Nietzsche characterizes both his Apollo and Apollo's dark alter ego,

Dionysius, as protectors of illusion. Nietzsche describes Apollo and Dionysius as "a world of dream images" and "intoxicating realities" that "break forth out of nature itself." Every artist, Nietzsche writes, is an "imitator" of these "unmediated artistic states of nature." Nietzsche describes Apollo's eye as sunlike, which he describes as a "consecration" of the "beautiful illusion" of "higher truth." The "higher truth" of the Sun is not reality that is revealed but a performative "dream image" that serves as a perceived or representational reality.

In his book *Sincerity and Authenticity,* Lionel Trilling writes that sincerity is an affect of class—an economic quality. Through a literary analysis of Goethe's *Sorrows of Young Werther,* Trilling shows that the alienation of self away from self as described by Hegel— the alienation of social existence—is fundamental to Europe's early liberalism. *Sorrows of Young Werther* is a story of performative authenticity, of an "honest soul" who ends in nihilistic suicide because Werther finds that there is no place for honest souls in his society. In *The Presentation of Self in Everyday Life,* Erving Goffman writes that liberal societies are held together by modes of everyday theater. In Goffman's analysis, the presentation of a social face or mask relies on the existence of a hidden backstage in which actors can relax and prepare, negotiate, and critique their roles, e.g., the kitchen of a restaurant, a girl's bedroom, or the servants' quarters. "The performance of an individual accentuates certain matters and conceals others," writes Goffman.

Like the chiaroscuro-lit figures of Caravaggio, performance relies not only on showmanship and light; it also needs shadows and concealment. In enlightened or liberal societies, which are also visual societies, some things are revealed while others are hidden. Mars writes that money alienates people from one another and from themselves. In liberal societies where identities are performative and surveilled, you're never sure that what you see is what you get. Within liberal societies, authenticity becomes elevated to morality. Liberal authenticity is always framed as opposing class structure. The liberal hero is always an honest soul, especially when they behave in reprehensible or socially antagonistic ways, while the liberal villain, as Trilling writes, "violates his social purpose . . . by covert acts, by guile. . . . He is a hypocrite, which is to say one who plays a part." The liberal hero is always an *honest* hero, even—or especially—when he does reprehensible things.

A neoliberal market is a speculative economy, meaning that it depends on finance as a spectacle. Naomi Klein puts it this way: "The stock market loves overhyped, highly managed moments that send stock prices soaring, usually provided by an initial public offering, the announcement of a huge merger or the hiring of a celebrity CEO." Klein calls the spectacles of the neoliberal economy "high-drama market events" and connects these events to the hyperinflationary bubbles that arise in third-world countries when foreign money floods in and government regulations step out.

After gold was mined out of South Africa and buried in the foundations of the finance capitals of New York and London, it was replaced with a finance that behaved like theater. Thabo Mbeki, Nelson Mandela's successor as president of South Africa, hoped to avoid market failure by coordinating with American mining interests. He reformed South Africa's economic policies according to free-market principles. In contrast, the Freedom Charter called that "land be given to all landless people" and that "the national wealth of our country, the heritage of South Africans, shall be restored to the people; the mineral wealth beneath the soil, the Banks and the monopoly industry shall be transferred to the ownership of the people as a whole; all other industry and trade shall be controlled to assist the well-being of the people." However, instead of nationalizing the mining industries and redistributing wealth to Black South Africans in accordance with the Freedom Charter, President Mbeki called for more privatization, removed labor protections, and effectively orchestrated a high-drama market event in which

South Africa's land and labor power became available for foreign purchase. Reassuring Western powers that he was a Thatcherite, Mbeki turned South Africa's material resources into a South African financial spectacle.

As part of a market event that depended upon "hype" and theater in order to generate value, Mbeki also constructed a backstage for him and his closest colleagues by swearing those working on the reform with him to secrecy and insulating the project from popular pressures. The audience for Mbeki's high-drama market performance, then, was not South Africa but investors in America and Europe. Mbeki advertised South Africa as a neoliberal economic force ready for development. Under neoliberalism, the global market is a theatrical stage upon which national identity is performed. On this theatrical stage, Mbeki performed a South African nationalism for the benefit of private Western corporations. The result: rather than prioritizing wealth over markets, South Africa continued to make payments on apartheid debt for more than a decade after apartheid had ended, fearing that not doing so would harm South Africa's credit rating. This resulted in economic policies in which Black labor continued to pay white business owners while not receiving reparations in land or resources. In a landscape that sees the spectacle of financial theater as more real than production or natural resources—a landscape afraid that drops in the value of gold stock would be more detrimental to the nation than the real exploitation of Black laborers in the mining industries—capital is more real than life.

The Sun is an aura. Auras light up some objects and conceal others. Auras make a new reality. Light becomes an aura when it dramatizes reality. Some things become more real than others. Finance is hyperreal because it is more real than anything else. The hype of finance realizes its own reality at the expense of almost everything else. When we talk about "real property" or "real estate," the word "real" is not derived from Latin *res,* or "thing"; it's from the

Spanish *real,* meaning "royal" or "belonging to the king." Reality emerges from sovereignty—from capital.

Guy Debord compares the spectacle with the Sun, writing that spectacle is "the sun which never sets over the empire of modern passivity" and that it "covers the entire surface of the world and bathes endlessly in its own glory." The spectacle, Debord writes, alienates people from one another and orients them around a center. Like the colonizers who broke down relations between colonized peoples and reoriented them toward cultural centers of power, the spectacular commodity alienates people from their own existence and reorients them to face power. In a spectacular society, visibility does not emerge from existence but from the orientation toward power.

Walter Benjamin writes that within industrialized societies that mechanize art making, auras disappear. These auras, which are no longer religious, stand for originality and authenticity. Objects in a mechanical society have no aura, as everything becomes endlessly reproducible. Isabelle Graw elaborates upon this notion by suggesting that, rather than disappearing entirely, auras have become a fabricated feeling that is produced when actors perform authenticity. Artists that produce work in a mechanical age engineer feelings of authenticity and originality around their work, Graw writes, by positioning themselves as antagonistic to the market. These engineered feelings of authenticity help art retain its position as a luxury object.

By refusing to price itself, art's engineered authenticity ensures that it has a priceless value. In this way, art's value can rocket upward toward an endlessly distant ceiling. Artists such as Rauschenberg, who found that his works increased in value when he protested their sale, and Courbet, who wrote that "the action that I took in this revolution [meaning his displaying of his own work when he was rejected by the Salon] has caused the prices of my paintings to triple," establish their own authentic positions and value by defining themselves as contrary to the market. When liberal subjects perform authenticity, they elevate their value and morality by making some things more real than others. Liberal authenticity, even authenticities that frame themselves as revolutionary or antagonistic to the market, are always highly managed spectacles that reframe the image of the real as a contrast between light and dark or the seen and the unseen. Liberal authenticity is a strategic centering of power.

Authenticity is a symptom of liberalism because, within liberalism, individuals are self-governing, self-regulating, and self-surveilling. This creates what Habermas calls the public sphere and, with it, the private sphere. Habermas writes that this private sphere is really a performative entity because its existence can only exist in relationship to the public. Privacy, and the authenticity that lives within privacy, is a performative element of public existence. Liberalism is a totalitarianism of private interests and private spaces. A liberal world is not a public world but a private one. A privatized world produces visibility through surveillance. There is no reality in a privatized world but only hyperreality, since finance is the only reality. Finance as hyperreality is a line of sight that orients everything toward power.

Aura

Sara Ahmed writes that whiteness is an orientation. Ahmed examines Husserl's statement that "if we consider the characteristic way in which the Body presents itself and do the same for things, then we find the following situation: each Ego has its own domain of perceptual things and necessarily perceives the things in a certain orientation," and in response she postulates that whiteness is a way of perceiving abstract and material objects as behind the times, as progressive, as on top, as below, and as sidelined. Orientations, to Ahmed, are about backgrounding and foregrounding. To orient yourself to a certain perspective means you consider some things to be subjects and other things to be objects. Relating Frantz Fanon to whiteness as an orientation, Ahmed writes that Fanon shows the body in the moment when it is "made black by becoming the object of the hostile white gaze." Fanon begins this passage by writing, "And then the occasion arose when I had to meet the white man's eyes." In this passage, Fanon constructs a scene in which the white gaze is the subject that makes Fanon into an object.

In Foucault's famous passage about the panopticon or inspection house in *Discipline and Punish,* he traces what he calls the modern disciplinary society through the architecture of an asylum. The panopticon prison is a series of cells constructed in a circular shape, all of which face the middle of the fortress. In the middle of the circle is an extended surveillance tower. Foucault writes that because the cells within a panopticon are constantly visible to the tower, but there is no way for someone within the cells to tell whether there is someone inside the tower, the architecture is able to create an omnipotence of surveillance in which prisoners understand that they might be observed at all times, even if there is never any actual guard within the tower.

Benedict Anderson describes in his book *Imagined Communities* how the nationalisms of the third world and the former European colonies were originally cultivated by colonial powers, specifically through educational and administrative policies. The colonies, which were carved out according to European contact, were not responsive to preexisting differences in language, culture, or geography. The lines that European powers drew in the colonial world frequently divided communities into pieces and reorganized them under colonial names. Colonial subjects, who were often described as "Indigenous" or "native," were contrasted with "nationals," who could only be imperialists. However, as Anderson writes, "the late-nineteenth-century empires were too large and too far-flung to be ruled by a handful of nationals."

In the late nineteenth century, colonial schools and maps became increasingly standardized. Students no longer studied in their local villages but were sent to cultural centers of power, where they pursued a Western higher education. The colonies were encouraged to develop a unique national identity fostered by the emerging local intelligentsia. Through colonial education, "natives . . . could come to see themselves as 'national,'" Anderson says. As Anderson writes, "the expansion of the colonial state which, so to speak, invited 'natives' into [the] schools and offices" became the bureaucratic colonial state. Colonial powers cultivated a sense of nationalism within their colonies, which originally did not identify themselves through nation-states, in order to better manage their power. Thus, third-world nationalism oriented former colonies to their colonizers through the construction of cultural centers of power. As Altaf Gouhar put it, under third-world nationalism, "It did not take long for the people to discover that all that had been changed was the color of their masters. . . . For the masses the achievement of independence was the end of their struggle and also the end of their dreams."

In other words, the third-world nationalism that American imperialism is often tasked with controlling does not develop naturally and spontaneously. Rather, nationalism was cultivated within the colonies by their colonial masters through the orientation of the country toward urban centers through which foreign capital flowed. These new orientations to geopolitical power were then mapped by the colonizers so that every street and village could be surveyed through an omnipotent and all-seeing eye.

Surveillance is not neutral. Some gazes, when they see a thing, make it more real than other gazes. The gaze is a colonial encounter. Surveillance is the act of making things real by looking at them through white gazes and male gazes. These gazes are eyes from which rays of sight extend outwards.

The British empire was often imagined through the Sun. The British empire was a place upon which the Sun would never set. Japan, after Westernizing during the Meiji era, was also described through images of the Sun. Both empires used the Sun to describe empire as a thing that emanates outward. Both saw their empires as multicultural. Empires see themselves as the organizers of multiculturalism. The British empire saw themselves as the organizers of a multicultural empire that ranged from the Pacific Islands to the Americas. Japan described their nation-state as multicultural, with Chinese, Korean, and Russian influences. As a multicultural nation-state, Japan saw itself as uniquely positioned to unify Asia and bring it into modernity. The American empire, too, describes itself as a multicultural empire and often propagates images of "good" multiculturalism next to images of "bad" Indigenous ethnic purity. All empires, including ancient Persia and Rome, have described themselves as multicultural.

Multiculturalism is not neutral. Multicultural empires exist at the expense of Indigenous sovereignty. "Natives" cannot be multicultural, while "nationals" can. The multicultural empire is oriented toward power. Multicultural empires often frame power as representational while simultaneously wielding power through surveillance. Multiculturalism, because it describes difference in terms of race, is also a theater game that is controlled by its orientation toward the white gaze because race is a vocabulary of being controlled by white power. Visibility as power, or race, reveals some things while hiding others. Race orients the world toward the white male gaze. As in Foucault's panopticon, these gazes are lines of sight that are imagined to emanate from cultural centers of power but often control events even when the surveillance towers are empty. Fanon "had to meet the white man's eyes." Colonial subjects are trained by colonizers to see themselves through the eyes of the colonizer—as "nationals" rather than "natives." These "nationals" orient the former colonies to the West and toward modernity.

Why do people describe themselves as "nationals" instead of as "natives"? Why do countries perform good multicultural nationalism on the international stage rather than bad indigeneity? Why do countries sell their land and labor to wealthy Western corporations in order to raise their economic standing? Why do we orient ourselves to the white gaze?

When people orient themselves to power, they are not only orienting themselves to capital but also to the *future*. The Sun is a chariot that moves in a circle, representing time. Heaven is a future utopia. The Sun projects power by dreaming of future utopias, future Elysiums, and future heavens. In finance, the future is not only abstract but also material. Debord writes that the visibility engineered by orientations toward power in spectacular societies are "actual" and "materially translated." The finance world literally trades "futures." Futures are traded when investors decide whether the future viability of a thing—whether that thing is a person, a land, or a community—exists. Crops are traded as futures before seeds are even planted. Businesses prove their economic viability, or future, before they manufacture a single product. Capital is not just a hyperreal object; it is also an object that becomes real in the future. Objects that cannot be realized by capital—objects that are not hyperreal—are also objects that have no future. We have futures when we have capital, and when we do not have capital, our futures are also at risk. "At risk" youth are also youth whose futures are neglected by capital. Because it is often impossible to imagine a future without capitalism, it is also impossible to imagine our own futures without capital.

In 2018, Douglas Rushoff wrote an article about an experience he had when five of the world's richest people paid him six figures to talk to them about the future. These five men were primarily concerned with questions of how they would retain an armed security force when money becomes obsolete: "How do I maintain author-ity over my security force after the event?" Rushoff writes that "the future became less a thing we create through our present-day choices or hopes for humankind than a predestined scenario we bet on with our venture capital but arrive at passively" and that "for all their wealth and power, they don't believe they can affect the future." For all of the wealth and power that the world's five rich-est men have, they don't believe they have the power to affect the future. We don't feel like we have the power to imagine a future that is not also oriented toward capital.

These five richest men don't have the power to affect the future because they're just five men. When capital becomes obsolete, people affect the future. Five men are not people. They're afraid of *us*.

Neoliberals are concerned with liberty. Conversative neoliber-als are concerned with free markets, and liberal neoliberals with freedom of choice. Freedom is the power to imagine the future. The astrological Sun, imbued with this power, is Fate. Fate, like finance, is an abstract utopia that liberates the world from its material con-straints. Fate is the power to describe the future. In a neoliberal world, capital realizes things that orient themselves to the white, male gaze while concealing and erasing things that cannot be real-ized by the white, male gaze. Things become real when they realize capital; things are unreal when they do not. Unreal things are not seen to control Fate and exist without futures. However, it is pre-cisely the unrealized things that sometimes affect the future.

2

ETYMOLOGY OF THE MOON

Coinage, Metallics, and Luminance

The origin of money is religious. Herman Borisonik writes that the original purpose of money was not for exchange, or even barter, but as "a means of repaying debt between men and gods." The first banks were temples, where sacred gold was stored. The temple was also the commerce center of the city, where merchants and sex workers clustered. If Saturn is the (agri)cultural arts, then coinage is the fabricating arts.

Coinage has always had a relationship with the luminaries in the sky. Gold was attributed to the Sun, while silver was attributed to the Moon. The royal metals projected royal authority, influencing socioeconomics and politics. In the Roman Empire, the minting of both gold and silver were the exclusive right of the emperor. Both the Sun and Moon, then, are projections of power, specifically monarchical power. Only copper coins (Mercury) were controlled by the Senate and local authorities in the provinces and towns.

Before the Middle Ages, the precious metals that represented the luminaries functioned in different ways in Greek and Roman societies. Before ancient Greece, gold and silver were primarily stored in the temples and not circulated. Instead, the luminous metals, because they were precious, were used to measure value, while everyday transactions depended mostly on credit. In Egypt, every merchant had a copper coil that they measured credit by. Money itself was an imaginary system of accounts that, every so often and due to rebellions, the king would clear by forgiving all debts. Royal mercy was built on accumulation—the act of holding onto a lot of gold and silver but almost never spending it.

The Greek and Roman empires differentiated themselves from earlier ones by building an economy dependent on slave labor and mining for luminous metals. Because citizenship in Greek and Roman society was seen as inherently oppositional to slavery, these empires had to keep conquering neighboring lands to maintain a steady supply of foreign workers used to mine for streams of silver. Children of slaves born within the empire became citizens, and the constantly dwindling population of slaves meant that more and more foreigners had to be conquered. Before ancient empires, money was credit and was unattached to metallics. Within the empires, money became precious metals that were mined out of the ground—a process that created a specific social hierarchy in which citizens were represented and foreigners were exploited.

In the Middle Ages, much of the gold was hoarded by the church, and the people returned to using mostly invisible accounts of credit. If gold is a metaphor for the Sun, or God, then God's power was guarded by the church. However, local kings in their independent domains were allowed to mint silver coins. Silver, a lunar metal, became more representative of local means to control the economy, while gold became once again sacrosanct, much as it had been before Greek and Roman times. However, both metals were still considered royal. All coins, like the coins of ancient Greece that bore the symbols of gods, bore images of kings, even if they were not of royal origin and were only used in specific cities. If the Sun, and gold, stood for God's power, then the Moon, and silver, stood for local power.

Medieval Europe developed a fetishistic relationship to coins. The word "fetish," according to Charles de Brosses, has an etymological origin linked to "enchantment, with amulets, or other objects possessed by superhuman, sacred forces." Part of this influence was Islamic. "It is clear that the great contribution of the early medieval Muslim world to the history of magic is the concept that the power of celestial bodies could be drawn down ritually into material objects, fashioned of suitable materials and inscribed with appropriate signs," writes Ronald Hutton. "We still preserve the distinctive Arabic word for these objects: talismans." Alternatively, Giorgio Agamben attributes the etymology of the word "fetish" to the Latin verb *facere,* which meant to fabricate. In use, fabrication, such as the painting crafts, was considered to be more fictional than the productive arts, which linked culture to agriculture.

Thus, the significance of coins to the lords, merchants, and peasantry of the Middle Ages was at once linked to their royal power, a foreign magic, and a fictional production. Alchemy tried to create gold at a time when it was believed that God's power resided in the metal itself, not just due to the political authority of the Church. Alchemy attempted to use the powers of fabrication to invoke and provoke the institution.

Because money was a fabrication, it was seen as having a type of value that had no prestige. The possession of money was respected far less than the ownership of land. Saturn, ruler of carbon and black soil, had sole domain over the real source of any wealth: the land. For the Greeks, land as property was distinguished from all other types of property because land was the only possession that granted its master citizenship. For the Romans and the Germans, land was never a private possession, because landownership was never a matter of buying but of inheritance. The ownership of land was not given to those with money; it was given to those who had earned a special importance within the community. Landownership was the membership of an individual in his larger community or clan as well as his continuity with his ancestors, rather than a matter of individual accumulation. Ownership of land was always a social dignity. If possession of land is a matter of state authorization, and sovereignty can only come from the state, then the possession of money did not necessitate the same relationship to government, community, and citizenship. Thus, the French sayings Marx quotes in volume I of *Capital:* "No land is without its lord," and "money has no master."

A Note about Gender

Within Hellenistic astrology, the Moon had another meaning besides the market. The waning and waxing of the Moon symbolically stood for pregnancy. The Moon in Babylon was thought of as a triplicity, and the positions of the crescent, full, and new moons symbolized gods who reigned under the earth, along its horizon, and from high above. The lunar gods who ruled these three celestial zones were Ea, Anu, and Enlil. The Greeks and Romans adopted the Mesopotamian practice of imagining the Moon as a triplicity but imagined a trio of female goddesses rather than male gods. Artemis, the virgin, stood for the crescent moon; Diana, the married or conjugated goddess, for the full moon; and Hecate, the old woman or witch, for the new moon. A full lunar cycle stood for sexual life, beginning from youth and wildness, culminating with the union of adulthood, and ending with the darkness and mystery of the darkest kind of night. The cycles of the Moon, which average twenty-eight days in length, also align with menstruation and seem to link the Moon with female reproduction.

It is important to note that, while it may seem that the Moon is implicitly linked to femininity on account of the timing of its cycle, the Moon's construction as a feminine symbol is only made explicit within modernity. Modern analysts and neopagans, such as Carl Jung and Robert Graves, write of the Moon as the Triple Goddess. Jung described the Triple Goddess as a Maiden, a Mother, and a Crone. Graves writes in his book *The White Goddess,* published in 1948, that "as the New Moon or Spring she was a girl; as the Full Moon or Summer she was woman; as the Old Moon or Winter she was hag."

While the Romans may have represented the Moon as a Triple Goddess, the meanings of these goddesses were inferred from the male gods Ea, Anu, and Enlil. The new moon was linked to the Underworld not because of the modern associations we might have with crones, hags, or old women being witches; rather, it was because Romans and Mesopotamians were aware that, during a new moon, the moon shifts to the other side of the earth at night and is literally positioned underneath the ground. The new moon was Enlil, who lived under the earth. The crescent moon moves along its path close to the horizon and symbolizes the emergence of the material world. The full moon is the most sunlike moon as this moon is stationed up above. The Moon, then, prior to modernity, derives its meaning *solely from the basis of its relation to the ground.*

While the Sun was always associated with abstract Fate, the Moon was always associated with material Fortune. While solar Fate ruled over invisible forces such as political power, philosophical oration, and sight itself, lunar Fortune ruled over everything material, including the physical body, cultivation of the land, and material wealth. While this binary between abstraction and materiality is gendered, the Moon's Fortune could also be represented by male gods rather than female goddesses. When the Egyptian astrologer Rhetorius writes that "the Moon is the Fortune of us all," he is saying that everything manifests through lunar Fortune because we are bound to a material existence. We all have a body. The materiality of the Moon was not seen through modern concepts of womanhood, fertility, and reproductive labor but rather through the concept of Fortune. This means that the dynamics between Fate and Fortune often conflict with modern sensibilities concerning gender, and those gender sensibilities cannot be relied on to analyze the Sun and the Moon. For example, in contrast to what modern sensibilities about gender and labor might assume, Romans saw stonemasons as more lunar (and more feminine) than poets because stonemasons work with material, while poets work with abstraction.

When thinking about the Moon, it is important to not begin with modern myths about femininity. The myths about femininity as we understand it now did not exist before modernity. Analysts who looked for a primordial womb within the Moon, such as Jung or Graves, were responding to the perceived loss of cultural inheritance as a result of industrialization. Only in industrial societies is femininity perceived to be more archaic than masculinity. Only after industrialization does lunar imagery become strongly associated not only with Fortune and materiality but especially with womanhood and reproductive labor. Before industrialization, the Moon stands for markets, borders, and foreigners. The association between the Moon and reproductive labor within modernity, as we will see, does not bypass the Moon's association to materiality and the market; rather, it travels to diversely gendered bodies through the market. The type of reproduction that the Moon stands for is not a gender but a type of labor. The Moon is a body thing, and genders don't come from bodies but from social agreements. While the concept of Fortune was gendered, it did not describe gender as sociopolitical identity as Venus might but rather as an economic entity. The contrast between Fate and Fortune applies to all life forms, not only human ones, and these materials move across the world through the market.

Moon Merchants

In contrast to Saturn's ideal of property ownership and immobile wealth, the Moon was associated with mobile wealth. It is wealth that the owner can flee with if necessary.

From Roman times and into modernity, the Moon was associated with mercenaries. Mercenaries traveled by water, which is controlled by the Moon, and they had to keep their noses finely attuned to the changing trends and appetites of the times, always responding to the market to bring new items to the table. Their rapid movements were compared to the always-changing faces of the Moon. Merchants were seen as untrustworthy and as having duplicitous faces, because of their lack of commitment to any one community. If the Moon pulls the tides, it also rules the markets. Paul Virilio writes that "the first marketplace was the beach. The Phoenicians pass by in boats (same thing for caravans), they leave an object on the beach, and later they come back to see if anyone has taken it, if anyone has put something else in its place." The astrological Moon has always stood for the commercial market, which resided along capital's fringes, near riverbanks, where mercenary boats could come and go.

This association between mercenaries and duplicity is deep and old. In 1610, the playwrights Thomas Dekker and John Webber wrote, "He that would grow damn'd rich, yet live secure/Must keep a case of face[s]." This case of face(s), which allowed the emerging middle class of the time to sell goods at different prices to different buyers, came directly from the association between the seller and the moon—that thing in the sky that shows us a subtly different face every night. Richard Campbell writes in *The London Tradesmen* in 1747 that a merchant must be "a perfect Proteus, change Shapes as often as the Moon, and still find something new" to keep with the "continual Flux and reflux of Fashion."

The Moon, then, and the merchant with it, was the original two-face. The merchant is a circulator of goods, buying items from one region and representing them in a new way in a cultural context unfamiliar with the production of the item. Merchants do not produce commodities, but they do produce race and exoticism. P. T. Barnum, who traveled with a collection of freaks, displayed a "Feejee" (Fiji) mermaid and a Black woman whom he claimed to be

George Washington's wet nurse. In his cabinet of curiosities he displayed what he called "Circassian girls"—a race thought to embody pure, white beauty—who were actually mixed-race women.

Georg Simmel, a Jewish scholar living in the Weimar Republic, writes of this association between the social outsider and trade: "The basic interest in money expresses itself first and foremost in trade. For good reason, the trader is usually a stranger at the beginning of economic development." He goes on to say that "the role that the stranger plays within a social group directs him, from the outset, toward relations with the group that are mediated by money, above all because of the transportability and the extensive usefulness of money outside the boundaries of the group." Simmel finds a historical basis for the connection between money and the political outsider in Rome:

> *The emancipated Roman slaves were predisposed towards monetary transactions because they lacked any chance of achieving complete citizen status. Already in Athens, at the very inception of pure monetary transactions in the fourth century, the wealthiest banker, Pasion, had started his career as a slave. In Turkey the Armenians, a despised and often persecuted people, are frequently merchants and moneylenders, as, under similar circumstances, were the Moors in Spain. In India these circumstances are a frequent occurrence. On the one hand, the socially oppressed and yet cautiously advancing Parsee are mostly money-changers or bankers, while on the other hand in some parts of southern India, money business and wealth are in the hands of the Chetty, a mixed caste, who, because of imperfect caste purity, have less prestige. Similarly, the Huguenots in France, like the Quakers in England, applied themselves with the greatest intensity to money acquisition because of their exposed and restricted position. To exclude someone in principle from the acquisition of money is almost impossible because all possible paths constantly lead to it. . . .*
>
> *Dispersed peoples, crowded into more or less closed cultural circles, can hardly put down roots or find a free position in production. They are therefore dependent on intermediate trade which is much more elastic*

than primary production, since the sphere of trade can be expanded almost limitlessly by merely formal combinations and can absorb people from outside whose roots do not lie in the group.

Because strangers are socially excluded from obtaining citizenship, holding office, and owning land, money and commercial activities became the means for strangers to achieve some influence. Moreover, because the mercenary is often a stranger, the market became the means through which exotic objects were introduced into a community, and exoticism became defined. The Moon is the market, and the market is the foreign. Money, far from being neutral, is actually an inherently antinationalist symbol of exchange. The interests of money work to redefine those of the nation.

Within settler colonialism, the dichotomy between who was allowed to settle and who was considered to be transient was decided upon by race. Indigenous Americans, Africans, Mexicans, Chinese, and Irish bond laborers (up to a certain period) were legally considered to be transients. Transiency, the legal status of not belonging somewhere, was punishable by law in the 1800s. Only white Americans were legally allowed to settle in early American history—to exist in a space without the fear of being criminalized and incarcerated. The condition of enslavement was especially related to strangeness. As Achille Mbembe writes, "concerning the law, slaves occupied the position of the foreigner within a society of fellow humans."

In her book *Living a Feminist Life,* Sara Ahmed writes about her education of the stranger. Because Ahmed attended a predominantly white institution, she was taught to protect herself from stranger danger along with her fellow classmates. Later, when Ahmed is parked in a suburban neighborhood in her car, she has an experience where a police officer asks her whether she is Aborginal or if she "just has a tan." Ahmed writes that, in that moment, the officer was really asking Ahmed whether she is a stranger. Ahmed defines the stranger as "not simply those we do not recognize" but as those "who we recognize as strangers, not only those you do not know but those you should not know." The stranger is a racialized thing. Under white patriarchal capitalism, the strange is a *familiar* figure: "The stranger becomes a container of fear."

Cancer, Carnage, Cockaigne

Trigger warning: this section contains dehumanizing language, sexual fetishization, and descriptions of white on Black cannibalism.

In the myth of Saturn and Jupiter, during Jupiter's exile he was nursed to a supernatural strength by his foster mother Amalthea, the nurturing goddess. Amalthea was a goat goddess with two horns, and she was the Greek version of older mother archetypes. One day, while playing, Jupiter accidentally broke off one of her horns, and this horn became the cornucopia, a mythological object from which a never-ending flow of abundance and nourishment spilled.

The Moon is always interpreted through Saturn, and vice versa. Not only do their movements in the sky parallel one another (a twenty-eight year cycle for Saturn and a twenty-eight day cycle for the moon), but they have rulership over oppositional signs—Cancer and Capricorn. In contrast to Saturn's capricious and stingy rule over nature, the cornucopia generously provides an abundance that never keeps score of what has been given. Like the crab (the Moon rules Cancer), the cornucopia has a hard shell and yummy insides.

Because Saturn often stands for a time and place located before history, Saturn is prehistorical. If Saturn is defined by the mythological golden age that came before the metals and races degenerated, then the Moon is defined by the mythological Land of Cockaigne. Cockaigne, which was not a real place but one that showed up in medieval poetry, was as much a dystopia as a utopia. It was a land of abundance frequently represented by the cornucopia, which the peasant yearned for during scarce times. It was also a land of grotesque abundance—a critique of human vices.

Not only was Cockaigne a land where "roasted pigs wander about with knives in their backs to make carving easy, where grilled geese fly directly into one's mouth, where cooked fish jump out of the water and land at one's feet" (according to Herman Pleij); it was also a place where normative power dynamics reversed themselves. Monks beat abbots, women dominated men, nuns were sexually licentious, and the last runner to cross the finish line in a race was the winner. Cockaigne differs from Saturnalia in its perversity. While the golden age is imagined as an original perfection that precedes degeneracy, Cockaigine had a connection with savagery. The reversals of power in Cockaigne were reacted to with as much revulsion as desire, since they represented the consequences of moral degeneracy. While Saturn's golden age was a utopia, Cockaigne, as a celebration of the grotesque, was a dystopia.

Historian Peter Burke writes that "Cockaigne is a vision of life as one long Carnival, and Carnival is a temporary Cockaigne with the same emphasis of eating and reversals." The European tradition of Carnival, which has its root in the word *carne,* or flesh, happens right before Lent and is a reaction against asceticism. During Carnival, foods prohibited during Lent are consumed in excess, and traditional gender roles are subverted in theatrical games. Masks are worn, not to hide one's face, but to transform the entire community into a game of theater. In contrast to the Saturnalia, which was celebrated by Roman senators, Carnival was for the peasants.

In 1869, Charles Baudelaire retells the story of Cockaigne in his prose poem, "The Invitation to the Voyage," beginning the poem with:

> *It is a superb land, a country of Cockaigne, as they say, that I dream of visiting with an old friend. A strange land, drowned in our northern fogs, that one might call the East of the West, the China of Europe; a land patiently and luxuriously decorated with the wise, delicate vegetations of a warm and capricious fantasy.*
>
> *A true land of Cockaigne, where all is beautiful, rich, tranquil, and honest; where luxury is pleased to mirror itself in order; where life is*

opulent, and sweet to breathe; from whence disorder, turbulence, and the
unforeseen are excluded; where happiness is married to silence; where
even the food is poetic, rich and exciting at the same time; where all
things, my beloved, are like you.

    Do you know that feverish malady that seizes hold of us in our cold
miseries; that nostalgia of a land unknown; that anguish of curiosity?
It is a land which resembles you, where all is beautiful, rich, tranquil,
and honest, where fantasy has built and decorated an occidental China,
where life is sweet to breathe, and happiness married to silence. It is there
that one would live; there that one would die.

The poem ends with:

These treasures, furnishings, luxury, order, perfumes, and miraculous
flowers, are you. You again are the great rivers and calm canals. The
enormous ships drifting beneath their loads of riches, and musical with
the sailors' monotonous song, are my thoughts that sleep and stir upon
your breast. You take them gently to the sea that is Infinity, reflecting the
profundities of the sky in the limpid waters of your lovely soul; and when,
outworn by the surge and gorged with the products of the Orient, the
ships come back to the ports of home, they are still my thoughts, grown
rich, that have returned to you from Infinity.

This "China of Europe" or "occidental China," is the mythological land that resides only within an European poetic tradition.
The Asia that Baudelaire speaks of is not the real Asia but the fantastical Asia within European imagination. Baudelaire is not the
only literary figure who describes this imaginary Asia ironically.
Oscar Wilde, writing about Japan, asks: "Do you really imagine
that the Japanese people, as they are presented to us in art, have
any existence? . . . If you do, you have never understood Japanese
art at all. . . . The Japanese people are the deliberate self-conscious
creation of certain individual artists. . . . The whole of Japan is
a pure invention. There is no such country, there are no such
people."

For Baudelaire and Wilde, China and Japan are fantasy lands. These fantasy lands are not located outside of Europe at all. Rather, they live within Western minds and even within Western landscapes. Wilde writes that "the Japanese people are, as I have said, simply a mode of style, an exquisite fancy of art. And so, if you desire to see a Japanese effect, you will stay at home, and steep yourself in the work of certain Japanese artists and then, when you have absorbed the spirit of their style, and caught their imaginative manner of vision, you will go some afternoon and sit in the Park or stroll down Piccadilly, and if you cannot see an absolutely Japanese effect there, you will not see it anywhere." When Baudelaire finishes his poem by evoking traditional lunar imagery of ships and ports, he is referring not to an Orient that actually exists but an Orient that the West encounters—an Orient wrapped up in older, Western associations between material generosity, the market, and duplicity.

Baudelaire's Cockaigne is Shangri-la. Shangri-la, materially abundant and exotic, is a fantastical place rather than a real one, where hordes of Asian sex workers with strange faces and names are open and available for business with European clientele. It is a place where anyone can become rich, provided that they are white, or can at least go home with an excellent story to tell of some wild escapade, a place where sexual codes are liberated and the land is open to be plundered. Shangri-la is more than just the Asia of Western imagination, replete with mixed cultural elements from all over Asia. It is Asia, with silk, tea, and ink—Asia as abbreviation for the market itself.

Not only was the Carnival a celebration of life and Cockaigne; it was also a flesh festival that aimed local aggression toward political outsiders, such as nearby Jews. When charged with usury, the making of bad money debts, local medieval lords often pointed to what they called "their Jews" or Jews under their so-called protection. While most of the bad moneylenders were actually not Jewish, and Jews themselves were excluded from most realms of business, lords used Jews as scapegoats for their own predatory lending prac-tices. In this way, Jews and the foreigner became synonymous with bad debt and the tricky quality of money. By the nineteenth cen-tury, Jews were not only seen as owners of money but as synony-mous with money itself and responsible for the economic crisis, social alienation, and loss of tradition that resulted from industri-alization. Iyko Day writes in her book *Alien Capital* that "Jews not only were identified with money but became a personification of the destructive nature and abstract domination of capital."

Money, like the foreigner, is a story. Simmel writes that money, like the foreigner, is something that is "never completely unreal and never completely realized." Because the foreigner is always some-one who is unknowable but is knowable in that unknowability, they are the story that tells itself, or the symbol that stands for itself. Money is a metaphor for the foreigner because money is used in the exchange between the known and the unknown. It is the sign that becomes emancipated from representation. If money is a symbol, it is one that mediates relationships between the familiar and the foreign—the imagined and the unimaginable. Money is a theater.

Cockaigne was an anthropological feast. What is consumed in Cockaigne is not only food but also ethnicity. Americans literally consumed Black people in the 1800s. As Vincent Woodards writes in *The Delectable Negro: Human Consumption and Homoeroticism within US Slave Culture,* "the social consumption of the enslaved person was such a concern in the colonial United States that sena-tors, religious leaders, and abolitionists heatedly debated whether America was becoming something akin to a cannibal nation." Woodards archives histories in which white people literally ate Black people: the white plantation owner Lilburn Lewis quartered and cooked the enslaved person George, whites boiled the body of Nat Turner and ate it, and those on the *Essex* whaleship killed and ate their Black shipmates. In many modern astrology books, the Moon is linked to hunger, needs, and consumption. However, the consumption that is associated with the Moon is not an apolitical eating but the consumption of the social other. It is ethnic consumption—what Maria Thereza Alves and other postmodern scholars call the anthropological feast.

In her essay "Cannibalism in Brazil since 1500," Alves asks, in the anthropological feast, who is eating who? In the fifteenth century, Germans depicted Jews as cannibals, specifically in the murder of Simon Trent. Early American settlers depicted Indigenous people as cannibals, and the name of Shakespeare's character Caliban even comes from the word *cannibal*. In a reckoning with the cannibalism found in Brazil, Alves writes that "Euro-Brazilians' continuous fascination with cannibalism might perhaps be a subconscious acknowledgement of the genocide committed in Brazil against the native population. If you consider who is eating who, the level of cannibalization was astounding."

For both Alves and Woodard, the white consumption of Black flesh is both organized and institutionally sustained. When Lilburn Lewis' wife asks him where the screams she heard on the evening he ate George came from, he answered that "he had never enjoyed himself so well *at a ball* as he had enjoyed himself that evening." A "ball," from the Italian *ballo,* is a public-facing formal dance originally done in a court, where elite members of society performed for one another and for those who bought tickets that allowed them to watch. In other words, Lewis sees his own cannibalism as a public spectacle—as an act that aligns his private desires with public feelings around eroticism, play, and appetite. The anthropological feast is not a private act of consumption hidden from the public but an eating that happens in the public. White appetites—social, sexual, and physical—work as public theater.

In his book *Bunk,* Kevin Young writes that both the modern and the romantic hoax are scripted and coded realities. The script of the hoax is as follows: it begs to be caught, denies, redirects, then excuses itself as irony. In the final stage, the hoax is confessed to, frequently in the form of a long autobiographical memoir, and the confession of the hoax is just as cathartic as the hoax itself. Even when the hoax is revealed, it continues to go viral. As lovers of the hoax, we want to be duped. We continue to spread stories that we know to be false even when, or especially when, it is revealed that they are fabrications.

Young goes on to write that the codes that create the hoax are limited. These social codes always exaggerate or exasperate assumptions around race and gender:

"For the hoax, the symbolic 'store' is the stock set of images, race and gender stereotypes, grotesque and fake horrors, that get returned to again and again. . . . British and American, such archetypes enact racial and sexual, if not violent, fantasies. . . . The hoax is rather a kind of coded confession, revealing not only a deep-seated cultural wish but also a common set of themes—or feints or strategies—that add up to a ritual. This is why we often are not just fooled, but made fools of, by the hoax—indicated by its revelations, not of what's true but of what we truly believe."

Race is a hoax. It is a "coded confession" that makes us into fools, enacting fantasies and revealing what we believe in. Race, which began as a state of criminalized transiency or strangeness, is not attached to any biological reality but is an economic fiction. Like money, race is "never completely unreal and never completely realized." Racialization is not a real state of existence but a game of theater controlled by white people. Racialization is social consumption. To live as a racialized person is to live within a white capitalist patriarchy in which your safety and sanctity are perpetually threatened by the race play of those who have comfort. It is to be flesh that is always being eaten.

The Global Market

The story of the global market begins with silver. Silver was the first global currency. It was mined from the Americas by Indigenous and Black slaves. Before the plantation, mining was the basis of the American economy. The mining industries created what would become industrialized slavery. The silver mined out of the Americas first went to Europe, which used it to trade with China. Most of the silver in the global market ended up in China, since Chinese emperors did not recognize any other currency as money. Until the Opium Wars, China would control 30 percent of the world's silver.

Plotemy describes the Moon as a sinister planet. The word *sinister* means left-handed. On a natal chart, which is the way most early civilizations oriented themselves, left is east. Another word for "eastern" is *Oriental*. If the Moon is sinister, then it is also Oriental. Silver, as the Moon's metal, became associated with the global market but also with the Orient. If Orientalism is not only an institutional orientation but also an economic one, then the Orient stands for the global market for the European imagination, and silver becomes its mediator.

In the 1600s, Britain, Portugal, France, and the United States replaced silver as the currency that mediated East-West relations with opium. In India poppy was grown as a cash crop (at the expense of land used to grow food, which resulted in mass famine for Indians) and used to manufacture opium, and it was sold illegally in China. Efforts to enforce China's ban on opium resulted in the Opium Wars. As a result of the opium trade, a large portion of the silver that ended up in China from global trade went back to Europe. Later, in the 1930s, more of the silver in China would flow to the United States when Roosevelt supported policies proposed by the "strong silver" coalition. These silver speculators wanted to raise the value of silver, so they encouraged Roosevelt to buy silver at a high price point. At the time, Asian countries used silver as their national currencies. Silver was so associated with Asia that Milton Friedman would write that "silver is the money of all Asia."

Because silver was cheaper and less stable than gold, it became closely linked to speculation. William L. Silber writes in *The Story*

of Silver: How the White Metal Shaped America and the Modern World
that the history of silver is also the history of speculation. Both
Jewish and Asian people have been associated with alien capital.
As the *Atlantic Monthly* declared in 1900: "No Jew can smell out with
keener instinct an opportunity where money can be made to grow
than can a Chinaman." Because silver is associated with speculation, it acts as a dream agent within the world of abstract capital.
When the value of silver went up, silver was smuggled out of Asia
and into the United States. Silver coins stamped with Sun Yat-sen's
image were melted and processed into silver nitrate, which was
used then to make film.

There is a dreamlike quality to the way we imagine the Moon.
While the Sun's rays of light clarify and cleanse, the rays of the Moon
disturb and distort. The Moon promotes unclear visions and fits of
lunacy. This dreamlike quality arises from the relationship between
the West and the foreign, which is mediated by hallucinations, opium,
and film. In her essay "Shine: On Race, Glamour, and the Modern,"
Anne Anlin Cheng finds that yellow women are perceived to be
"gleaming," "golden," "chromatic," "metallic," and "inorganic" when
they are depicted on film. The woman of color is a metallic woman.
Her flesh is inhuman or subhuman. She becomes imbued with the
qualities of silver and other metals that have monetary value.

The Moon is the body. The body isn't just a physical thing but
an imagined thing. The Moon is the somatic body. As Kyla Schumer
writes, some bodies are perceived to be, and because of that perception, are experienced as being more vulnerable than other bodies.
White bodies are perceived to be and are experienced as being
more vulnerable than other bodies. White bodies are deemed to be
impressionable, sensitive to the effects of contaminating influences
or foreign elements, and in need of protection.

The somatic body, which is the Moon, is an imagined thing
and a political reality. We all have wounds on our somatic bodies.
These wounds are inflicted by institutions, states, and communities.

Because these wounds anticipate losses or pain, our somatic bodies sometimes react to imagined and political realities. The Moon—the celestial one—is deeply scarred. While Cheng specifically studies film depictions of women of color, the bodies of people of color of all genders are perceived to be resistant or hardened, in contrast to the vulnerable white body. Even though the bodies of people of color are represented as metallic or gleaming, as seeming to resist everything including light, we experience our somatic bodies as scarred. We react to old, ancestral wounds.

The somatic body is race. The somatic body, as a set of reactions and responses to political and social triggers, is race as a body. Somatic bodies carry our histories of pain, which feel very, very heavy. Race is a fiction—a theater controlled by white power. The way that women of color are staged as inhuman and metallic within film is a fiction. However, race has real consequences for real bodies, and somatic bodies produce biological consequences upon biological bodies. While the white woman's reproductive power is protected and accounted for within the nuclear family, the woman of color's reproductive power is compared to economic factors and to profit—accounted for as population.

Mbembe writes that colonization alienates the colonizer from other bodies because the colonizer sees their own body as living and the bodies of others as things: "Colonizing broadly consisted in a permanent work of separation: on one side, my living body; on the other, all those 'body-things' surrounding it; on one side, my human flesh, through which all those other 'flesh-things' and 'flesh-meats' exist for me." He also writes that people of color are often accounted for en masse, as great weights and burdens. Antoine de Montchrestien wrote in the seventeenth century in colonial France that "a large number of men who live in idleness here, and represent a weight, a burden and do not relate to this kingdom." By calling people of color "a weight," Montchrestian implies that racialized people are not people but things—weighted, measured, and stocked.

Within the race theater of white capitalist patriarchy, women of color do not produce living bodies when they reproduce but body-things that amount to great masses that weigh and burden society. These body-things (children) must, in the words of Monstchrestien, be "put to work," "removed from idleness," and made to produce "good merchandise." Not only is the flesh of the woman of color compared to gleaming silver; her offspring is compared with "good merchandise." Reproduction under colonialism likens the repro-ducing body to metal and the reproduced body to merchandise. The woman of color becomes a metaphor for the market. If silver is the Moon's metal because it is a signifier of the market, then bodies that also become signifiers of the market are represented as metal-lic. The Moon begins as the market and becomes the reproductive body through race theater. Reproduction under capitalism does not produce life but things.

The Interests of a People Possessed

Trigger warning: this section contains dehumanizing language, mentions slavery, and discusses sex work.

Deism, the Enlightenment theology that presupposed the alien-ation of God from the world, combined with Cartesian philosophy to imagine a world that works like a machine with all individual parts being alien and equal. The absence of God is really the absence of debt forgiveness, without which we rely only on the mercy of the creditor. Like an absent God believing the world will serve its own interests most efficiently without regulation or divine intervention, we put our faith in an economy that runs, like a perpetual-motion machine, automatically and on its own. Money is a machine. Under capitalism, we don't have faith in God; we have faith that money as a machine will continue to reproduce itself.

Aristotle once decreed that it is unnatural for money to create more money. Following a renewed attention to Aristotle in the revival of classical texts during the Renaissance, and under the influence of Al-Ghazalli and Ibn Sina, it became known that to treat money as a living thing, something that could bear fruit or offspring, was unnatural. Before industrialization, the central economic tension was between the debtor and the creditor, since peasants were kept in labor contracts due to their debts to their feudal lords. Interest on a loan was defined as thievery. It was understood that money, being inflexible due to its connection with gold and God, was not a productive power but an abstract one.

Usury, the loaning of money with interest, could only be committed against those who were foreign and with whom the lender has no kinship. Deuteronomy 23:20 decrees that "you may charge a foreigner interest, but not a fellow Israelite, so that the Lord your God may bless you in everything you put your hand to in the land you are entering to possess." When you use people as a means to extract profit, you are treating yourself as if you have no kinship.

The word for *interest* in most Mediterranean languages was the same as the word for *offspring*. The taboo on interest was also a moral cause because the growth of money was intrinsically tied to slavery for the ancient Greeks and Romans and for modern Europe. In Ireland, female slaves, or bondmaids, were actually a dominant currency used to appraise everyday exchanges, like gold or silver. David Graeber writes that when buying a woman, it is not the woman who is being bought but the right for the buyer to call her offspring his own. The growth of money through interest is an institution modeled on the owning of fertile bodies.

By 1748, Benjamin Franklin writes in his *Advice to a Young Tradesman* in complete contradiction of Aristotle's advice: "Remember, that money is of the prolific, generating nature. Money can beget money, and its offspring can beget more, and so on. . . . He that kills a breeding sow, destroys all her offspring to the thousandth generation. He that murders a crown, destroys all it might have produced, even scores of pounds."

It is clear, due to the context of writing in the United States, that Franklin was not talking about the sow breeding industry but human breeding, the slave economy being more integral to the formation of the United States than the sow economy. From this quotation, we can see that chattel slavery was not merely a labor force or even a market but an entire financial sector that changed the mechanism of money forever. The United States welcomed the growth of money through interest because it was a slave economy. In this sense, chattel slavery is responsible for modern investment, the independent financial sector, and the speculative market—the very idea that the market, like a living thing, will and should grow larger and more profitable naturally. Money's basic unit is that of the human body, and its growth potential relies on the exploitation of reproductive power. Thomas Jefferson, relating profitability to reproduction, was more candid than Franklin: "I consider the labor of a breeding woman as no object and that a child raised every two years is of more profit than the crop of the best laboring man."

But the incorporation of reproductive powers into the money economy was not natural or automatic. White people have enslaved their own for centuries, even in Aristotle's time, who was vehemently against the idea that money could breed itself like a crop or a cow could.

Slavery is not only the transformation of a human into an object but also the ripping away of an individual from their cultural context. Settlers chose to import labor from Africa rather than enslaving Indigenous Americans because it is impossible to enslave someone in their own home. For slavery to happen, home must be taken away. By taking children away from kinship networks, alienating parents from children, isolating prisoners from kin, and sterilizing prisoners, the prison-industrial complex destroys Black and brown communities and turns a social body situated for political power into one that can be exploited. In her essay "Slaying the Dream: The Black Family and the Crisis of Capitalism," Angela Davis outlines social programs that attempted to break Black families under the Reagan administration. In her analysis, she demonstrates how the ideal of a male supremacist nuclear family was detrimental to real communities that already existed.

In *Carceral Capitalism,* Jackie Wang explores the type of capitalism that the prison-industrial complex creates, from a propagandized science of race to a police state that exists to serve the financial sector. In comparison, the African kings who sold other Africans during the early days of the transatlantic slave trade used similar tactics of isolation and suppression. Local kings imposed severe punishments for small infractions so that offenders would be enslaved for minor misdemeanors. By using the justice system to service slavery and enforcing a highly surveilled police state, the kings of the seventeenth and eighteenth centuries alienated community members from one another. This made individuals vulnerable to penalization. For enslavement to occur, community and social relations must first be broken.

White reproduction is always situated within the nuclear family. Colonized reproduction is not framed as happening inside the protected space of the family but is instead accounted for as reproduction without kinship. Reproduction without kinship is not a natural state but a sociopolitical reality enforced by a police state that breaks up communal ties and social relations. Within this context, the white nuclear family is not only a buffered zone that seeks to protect itself from racialized others but also an active threat that destabilizes existing communities. Patriarchy, in the form of both the white family and the police state, destabilizes the connections and the power held between women of color.

The collision of biopower and machine manufactures financial power. The Moon, which originally stood for the market, is related to reproduction as profit. Money often has characteristics that make it behave as if it were a living thing. However, money is not a living thing but an abstract thing that exists within an industrialized reality. Money is only able to behave as if it were living when it appropriates reproductive—fucking, birthing, caring—power.

In the field of sex work, theorists and critics often find metaphors for the abuses of capitalism, exploitation, and the power dynamics that arrange social relations. However, sex work is not a metaphor. It is an institution that affects everyone. Sex works affects everyone's sex lives and economic lives.

Liberal critiques of sex work often frame it within questions relating to consent. Does a sex worker consent to work? These critiques ignore issues of consent within other industries. Does any worker consent to work? This happens because liberalism considers freedom in terms of choice. Many liberal critiques of sex work focus on the way sexual practices change when sex becomes work, as if there exists a mode of nonproductive sex that has not become work yet and as if sex work is a contained industry in which workers are paid for sex. This separation of sex from work is only possible when the sexual labor of fucking, birthing, and caring produces no value for the market. However, sex always produces value for the market. In this context, sex is any act that creates kinship. It is the work of fucking, birthing, and caring, though sex is still sex when it does not include all of the above. While the work of fucking, birthing, and caring are not counted in the production of GDP, value can only be produced when people fuck, birth, and care. Sex always produces value in some way or another. Sex as work is not a contained industry that anyone who does not consent to sexual exploitation can opt out of to seek nonexploitative sex. Rather, sex enacted under capitalism is often work whether it is paid or not.

Sex work not only changes the nature of sex; it also changes the nature of value and money as a signifier of value. The self-breeding nature of money is not possible without sex work. This sex work is done primarily by people of color and transpeople who do the work of fucking, birthing, and caring.

People who do sex as work, being seen as metaphors for money, are criminalized in public spaces. When a sex industry formed around the American military presence in the Philippines in the 1940s, Filipinx women were assumed to be sex workers when they appeared in public and were criminalized for inhabiting public spaces. Women who appeared in public were criminalized as sites of infectious disease. Haitian refugees who tested positive for HIV were imprisoned in Guantanamo Bay in conditions that exposed them to the elements, denied them medical treatment, and forced them to eat foods that were rotting and full of maggots. When the West characterizes those who do or might do sex work as diseased and corrupted, this characterization actually perpetuates conditions that make sex workers vulnerable to disease. Americans GIs infected Filipinx women, and American soldiers enforced conditions that exposed immunocompromised Haitian refugees to disease. Fanon wrote that, within neocolonialism, colonies become "brothels" for the West, characterizing colonies as sites of corruption. The racialized fantasy of the brothel is also the racialized fantasy of what Ahuja Neel calls the "fallen city," or the city that needs intervention to be saved. He writes that the source of corruption is the American dollar.

The Moon is a body. This body is a social relationship. In astrology, the Moon is often associated with fertility. However, the fertility symbolized by the Moon is not a biological reality but a neoliberal reproduction. This also means that the Moon is not about gender or sex but labor. Often, labor is sexualized or gendered, but people of all sexualities and genders perform reproductive labor. Reproduction happens in contexts where communal and kinship ties are continually broken and produces not living bodies but body-things that accumulate in population graphs. Exploited reproduction imbues money with reproductive power. The self-breeding nature of money has continued to influence how we expect the financial sector to behave: as a thing that must constantly grow and produce more. A capitalism that must grow to infinity can only exist by appropriating reproductive power, because capital has no life outside of what it subsumes.

Money is liquid capital, liquidity being the capital that appears when we treat one another as strangers. The body becomes the medium of capital, because if capital is mobile property, the body is the thing that we can always take with us when running away. Liquidity is the privilege of the mobile and private citizen. The liquidity of capital is an antisocial and neoliberal feeling. It is a liquid Moon that exists only in the private sphere. It is said that possession is the taking over of the body by outside spirits. The spirit that haunts the reproducing and exploited body today is the abstract value of a money economy based on exploitation. In this way, not only does money become an extension of the body, but the body also becomes an extension of money.

Money seeks to exploit the foreign body over the native body because capital can only emerge with usury (the taking of interest), and usury can only be done against foreigners. When usury is normalized, we all become strangers to one another. The story of the Moon is the story of the emergence of the market, which develops from exploited reproduction and the anthropological feast. This market becomes liquid through foreignness, fertile through exploited reproductive power, and luminescent through inhumanity. What the market reproduces is not capital but the anthropological feast. In this anthropological feast, bodies become strange.

3

ETYMOLOGY OF SATURN

Saturn and the Golden Age

The golden age is never something you find yourself in the middle of. It always shows up in reminiscences, in the golden years of one's life. The golden age, then, is not an experienced reality but a type of eye or viewing—a type of memory.

In Roman times, the archetype of the golden age was a poetic metaphor used to comment on, contrast with, and satirize current events. The golden age was understood to be a mythical time that predated history. If the world of the present was busy with war, then in the golden age "no armies, no rage to kill, [and] no war existed," Tibullus wrote (1.3). If the present day was scarce in resources, then in the golden age "oak trees dripped honey, and ewes, voluntarily coming forward, gave free-flowing milk." If, in the present day, property laws were unfair, then the golden age had "marked fixed limits to the farms" that discouraged hoarding. Rather than referring to a real historical period, the golden age represented political commentary. It was a satirical, and literary, tool.

What remains consistent about this golden age is that it is always a time when Saturn, the old god, is king. It is also always an agricultural place. The Greco-Roman version of Saturn merged indigenous agricultural gods. As the slowest-moving consistently visible planet, Saturn represents a state of being that precedes political power. In other words, he represents the land. In Rome, Saturn came to represent an idyllic time of complete agrarian dependency, before governments were formed in centers of power. This mythological time period, one of naïve farming, implies a simple existence before Jupiter came to create government and sovereignty. In Saturn's domain, there is no recorded history and only cyclical turnings of the land.

Saturn was worshipped through gambling. Farmers played dice games after seeds were sown and nothing more could be done to ensure a good harvest except to wait and see if Fate and Fortune were pleased with them. The dice represented the precarity of nature. No matter who you are born as, no matter your social station, and no matter your momentary wealth, the dice reminded you that Saturn could take it all away on a whim. In an agricultural sense, there is only so much work you can do to make your crops grow. Ultimately, farming is a gamble by humans against nature and the gods. In mythology, Saturn was the all-or-nothing god who didn't know how to create hierarchies of government in order to solidify his rule and thus was overtaken by Jupiter, who understood delegation. Saturn, god of chance, either gave you everything or took it all away. Saturn, ruling Capricorn, has a capricious aspect of nature. Rather than justifying what he gives and takes through reason, morality, or laws, Saturn is a reality that precedes politics.

In Roman cities where the farmer was a respected central figure, games of dice were played at the Saturnalia. In these games, every man would take off the clothing that represented his station in life, whether that was high or low, king or slave, and wear the toga that represented Roman citizenship. Unmarked by his status, he would play to see if his Fortune was good or bad. Fortune, ruler of a time before Jupiter/Zeus came to delegate power in a hierarchical manner, was capricious and pure. The Saturnalia represented the naïveté and precarity of the agrarian golden age, where there were no systems of power and humanity was wholly dependent on nature.

Saturn, then, was almost always associated with Fortune, which was a lunar concept in Roman times. As Rhetorius states, "The moon is the fortune of all." Astrologer John Foster relates this statement to the etymology of Fortune: Fortune is where forms are constantly changing, and the Moon, holder of form, is the body. Fortune, then, was a biological concept related to whether the needs of the physical body would be met by nature. It described how the physical body aligns with the physical world. To be fortunate is to be aligned with nature. Because Saturn is the ruler of agriculture, the connection between the Moon and Saturn was about the unpredictability of the harvest and, with it, our adjusting appetites. Culture arises from hunger.

Bruno Théret writes about a concept called "primordial debt," which is the feeling that humans, by being alive, owe their entire being to nature. Primordial debt describes "birth as an original debt incurred by all men, a debt owing to the cosmic powers from which humanity emerged" and goes on to say that "this initial belief-claim is also associated with the emergence of sovereign powers whose legitimacy resides in their ability to represent the entire original cosmos." Thus, the farmers who gamble with Saturn are not playing to outsmart natural forces but to express an understanding of primordial debt. They played with the awareness that fickle nature could take lives and livelihoods away with one bad harvest and that, being human, they owed it to nature to let that happen.

Writing about Romans and agriculture, Hannah Arendt says that "as far as Roman usage is concerned, the chief point always was the connection of culture with nature; culture originally meant agriculture, which was held in very high regard in Rome in opposition to the poetic and fabricating arts. . . . It was in the midst of a primarily agricultural people that the concept of culture first appeared, and the artistic connotations which might have been connected with this culture concerned the incomparably close relationship of the Latin people to nature, the creation of the famous Italian landscape."

Arendt continues her essay on tradition and hierarchy: "Contrary to our concepts of growth, where one grows into the future, the Romans felt that growth was directed towards the past. If one wants to relate this attitude to the hierarchical order established by authority and to visualize this hierarchy in the familiar image of the pyramid, it is as though the peak of the pyramid did not reach into the height of a sky above (or, as in Christianity, beyond) the earth, but into the depth of an earthly past." Within this interpretation of Roman hierarchy, the authority that we typically associate with Saturn doesn't come from higher powers but from lower powers. The authority of Saturn is not the elevated, elite authority of a social pyramid structured by prescribing the correct places and roles for its components but one that comes directly from the land. The authority of Saturn doesn't come from government but from the traditions that connect our experiences in the present to the records of our ancestors. This same authority is what the structure of civilization builds on. In other words, governments don't have authority over people. Rather, authority is fundamentally located within the people and their relationship to land. This authority is then collected in centers of power, and it constructs the government of the land. The myth of Jupiter superseding Saturn is really a myth about political power wrestling natural sovereignty away.

Though Saturn was a king, Saturn was the king of no land. In Roman times, Saturn was the one true king of an imaginary golden age, a rhetorical symbol of nature that existed to criticize existing government powers. No human rulers struggled over power in the golden age because civil government did not exist. Instead, there was no struggle since nature swallowed all struggle the same way

Saturn swallowed Jupiter. Without government, humankind relied on the whims of nature to meet their needs. Saturn was a wish for utopia (where the present-day government did not exist) and a fear of dystopia (where humanity was subject to the whims of nature unshielded). At its core, Saturn is a reminder that authority is the result of a stable relationship between humans and land as well as between (agri)culture and nature.

A Note on Gender

It's important to note that Saturn, the agricultural god, is always gendered male. Although there are feminine gods associated with the land in general, Saturn is a patriarch. This is significant because Saturn was used precisely to contrast rural life with the urban centers in the ancient world.

This goes all the way back to pre-Greek and even pre-Persian civilization. As we said before, Saturn is a compilation of various older agricultural gods dispersed around what became the Persian empire, then Greek, before finally becoming Roman. Urban centers in Sumeria, including cities like Babylon, Uruk, and Lagash, were always centered around the temple. Ancient temples themselves were the red-light districts of ancient cities. Their surroundings were full of sex workers, dancers, and gender play. Sex work had a sacred significance, and the temple was related to gold and silver.

In contrast, the agricultural gods that would later influence how we picture Saturn were worshiped in the outer fringes. The pastoral groups living away from cities were often political outsiders, forced out of commerce and into exodus. David Graeber writes that "resistance, in the ancient Middle East, was always less a politics of rebellion than a politics of exodus, of melting away with one's flock and families—often before both were taken away. . . . The pastoral fringes, the deserts and steppes away from the river valleys, were the places to which displaced, indebted farmers fled." The Saturn imagined by Romans was not only a lost golden age made up by poets and dramatists but also a direct reference to life outside centers of cultural power and to people displaced by emerging empire. The nostalgia of Saturn was not just a nostalgia of a lost age but a nostalgia of lost roots, people, and community.

Patriarchy was reasserted within exiled pastoral groups as a direct reaction to the perceived cosmopolitan culture and feminization of urban life. In fact, as Graeber writes, "'patriarchy' originated, first and foremost, in a rejection of the great urban civilizations in the name of a kind of purity, a reassertion of paternal control against great cities like Uruk, Lagash, and Babylon, seen as places of bureaucrats, traders, and whores." These bureaucrats, traders, and whores were wrapped in the sex industry, since sex work was a religious, commercial, and sexual practice. Saturn became a grandfatherly figure due to the efforts of fringe groups who wanted to contrast their own values against the values surrounding the urban temples. The Hebrews, who were one of these fringe groups, often compared religious deviations from Yahweh to the buying of sex, and cities to prostitutes: "Plead with your mother, plead: for she is not my wife, neither am I her husband: let her therefore put away her whoredoms out of her sight, and her adulteries from between her breasts. Lest I strip her naked, and set her as in the day that she was born. . . . For she has played the harlot" (Hosea 2:4-7). The patriarchal values we associate with Saturn, then, are patriarchal as a reassertion of cultural purity by displaced or nomadic groups against centers of urban and political power and cosmopolitanism.

The Mythological Golden Age and Utopianism

One man, almost minuscule, stands on a cliff and gazes upon a great expanse of fertile land. To liberal dreamers, this land represents fertility and wealth as much as it does freedom. The free white man is apparently entitled to this land. By possessing land, this free white man—the common man—owns a piece of his country and achieves the liberty of self-government. The dream of the self-governing agrarian free white man is a sublime one.

This agrarian dream, a Saturnian dream, is almost timeless as it situates itself outside of history. As Umberto Eco writes on the sublime, "nature itself, as opposed to the artifice of history, appeared obscure, formless and mysterious: it would not let itself be captured by precise, clear-cut forms, but overwhelmed the spectator with grandiose and sublime visions." Kant contrasts the melancholic enchantment of the sublime to the more fleeting and feminine charms of beauty: "The dominant feature of the melancholic is the sentiment of the Sublime. Even Beauty, to which he is just as sensible, does not only tend to fascinate him, but, by inspiring his admiration, to move him. In him the enjoyment of pleasure is more composed, but no less intense for that; but all emotions aroused by the Sublime are more attractive to him than all the fascinating attractions of Beauty." The sublime is a melancholic and masculine aesthetic. Edmund Burke, in his work *A Philosophical Enquiry into the Origin of our Ideas of the Sublime and Beautiful,* also associates the sublime with masculinity and beauty with femininity.

The melancholic yearning that Eco, Kant, and Burke describe is a cultural nostalgia closely associated with Saturn. For nations that construct identity through the sublime, the homeland is always a nostalgic place. Because the nation is always a work in progress, the yearning for this homeland is never fully actualized but is always yearned for and aspired toward. As an image, the sublime is never solid or clear but always as ambiguous and distant as Saturn's archaic realm. As Eco also writes, "the first German Romantics broadened the scope of the indefinable and of the vague covered by the term 'Romantisch,' which came to cover all that was distant, magical, and unknown, including the lugubrious, the irrational, and the cemeteries. Above all, what was specifically Romantic was the *aspiration ('Sehnsucht')* to all this."

In Greek and Roman civilization, property or the possession of the land was seen as more important than any other commodity, even if its value was the same. This is because while foreigners and former slaves were able to possess and create a fortune with money, only citizens of the land were able to engage in that highest aspiration: the cultivation of that "famous Italian landscape." Landownership was inherited by those with a special status within the local or national community. The selling of one's land was seen not only as a betrayal of one's country but of one's own ancestors. The stability of the relationship between the individual and the land was also the stability of the nation as a clan. Saturnian wealth, then, is immobile wealth. Saturn's wealth resides within property, belonging, and citizenship. Roxanne Dunbar-Ortiz, commenting on the work of Esther Kingston-Mann, who studies Russian peasantry, finds that the ownership of land within a modernizing Europe was elevated into a "sacred status."

The Germans, when defining national identity for the first time against a mess of sprawled-out local alliances, adopted ancient Roman ideals of landownership as analogous to citizenship. The United States also linked landownership with citizenship during the transcendentalism movement, because powerful writers like Ralph Waldo Emerson and politicians like Thomas Jefferson were fascinated with Germany, masculinity, and having a pure racial stock. Roman agrarian ideals influenced both Nazi and American utopianism. In modernity, Roman agrarianism lives on as a dream within a dream. This dream within a dream is exactly early American liberalism. John Locke thought that the despotism of state power could be limited by giving individual landowners voting power. This is the same ideal that Jefferson, purchaser of Louisiana and most of the American Midwest, subscribed to. For Jefferson, the self-governing farmer was the ideal citizen, and agrarian liberalism and its landowning farmer represented a break from monarchy and feudalism.

Hitler's dream of Germany was also an agrarian ideal. National socialism was very much a utopian project. Hitler prioritized the invasion of Ukraine because of its rich, black soil. Nazi agrarian romanticism saw the peasantry as the foundation of German national identity. Blood was connected with soil, and both were representative of a "natural order"—one that contrasted with the "asphalt culture" of cosmopolitanism, universalism, and internationalism. Nazi Germany's agrarianism was a reaction to what Nazis perceived to be a city-centric and business-minded international order. Like the displaced people of ancient Mesopotamia, the National Socialists advocated for cultural purity and contrasted the simplicity of agrarian life with tainted urban politics.

Both the United States and Nazi Germany glorified the simplicity of rural life and likened urban centers to a type of foreign cosmopolitanism that the common folk had become alienated from. Both tried to construct a utopian and agrarian golden age free of intellectualism, in reaction to Jupiterian struggles for power upon which ideology after ideology argued and negotiated. If Jupiter is political struggle, then utopianism transcends political struggle by returning back to the land and back to Saturn. The United States distanced itself from fast-talking city dwellers and idealized the sturdy and silent farmer. Nazi Germany's anti-Semitism conflated Jews and queers with cities and saw cultural sharing as cultural pollution. Both powers pined for a return to Saturn's domain—that of the agricultural golden age in which every citizen found freedom by taking off the markings of their social class.

However, it is important to note that while Mesopotamians and Romans framed Saturn as an existence that precedes religious political life, the English, Americans, and Germans saw Saturn as an existence that precedes commercial life. As John Brewer writes in *Pleasures of the Imagination:* "Barbarism, which had long been equated with the absence of Christianity, was now defined by the absence of commercial society." In England, Saturn's utopianism manifested as an artistic and literary invention known as the "pic-turesque." English Romanticism oriented itself around its own peasant class and emerged from enclosure—the accumulation of public land by private interests. The picturesque was a vision of the English landscape as a painting.

In the 1700s, tourists from cosmopolitan centers embarked on journeys around the English landscape, hoping to glimpse a life untainted by commercialism. While these tourists looked for autonomous rural farmers, the existing farm laborer-tenants were already commercially minded. The landscape that tourists yearned to see was not the actual state of the country but an anachronis-tic image of a landscape that precedes commercialization. Tour-ists brought with them frames for viewing the landscape, which they could use to crop out elements that contradicted their liberal notions of rural simplicity and autonomy. Nature seemed to move further and further away from England as enclosure took more and more land away from the peasants. As Brewer puts it, "nature was defined as both a precursor and a residue: it existed prior to the cultivation that consumed it, and it was what was left over when modern society, culture, and economy had gobbled up the rest. The rise of arts and sciences had expelled raw nature to the margins. No longer an integral part of human society, it was now confined to those places . . . which escaped human improvement."

Both Hitler's and Jefferson's agrarian dreams needed fertile land. As Sakai writes in *Settlers,* American colonization happened because there was a land shortage in Europe. As Dunbar-Ortiz writes on page 1 of *An Indigenous Peoples' History of the United States,* "Everything in US history is about the land—who oversaw and cul-tivated it, fished its waters, maintained its wildlife, who invaded and stole it; how it became a commodity ('real estate') broken into pieces to be bought and sold on the market." While English Romanticism arose from taking land away from peasant farmers, the United States and Germany seized land from Indigenous people, Ukraines, and Poles. To Jefferson, the Indigenous people of the Americas were incompatible with hierarchical capitalism. To Hitler, Ukrainians and Poles could be kept as a temporary rural workforce that would eventually be replaced by German farmers while Jews were exterminated from urban centers.

The agrarian visions of Nazi Germany and the United States are still alive today. These myths embody white supremacy and efficiency. When we think of the Nazis, we still picture them as they wanted to be represented—a strong, white machine. We still picture the expansion of America as the spread of a strong, pioneering people of Saxon or Nordic stock. Even as we critique the atrocities committed by the German and American empires, we believe in their almost religious veneration of agrarian idealism.

However, neither Germany nor America were independently governed agrarian nations but always existed as commercial enterprises in which the dream of rural autonomy coexisted with modernity and capitalism. The truth about Germany during World War II was that Hitler could never convince enough Germans to become the farmers that he idealized so much. He did not have enough laborers willing to colonize the black soils of Ukraine, so he could not enable his economy to stop using ethnic non-Germans as a working underclass. Nazi Germany's economy was kept afloat with capital seized from Jewish businesses. The United States was lifted out of economic peril again and again through the conquest and government sale of newly stolen land to new, white immigrants. The most common American worker was not the white, self-governing ideal citizen but always the slave. Jefferson's self-governing citizen was never the farmer, because the citizens of the Southern states he represented did not farm their own land, but always the capitalist and slave owner. The American economy never relied on Jefferson's agrarian ideals but, as in Nazi Germany, on a racial underclass, the constant seizure of new land and resources, and the constant proliferation of a money economy. Neither the United States nor

Germany were ever free from financialization. Agrarian idealism did not work on its own but relied on financialization and theft.

In Rome, and later the United States and Germany, the golden age was a cultural symbol more than a systematic treatment of land. Gianni Guestella writes: "Generally, Romans did not represent the original perfection [of an agrarian golden age] as a natural model; rather it, too, was a cultural model which had gradually degenerated." The original perfection of Saturn's golden age was used to contrast the degeneracy associated with what the Romans thought of as fabrications, which included all cultural forms apart from agriculture. Both the United States and Germany eventually expressed the Western anxiety about degeneracy through fears of racial mixing. Both nations defined utopia as a fundamentally white state. England's Romanticism shows that utopianism is not just a racially pure ethnostate but also a memorialization of the peasantry by the elite classes at a time when rural autonomy was at a decline. Utopian states glorify images of the folk or *Volk* and feed depictions of working-class people to themselves through print media and, later, the television, while their actual policies always supported the elite capitalist.

In his book *The Invention of the White Race,* Theodore Allen finds that whiteness as a social identity did not exist prior to Bacon's Rebellion, which took place in Virginia in 1676. Bonded laborers from both Ireland and Africa were bound by similar contracts. For the ruling class, the disproportionate number of laborers in relation to landowners made rebellion a constant social threat. Wealthy landowners were outnumbered. As bond laborers began to rebel against their owners, landowners invented whiteness in order to create a buffer class so that white laborers aligned themselves with their exploiters and against their fellow laborers, in order to guard their white privilege. While Black laborers were enslaved generation after generation in chattel slavery, white laborers were given freedom and plots of land after their years of contracted service.

These land policies were also policies of genocide, since land was taken from Indigenous people. Dunbar-Ortiz says these policies continued in "the dance between poor and rich US Americans ever since under the guise of equality of opportunity." This dance between rich and poor extended the American nation westward. The mythological essential white worker, who always seemed to need protection from foreign elements, is actually a buffer class generated by the land-rich classes in order to protect themselves against rebellion. Whiteness is hypervisible in the working class since the owning classes do not need to make their whiteness visible to maintain their privilege. American hypervisible whiteness is closely associated with a pioneer class. This pioneer class enacts genocide to serve and protect the land-rich.

Saturn, for the Romans, was citizenship because Saturn was associated with the land, and landownership emerged from Roman ancestry and citizenship. If Saturn is citizenship, then Saturn is also whiteness. Whiteness is a property that, once possessed, provides a clear path toward cultural belonging and citizenship. As Sara Ahmed writes, "whiteness may function as a form of public comfort *by allowing bodies to extend into spaces that have already taken their shape.*" This extension of white comfort is colonization. Saturn is also whiteness because whiteness is a utopia. If the utopianism of American agrarianism is a dream of land liberated from commercial interests, then whiteness is also the dream that workers can become liberated from having class interests.

The Laborer Who Is Both Noble and Savage

Trigger warning: this section contains descriptions of genocide.

While Saturn as whiteness is a utopia, Saturn is also a dystopia. As we have seen, in Roman times Saturn was a king even if he was an exiled king of a long-gone and timeless age. When feudalism became the dominant agricultural model in Europe in the Middle

Ages, Saturn's image changed from that of the old king to that of the old peasant. As the condition of the agricultural class worsened, Saturn's image, once linked to the rich Underworld that provided the surface world with abundance, became associated with ill fortune, miserliness, exile, and poverty. As Raymond Kilbansky writes in *Saturn and Melancholy: Studies in the History of Natural Philosophy, Religion, and Art:* "It is true that the other Greek gods, too, nearly all appear under a dual aspect, in the sense that they both chastise and bless, destroy and aid. But in none of them is this dual aspect so real and fundamental as Kronos (Saturn). His nature is a dual one not only with regard to his effect on the outer world, but with regard to his own—as it were, personal—destiny, and this dualism is so sharply marked that Kronos might fairly be described as god of opposites." Abu M'ashar, archiving the cross-cultural and diverse associations that the astrological Saturn had accumulated by the Middle Ages, writes that Saturn rules over both "owners of land" as well as "low-born people." Saturn's associations, as Kilbansky says, are oxymoronic. Saturn represents both wealth and poverty—both citizenship and disenfranchisement.

Saturnalia, the celebration of chance, was also a celebration of the relationship between chaos and organization. While Jupiter was seen as the organizing principle of civilization, Saturn was the organizing principle of nature that disrupted hierarchical powers and the social strata of society. Because nature mandates that all things die so that life can be regenerated, Saturn is a hungry god who demands sacrifice. Saturn is death. Death fertilizes the fields, but death is always the crops that fail. Death is regenerative but death is also a final ending. Death is sometimes the wealthy broker from the Underworld, and at other times, death comes in the form of the ragged and diseased peasant. The characterization of Saturn is also the characterization of death. Regardless of how death is characterized, it always shows up outside of life. It always exists outside of the institutions that seek to regulate and control life. Saturn is often pitted against Jupiter because Saturn, as death, disrupts political society.

In the Roman Saturnalia, slaves were served by their masters, and children were given gifts. The festival of Saturn, like the golden age it represented, was a reversal of society's power relations. Because slaves and children were not citizens nor part of the political realms governing life, they represented death. As Al-Wahid would later write, "one becomes a slave in situations where one would otherwise have died." The slave as political outsider and death were celebrated during Saturnalia as potential agents of chaos that could disturb the power relations of the day. Through death, the distribution of wealth and debt are overturned along with the land. The political outsider, likewise, seeks to disrupt the current distribution of natural resources.

Death, who used to be a king, became poorer during feudalism. The Grim Reaper, still agricultural as he carries a scythe, is starved down to the bones and wears a tattered cloak. Rather than being the king of a realm, the Grim Reaper is a drifter without a sense of belonging. Saturn, as death, became desolate. Likewise, the devil, a figure that consolidated a myriad of smaller demons and monsters, became a popular symbol within the intelligentsia during industrialization. The pagan celebrations of death as a regeneration principle came to be seen as antiprogressive, irrational, and evil. As a miser, Saturn's condition was directly affected by the condition of the working class of the feudal era.

What reformed feudalism in Europe was a combination of industrialization and colonization. As Europe's empires widened and wealth flowed through, the tendency to define the political outsider through Saturnian terms never went away. There are remarkable similarities between how the Romans saw Saturn and how humanist thinkers described the noble savage in the seventeenth century. The noble savage was almost always described as being poor, primitive, and naïve. Poorness, for the humanists, typically meant someone who was uneducated but also closer to nature. Primitiveness referred to a person who seemed to come from an earlier and more romantic time. Naïveté related to an innocence regarding the politics of the day. Like Saturn, the noble savage implied the disruption of social order.

Alexander Pope's *Essay on Man*, which contains a passage describing the Indigenous American, shares remarkable similarities to Tibullus's accounts of the mythological Roman golden age:

> Lo, the poor Indian! whose untutor'd mind
> Sees God in clouds, or hears him in the wind;
> His soul proud Science never taught to stray
> Far as the solar walk or milky way;
> Yet simple Nature to his hope has giv'n,
> Behind the cloud-topp'd hill, a humbler heav'n;
> Some safer world in depth of woods embrac'd,
> Some happier island in the wat'ry waste,
> Where slaves once more their native land behold,
> No fiends torment, no Christians thirst for gold!
> To be, contents his natural desire;
> He asks no angel's wing, no seraph's fire:
> But thinks, admitted to that equal sky,
> His faithful dog shall bear him company.

Pope's essay on the noble savage mirrors Tibullus's poems about the golden age. If Saturn as the golden age is the natural state of the uncultivated land, then Saturn as the noble savage is one who is "untutor'd" in power. If Saturn as the golden age is a time of agricultural utopia, then Saturn as the noble savage is of a "safer world," "happier island," and "simple Nature." If Saturn as the golden age is the time that existed before political power, then Saturn as the noble savage lives under an "equal sky." Saturn is dialectically opposed to power. Thus, the image of the noble savage is also the image of someone who is inherently unable to achieve any political power. As William Vance put it, "Indians and fauns and

Arcadian shepherds were all essentially of the same breed, sharing the animal life of nature." Indigenous people represented a mythological Arcadia to European settlers.

Whiteness is also the ability to control and shape race. Racialized depictions of simple agrarian existence were also featured within American and German propaganda. For Hitler, the perfect Aryan farmer handled "black soil," was hypermasculine, and had dark skin bronzed by the sun. In contrast, the Nazis depicted ethnic minorities within Europe as lighter skinned and physically weakened due to city life. After World War II, a utopianism arose in the United States that was surprisingly similar to the utopianism of America's defeated Nazi rival. This American utopianism emerged from the counterculture of the 1960s. Young and white self-styled bohemians, living in prosperous suburban sprawls, curated catalogues of books and clothing that represented a long-lost American masculinity. The *Whole Earth Catalog,* which heavily influenced the counterculture of the 1960s, described the "Cowboy Nomad," an idealized figure that existed within American utopia, in this passage: "The frontier days were land ownin [sic], putting down roots, self sufficient farmer stability. The cowboy was living in another life style, sacrificing comfort for freedom and stability."

In contrast, the *Catalog* describes contemporary society like this: "Society today is ambiguous, laws enforce static living patterns with voter residency law, drivers license state jurisdiction, states rights keep you in your place, in a civilization designed for mobility."

These passages compare "land ownin" with being "kept in your place," "self sufficient farmer stability" with "static living patterns" and "voter residency law," and "freedom" with "mobility." In other words, like the Roman poets evoking a lost golden age or Nazi propagandists romanticizing the *übermensch* who obeys the land rather than the the cosmopolitan world order, the *Whole Earth Catalog* rejected a political sense of power in exchange for an agrarian one. The *Catalog* encouraged readers to read Jack Kerouac, wear moccasins, and sexually liberate themselves. While the countercultural hippies of the 1960s saw themselves opposed to the asphalt culture of the suburbs, they actually extended whiteness outward. The small clusters of farming collectives that sprang up across the United States displaced Indigenous communities and replicated patriarchal gender norms.

If Saturn is connected with agrarian freedom, then agrarian freedom is not just available only to white people; it is also an appropriated image of the racial outsider that the white citizen can put on and take off at will. White utopianists don't just reproduce whiteness—they also reproduce whiteness that controls and reproduces Indigeneity. Whiteness is not a racial category but the evidence of power. The self-styled "Cowboy Nomads" that lived out their frontier fantasies also wore moccasins and feathers. The "Nomad" component of "Cowboy Nomad" comes from hippie appropriations of items associated with Indigenous Americans, such as moccasins and Indigenous prints. By acting out stylizations of both the cowboy and the Indigenous American, "Cowboy Nomads" reproduced the frontier as the site of genocide. The aesthetic opposition between the cowboy and the Indian is an aesthetic of death. American counterculturalists from the 1960s styled themselves with genocide as fashion.

The theatrical performance of genocide within the United States did not begin in the 1960s. Rather, the "Cowboy Nomad" counterculture was an extension of older traditions of what Philip J. Deloria calls "playing Indian." "Playing Indian" is a tradition that historically has heightened whenever the United States seeks to differentiate itself from Europe. Settlers create an original identity and differentiate themselves from their homelands by dressing up as and "playing Indian." Jodi Byrd says "playing Indian" is "a core process through which US nonnative national identities form." Michael Kammen writes that "the history of Native Americans only became useful when cultural resistance to Europe began to be important. Real Indians had largely disappeared by then from the mainstream view; so their legends could be approvingly used for aesthetic and symbolic motifs."

The Boston Tea Party, that mythological origin story of the American settler identity, is just one example of colonialists playing Indian to express economic dissatisfaction. Settler colonialists often put feathers in their hair, painted their faces, and ran around whooping and howling when they rallied for their economic interests. White American national identity emerged from Indigeneity as fashion. Even the bourgeoisie would wear working-class costumes with Indigenous embellishments to express their support of independent American nationality.

America was also called Columbia. In the early days of the American empire, Columbia was represented as an "Indian princess" through fashions of the Indigenous people of the United States, wearing feathers, often nude or partially nude, and associated with animals like parrots and alligators. She was frequently seen holding a cornucopia, symbolizing the land abundance of the Americas. Her image as an American Indigenous woman symbolized for the early American colonists both a break from British tradition and the wildness or availability of the new land. Later, Columbia became white. While she was still usually seen partially nude, she often wore garments made of the new American flag draped over a classically shaped figure. Her dress no longer resembled that of the Indigenous Americans or that of the American settler colonialists. Instead, Columbia wore garments that referenced classically Roman garments. In an 1872 painting by John Gast titled *American Progress,* Columbia is seen floating in the air and wearing a Roman toga while guiding covered wagons and steam engine trains westward. Columbia was more than a manifestation of destiny. She, as a representation of the United States, emerges from the appropriation of Indigeneity and becomes neoclassical, while remaining partially nude to assert her separation from Europe.

Not only did settlers put on Indigenous costumes to express nationalism; they also saw themselves as the inheritors of Indigenous culture. The Tammany Society of New York, named after the Lenape leader, saw their members as the inheritors of a kind of Indigenous nobility. This supposed Indigenous nobility helped Tammany Society members justify their positions as an urban political elite. Tammany's death was seen as a metaphor for the disappearance of the Indigenous peoples. Tammany, as a dead king, was appropriated so white settlers could frame themselves as the new kings of a new world.

Deloria writes that the May Day dance around the maypole was an European tradition that celebrated the death of the old king and the succession of a new one. When settlers danced around the maypole on American soil, they decorated the pole "with wild flowers gathered from the adjacent woods," circled around it to "perform the Indian war dance," and copied "many other customs which they had seen exhibited by the children of the forest." This ritual, which signified the end of one cycle and the beginning of a new one, was also a celebration of the "the destruction of the old cycle" and "the dawning of another era in which successor Americans would enjoy their new world." Deloria writes that the Tammany Society appropriated "the interior, aboriginal identity of the Indian . . . fused to a Greco-Roman history" and saw Indigenous people "as simply predead Indians who, upon dying, would become historical, locked in a grand narrative of inevitable American progress."

The cultural appropriation of Indigeneity by settlers would continue and heighten at certain moments when settlers sought to contrast America with Europe. During the World War era, amid anxieties that American boys were being raised by the "asphalt culture" of the cities, the Boy Scouts gave white boys the opportunity to create their own "tribes," choose their own "chiefs," and earn their own badges. In the 1990s, the Grateful Dead, whose name suggests that dead people are grateful, would perform to crowds wearing "paint, buckskin, even feathers" adorned with "chicory coffee, hummus and pita bread, skulls, bears, and roses, and the smell of patchouli oil on skin."

While the Sun is linked with a future, multicultural utopia where all races participate freely in the public spectacle of finance, and the Moon depicts a market where race is consumed, Saturn is not about race. Rather, Saturn stands outside of race. Jodi Byrd frames Indigeneity in parallax with race, writing that while multicultural settler colonial nations have often tried to integrate Indigeneity into the empire by conflating it with race, Indigeneity is not race, and Indigenous sovereignty is not compatible with the multicultural empire. She writes that "transforming American Indians into a minority within a country of minorities is the fait accompli of the colonial project that disappears sovereignty, land rights, and self-governance," and is a component of the assimilation project. In *Transits of Empire: Indigenous Critiques of Colonialism,* Byrd calls the "paradigmatic 'Indian tribe'" a "ghost in the constituting machine of empire" that exists as a "parallel" to the "foreign nation." She writes that the American empire "facilitates the colonialist administration of foreign nations and Indian tribes alike" and that "racialization and colonization should thus be understood as concomitant global systems that secure white dominance through time, property, and notions of self."

Race is a theater controlled and scripted by white power. In the race theater of the Moon, behaviors that came from white people— cannibalism, murder, corruption—were portrayed as originating from racial others. For Saturn, Indigeneity is portrayed as a race that settlers can reimagine their own identities through.

America tries to integrate Indigenous nations into empire by describing them through the language of race. As a "ghost in the constituting machine of empire," Indigenous people are often described through the aesthetics of death. When settlers integrate Indigenous people into the empire through race, we are also imagining

Indigeneity through the aesthetics of death because Indigeneity as a death aesthetic was foundational to the white American identity. American liberal culture tries to bury Indigenous nations by memorializing them. However, Indigenous people and nations are not historical but exist in the present and deal with contemporary issues. Gerald Vizenor calls the settler appropriation of Indigeneity a simulation that is also "an absence of the tribal real." These stimulations fit the Indigenous into the "melancholy of dominance" and arise from death. Vizenor opposes these simulations with a term he coined: survivance. Of survivance, Vizenor writes: "The conventions of survivance create a sense of Native presence over nihility and victory. Survivance is an active presence: it is not absence, deracination, or ethnographic oblivion, and survivable is the continuance of narratives, not a mere reaction, however pertinent. Survivance stories are renunciations of dominance, the unbearable sentiments of tragedy, and the legacy of victory." Of Indigenous stories and simulated Indians, Vizenor writes: "Shadow words and nicknames are survivance stories that seem to have an unstated presence in narratives; the reader hears the shadow stories."

Saturn as Revolutionary in Late Capitalism

When the Spanish conquistador Hernán Cortés came to rob the Aztec empire of all its gold, the story goes, he sat down with the king Moctezuma and played a game. The stakes of the game were high. Cortés was playing for gold, and he cheated. Moctezuma knew he was being cheated. Still, in all historical accounts of the event, each time Cortés won, however unfairly, Moctezuma dutifully paid up. Gold piled up on Cortés's side of the table until Moctezuma lost all he had. You see, while Cortés may have been playing for gold, Moctezuma never was. The gamble, for him, was deeply connected to Fate. As the story goes, if God did not wish for Moctezuma to keep his empire then he could not have given it away in a game of dice.

Gambling is an intrinsic part of Saturn worship. Saturn rules nature, and farming is a human bet against nature. Abundance and scarcity are ruled by physical properties described by Fortune.

Under late capitalism, gambling is a part of the economy itself. To participate in the economy is also to cast your dice in the stocks and bonds market, hedging a bet with the market. When you bet on the market, you take on risk. In other words, you bet on futures—on time itself. In popular American imagination, the stock market is dreamed of as an equalizer—an imaginary realm in which anyone can get rich quick if they are savvy and lucky enough. Every American can have a stake in corporate health if they invest in the stock market. The financial market acts like the dice games of the Romans; it is a ritualistic game that, supposedly, can turn the slave into a master and the master into a slave. American ideals about the equal and common man rely on the financial sector to provide a liberalizing of values. For the globally influential political economist Friedrich Hayek, liberty could only be achieved through a free market.

Bets against Saturn are also bets against nature. The dice games played by Romans were a symbol for the precarity of life in the face of certain death. In contrast, our stock markets are an effort to control nature and minimize the risk of being subject to Saturn's whims. We have stopped betting on nature and have industrialized the farms.

Saturn, however, happens to be a wrathful god and one whose consequences become more and more dire the more they are delayed. By refusing to gamble with the agricultural god and seeking to pathologize him as that which needs to be controlled, we have only postponed payment for our ever-increasing gamble with nature. Late capitalism is the end of capitalism due to natural forces. Industrialization, or creation of a risk-minimized developed world, only exports the consequences of a controlled environment elsewhere. Heavy minerals are mined in the third world, natural resources are sold and swallowed, and pollution is exported.

Climate change will devastate the third and developing world before it reaches the wealth-hoarding nations.

Saturn's sickle appears in Karl Marx's dreams of a classless society. Marx imagines that a revolution can reorganize and regenerate society, returning it to an original state. This dream of revolution has a traditional basis because the Saturnalia was always the ritual that yearned for classnessless. In communism, Saturn becomes revolution. Following the Saturnalia and the diverse forms of governments that Marx's revolution has inspired, the revolution becomes a symbol or ritual that is imagined in order to meet psychological needs created by political society. The ritual of revolution, like the ritual of Saturnalia, imagines death as fruitful, seeks to disrupt the corrupt status quo, and allies itself with political outsiders. The wish for revolution is also the yearning for a prepolitical and original state—the tabula rasa that Fanon described as a necessary stage of decolonization.

In her book *Shock Doctrine*, Naomi Klein finds that the concept of a revolution that remakes the world has been appropriated by neoliberals. The dream of a proletariat that rises up and destroys all social institutions to create a blank slate for another reality, although it has leftist origins, has been used by right-leaning economists to destroy formerly democratic and leftist governments.

Let's go back to the story about Cortés. The thing is, like all stories, it gives an overly simplistic and unexamined view of what really happened. It is inconceivable that Moctezuma, a great king of a great empire who must have had to plan his affairs strategically in order to keep his empire—a king who was planning reforms that would unify peoples that the Aztec empire had formerly alienated against the colonizers—would forsake all he had in a game of dice. To consider the possibility that he would stinks of colonial assumptions that Indigenous people are overly naïve and superstitious.

What really happened in the Aztec empire is a story familiar to all of us in the twenty-first century. Cortés, knowing that the large size of the Aztec empire had alienated several small groups around the region, exploited frustrations with the current regime to destabilize the region. To support his actions, Cortés described the Aztecs to his European backers as tyrannical and given to human sacrifice. He used these extreme descriptions to arm and ally fringe groups, stage a coup, and use the resulting confusion to mine gold from the region and enslave the people.

In the 1970s, the CIA would stage multiple military coups in Latin America and the Pacific Islands before installing neoliberal leaders who would then open the region to foreign interests. While these areas were formerly democratic and left-leaning, with stable local economies, the United States would opportunistically install dictators friendly to corporate interests when political or natural disasters occurred. The assets of Brazil, Chile, Argentina, Sri Lanka, and Indonesia were stolen from the people through fabricated revolutions. The way the CIA acted was eerily similar to Cortés, painting a current power regime as totalitarian or extreme before staging coups, privatizing natural resources, and selling the resources to Western powers. After these revolutions, periods of terror occurred during which those loyal to the old regime would have to be shocked, tortured, and erased.

When we think of revolution today, it is almost impossible to imagine one that is not bloody. We often think of totalitarian regimes in which the majority of the populace is brainwashed or complicit. We romanticize the small fringe group that takes the matter of insurrection into its own hands, wreaks havoc, and destroys all social institutions. Only afterward can society begin again with a fresh slate. We see this revolutionary template in almost every cinematic example of revolution, including *The Matrix, V for Vendetta,* and the *Divergent* series. Almost all of our cinematic examples of sudden revolution resemble not the populist and democratic leftist movements of anti-imperialism but the colonial and neoliberal coups that rob third-world countries of their natural resources.

Often, these revolutions are what Deloria calls liminal states—it is almost impossible to imagine the day after the revolution. Deloria calls liminality "a frozen moment of unpredictable potential in the midst of a process of change." Michael Bristol relates liminality to Saturnalia, writing that "liminality is the experience of the social 'other'" and that "it provokes an alibi and an excuse," creating a space for "the fulfillment of wishes that ordinarily cannot be satisfied, or, in other words, utopia." Saturnalia was a space in which Roman masters dressed as slaves. In the American liminal space, Indigeneity is worn as costume to create a settler's utopia where wishes that cannot be ordinarily satisfied can be satisfied—a space where anyone can do anything.

The liminal space is not revolution. Revolution is not an in-between stage where anyone can do anything. Revolution is not an event. Revolutions must be sustainable.

Arendt writes that:

No doubt human life, placed on the earth, is surrounded by automatic processes—by the natural processes of the earth, which, in turn, are surrounded by cosmic processes, and we ourselves are driven by similar forces insofar as we too are a part of organic nature. Our political life, moreover, despite its being the realm of action, also takes place in the midst of processes which we call historical and which tend to become as automatic as natural or cosmic processes, although they were started by men. The truth is that automatism is inherent in all processes, no matter what their origin may be—which is why no single act, and no single event can ever, once and for all, deliver and save a man, or a nation, or mankind.

Audre Lorde simply says: "Revolution is not a one-time event."

We believe that revolutions must be bloody to be effective because the current neoliberal system relies on violence to maintain itself. The type of revolution that Arendt and Lorde spoke out against—the kind that is always a bloody, one-time event that erases societies and tries to create a blank slate—is happening all of the time. In 1993, some of the world's most influential economists met, by invitation only, in Washington, DC. In their meeting they decided that, after seeing the effects of the American experiments in Latin America and the Pacific Islands, it is logical to engineer a crisis with the goal of pursuing economic revolution. John Williamson, the host of this meeting, said, "one will have to ask whether it could conceivably make sense to think of deliberately provoking a crisis so as to remove the political logjam to reform." As a result of this meeting, an oil-hungry Bush administration would, in fact, deliberately provoke crisis after crisis in the Middle East. Joseph Nye found that protest was central to American soft power. The United States culturally influences its colonies by defining and depicting protest and freedom. It then redefines its military actions as liberty. The United States describes itself as having a monopoly on liberty. However, what America actually holds a monopoly over is violence.

Instead of using revolution as a media symbol or ritual, always bloody, destructive, necessary, and final, Lorde asks us to sustain revolution. Saturn's questions, from the golden age to modern utopia to present-day climate change, are always questions of sustainability. What Lorde teaches us is that revolution is not something that happens and then is over. Rather, revolution must be sustained, protected, and cultivated.

Sustainability is the realization that authority isn't something that disciplines us from above but is what's given to us from the land. It is the realization that Saturn isn't what gives us authority over others but what we give authority to, in an attempt to distribute the resources we have for survival. The central question in matters of sustainability is the distinction between what we can live with and what we can live without.

The thing about revolution is that if the issues being presented are truly in the interests of the population and not a small elite, then there is no need for a single, shocking, bloody event in which ordinary civilians must be killed. Violence is the weapon of the few against the many. When the many are in solidarity, a simple reprioritization of what we collectively value is enough. A boycott of any corporation for a single day or week is enough to destroy it, if enough people get behind it. In fact, the boycott was the strongest weapon of those in support of the Freedom Charter in South Africa in the 1980s. Other tools that the many have against the few are community care (to resist privatized health services), farming (to resist corporate landownership), and the strike (which takes away capitalism's ability to exploit our production). In a status quo that *needs* violence to sustain itself, saying *no* to violence is often enough to disrupt. When the many of the world—the colonized, the Indigenous, the subjugated—move in alignment, the few will confront this peaceful movement with violence. When protestors gather without enacting violence, the police will stage violence and brutalize protestors first while the media describes the protestors themselves as violent. It is important to understand that, in a militarized state, the state holds a monopoly on violence. Violence is how the few discipline the many. Violence within revolution always comes from those in power.

But it goes deeper. Neoliberal economic revolution seeks to destroy social bonds because it, like the early utopianists of the Americas or the Third Reich, declares that an original state truly exists if only we can create enough destruction to unearth it. Neoliberal revolution sees revolutionary elements as something that comes from outside. The neoliberal revolution is only credible when idealized social relations of a make-believe utopia that exists before time itself takes priority over the actual messy social bonds that support our daily lives. There is no utopia but our relationships. A sustainable revolution, then, must value existing relationships instead of attempting to remake the world anew. A sustainable revolution must learn to live with the world we have. A sustainable revolution does not come from outside but from the protection and survivance of Indigeneity.

Colonization is often depicted as clean, as reform, and as liberating. Decolonization is often framed as destructive and as violent. However, Jodi Byrd writes that decolonization is not destructive. Rather, it is a grieving process that also restores life: "Rather than framing justice for American Indians as the fourth horseman accompanying the apocalyptic 'plague, pestilence, and famine,' it is time to imagine Indigenous decolonization as a process that restores life and allows settler, arrivant, and native to apprehend and grieve together the violences of US empire." Rather than seeing decolonization through the Western, biblical imagery of the Book of Revelations, we must expose the violence of colonialism as what it is. Byrd writes that "the story of the new world is horror, the story of America is a crime." When Fanon wrote about the necessity of violence in revolution, asking revolutionaries whether they plan to revolt using guns made by capitalist arms manufacturers, he was not describing violence as something that emerges from the colonized in protest; he was advocating for a revolution that *survives* the violence that comes from the colonizers.

In other words, revolution is not an event. Revolution lives. It is the remaking of culture. Culture is the cultivation of the land. Hawaiian nationalist Haunani-Kay Trask says culture is the center of politics and that "only Hawaiian culture comes from Hawaii. Every other culture comes from someplace else." Speaking in support of Hawaiian sovereignty, Trask says, "we did not come from Adam and Eve, or China, or Japan, or Korea, or the Philippines, and we will not be saved by the Christ child from Bethlehem. We came from this earth. We grew right out of this earth. And our survival depends, especially today, on understanding and connecting to this land of our ancestors."

Revolution grieves. Revolution restores life. There is no revolution without Indigenous sovereignty. Revolution is not death but life that survives the death distributed by the colonizers.

CAPITAL:
LUMINARIES AND SATURN

fate/fortuna/primordial debt

king after kings/the stranger/King before kings

gold/silver/carbon

capital/liquid assets/property

elysium/cockaigne/arcadia

crown and capital/borders and markets/blood and soil

center/border/citizenship

spectacle/reproduction/revolution

the surveilled/the slave/the noble savage

eye/coin/the sublime

Melting Light with Carbon an Alchemy

You have plenty of gold lying somewhere underneath your lands. Just issue notes promising your creditors you'll give it to them later. Since no one knows how much gold there really is, there's no limit to how much you can promise.

—THE DEVIL, in *Faust* by Johann Wolfgang von Goethe

I will always be too expensive to buy.

—ADRIAN PIPER

In modern astrology, Saturn is often described through systems thinking. When Saturn provokes us through a hard transit or a stroll into an angular house, we're often told to restructure. The Moon, on the other hand, is associated with biopolitical management. At full moons, there is something to release, and new moon brings a time of ceasing and rest. Their opposing domiciles, Cancer and Capricorn, are described through security. While Cancer is what seeks emotional or inner security, Capricorn seeks material or outer security.

Security itself is a neoliberal commodity. "It's security that matters more than peace," said Len Rosen, a prominent Israeli investment banker, to *Fortune Magazine.* The financial sector literally trades in securities. Our most recent financial bubble, inflating rapidly in the early 2000s, was a security bubble. In his book *Cultures of Financialization,* Max Haiven describes securitization as the neoliberal biopolitical ethos. Securitization is "a technique or technology for achieving moment-to-moment advantage by counterbalancing risks, and also the impulse to customize multiple (often conflicting and contradicting) forms of volatility and chance." Securitization, then, is the management of risk. Because neoliberalism sees us all as mutually competitive and alienated players in an economy that looks and feels like a game, our lives are structured by risk. Securitization literally trades in the future, predicting and managing any chance for risk.

Risk is a property of the Sun, the Moon, and Saturn, with all of their inconvenient ecological events and failing bodies. Certain populations (communities of color) are also "at risk." Securitization, then, is the policing of elements of risk in our society through logic and data. It is a policing of our communities, our futures, and our biorhythms. However, the securities that finance trades with are often shortsighted. Like the traders who encouraged poor and vulnerable families to refinance their homes prior to 2008, they often create risk just so they can manage it. Since most traders do not work past their thirties, their careers are often about mitigating risk, or putting it just far off enough into the future that they won't be around when things c o m e f a l l i n g d o w n.

Both Saturn and the Moon begin with the sickle or crescent. During its cycle, the Moon swells in size, becoming full with its own potential. As symbols of property and capital, Saturn and the Moon both begin with the symbol for labor.

But what is labor? Is labor really a force of will against the tendency of living beings to collapse into lethargy?

While industrialized countries tend to think of labor and leisure as resistant to one another, and of labor as will stretched over the framework of discipline, preindustrialized civilizations defined labor as a release of one's natural tendencies. Before Fortune had anything to do with capital, it was a concept that described the alignment of one's own pattern to that of the natural world. Fortune is the form that changes.

Labor is not hard. We are built by the world so that labor becomes easy.

One of the questions I asked myself as I began writing this book was: "Do money economies inherently support one ideology, or can money, as a medium, be used as a tool for liberation?" While I don't have the answer to that question—because I'm learning that writing is not the answering of the questions you begin with but the finding of new questions you have never considered—I have found that the ways in which we've come to define property and capital are unaligned with the land and the body; they are, in essence, unfortunate.

And! This! Is! All! Very! Bad! Luck! Capitalism is unlucky. White supremacy is unlucky. Patriarchy is unlucky. Ableism is unlucky.

Gold Is in the Details (Or, but what do you do about those with a lot of power?)

In Byzantine icons, small paintings of God made by anonymous monks, the light source of the image was always found within the image itself. The figure of God or Jesus was where light came from, as if He were the human embodiment of the Sun on earth. Light and God in the canvas is a metaphor for gold in the economy. The Church's reserve of gold was what created a standard of measurement for every silver or paper exchange.

By the time of the Renaissance, the paintings of Botticelli and and da Vinci are illuminated by a light source that comes from outside the frame of representation. If light, or the Sun, is a symbol of God, then he has left the picture, although the effects of his power still shine. Since God, in a religious sense, is a symbol for gold in the economic sense, then the Renaissance is when gold begins to leave the economic picture.

In Dutch still-life painting, there is almost never one light source. Because still life is usually painted indoors, there are often multiple windows or candles that create a multiplicity of lighting in the image. These light sources are also usually absent from the frame of the image. Using light as the symbol for the Sun and gold again, the removal of gold from economic life and the use of silver and domestic light—the distillation of gold sunlight into an almost lunar light—to represent daily life coincides with the birth of the financial sector. Dutch still-life painting also represents commodities, which replace people as the central subject of a market-based culture.

While the commodity replaced the person as the ideal citizen in early capitalism, the corporation has since replaced the commodity. The commodity was the image in vogue in early capitalism, but today it is the poststructure, the framework, or the concept. The corporation can be described as an artificial person. Today, corporations enjoy most of the rights that human citizens are allowed, if not more.

While God and gold standards have dissipated as a singular and true beam of light, it turns out that we still want something that feels real. We rely on an increasingly complex set of algorithms to create that reality for us. God is truly in the details—in details so minuscule and exact that only a machine can comprehend them. If God is found in light and the paintings of early capitalism show a dominance of domestic light, of light that is distilled in a room the way the Moon distills sunlight, then late capitalism needs no light but the light of a thousand screens. Luminance has paled so dearly that it is not only silver—it is electric.

Necropolitics and Vital Life Force

The history of modern democracy is, at bottom, a history with two faces, and even two bodies—the solar body, on the one hand, and the nocturnal body, on the other. The major emblems of this nocturnal body are the colonial empire and the pro-slavery state—and more precisely the plantation and the penal colony.... The colonial world, as an offspring of democracy, was not the antithesis of the democratic order. It has always been its double or, again, its nocturnal face....

As Frantz Fanon indicated, this nocturnal face in effect hides a primordial and founding void—the law that originates in nonlaw and that is instituted as law outside the law. Added to this founding void is a second void—this time one of preservation. These two voids are closely imbricated in one another. Paradoxically, the metropolitan democratic order needs this twofold void, first, to give credence to the existence of an irreducible contrast between it and its apparent opposite; second, to nourish its mythological resources and better hide its underneath on the inside as well as on the outside. In other terms, the cost of the mythological logics required for modern democracies to function and survive is the exteriorization of their originary violence to third places, to nonplaces, of

> *which the plantation, the colony, or, today, the camp and the prison, are*
> *emblematic figures.*
>
> —ACHILLE MBEMBE, *Necropolitics*

In *Necropolitics*, Mbembe describes the cultural center of power, or the capital, as a thing that distributes death. He describes sovereignty as "the power and capacity to dictate who is able to live and who must die" and writes that biopower functions "by dividing people into those who must live and those who must die." Kalindi Vora, in her study of surrogate birth workers, the organ industry, and call-center workers argues that colonialism is the extraction "not only of economic (monetary) sources of value, of raw materials and labor-power, but also of life itself." She calls the living material that is extracted from the colonies and sent to the imperial countries "vital life force." Vital life force includes stuff such as kidneys, lungs, babies, and energy.

The astrological luminaries are about capital. The Sun emerges from the sovereign or the center. While images of the Sun depict it as a cultural capital of power, as something that radiates life outward, Mbembe finds that capitals have historically distributed death outward. While the Sun is depicted naturalistically as a warm and golden sphere of light, it is also attached within modernity to an artificial and disinfecting light that kills life forms. When the Sun is depicted as an eye, it is also a technology of the state as a surveiller. The Sun is not just a force of life. It is also a dealer of death.

The Moon emerges from the margins. The margins, moving like tides, are perceived to be what is pushed out of the center. Vora finds that the margin is actually a site that regulates the extraction of life matter toward the center. The Moon is seen to be fertile but also as corrupt. The corruption of sites that are associated with lunar margins—the colonies, marginalized people, sex workers—is enacted by conditions perpetuated by the imperialists. Money, as a metaphor for the marginalized body, is also viewed as corrupt and as self-breeding because it absorbs the reproductive power of exploited peoples.

Within astrology, charts are divided into the night sect and the day sect. Those born during the day have a day chart and those born during the night have a night chart. The Moon is the nighttime luminary and the Sun is the daytime luminary. If the luminaries represent capital, then the Sun represents the daytime face of capital, while the Moon represents the nighttime power that works within capital. Mbembe calls this nocturnal body the colonial state and finds it within the plantation and the penal colony.

Both luminaries are also associated with theater—the Sun with a spectacle culture that emanates from the sovereign, and the Moon with the race theater staged by the public. As luminaries, the Sun and Moon stand for things that don't just act but also enact. Capital is not only a spectacle that is distributed from the center of power toward the margins but is also theater that is enacted from the public toward the sovereign. The theater that capital produces is race, which is a division between life and death—a division between who is allowed to live and who is allowed to die.

The dual theaters of the Sun and Moon create the illusion that the state is able to control life. Foucault writes that there are moments in which it is revealed that the state, in fact, cannot control life—that life is a series of processes that governmentality is unable to replace, control, or regulate. These moments happen when the security apparatuses of the state are revealed.

The government is unable to control life. The government is unable to control life. *The government is unable to control life.* This should be obvious, but it isn't. We authorize the government to deploy war, sanctions, and welfare when we believe that the government is capable of controlling life. Through war, finance, and welfare, institutions seek to control life and distribute death (when I talk about the welfare state I'm not just talking about welfare as social programs but the tendency for the state to act as a public client to private corporations, which is a tendency that includes social programs).

Because death is often associated with people of color, people of color are also sometimes called upon to perform good ancestry and to ritualize public encounters with the dead. Like food, ancestry is expected to occupy the social position of performing cultural authenticity. Ancestor rituals are supposed to be authentic, soul enriching, and connected to certain ethnic traditions. When we perform ancestry, we are also performing ethnicity. We are supposed to have sincere and unironic relationships with our ancestors and with our ethnicity. Ancestor rites are supposed to be real—not counterfeit. Above all, they're not supposed to be funny.

What Do You Do about Those with a Lot of Power?, Cont'd.

Sometimes, when I go back to China, my relatives and I visit my grandma's or great-grandpa's graves. We go to the hill they are buried on, facing the river because those who are buried with their backs facing mountains and their gazes upon waters are lucky. We bring with us masses of counterfeit bills, printed on flammable paper, and food that the spirits do not eat.

My uncle pours good wine into the ground, telling my grandma to have a drink with us while smiling like a trickster. None of the living drink. He lights three cigarettes (cigarettes are a nationalized industry) for my great-grandpa, and my mom complains that he died of smoking in the first place, so why force him to smoke in death? My uncle replies that, if he's already dead, to just let the man smoke. He lights three cigarettes for my grandmother. My mom asks him why, because she never smoked when alive. He brushes her off and says she should enjoy herself in death. Apparently, everyone smokes after they're dead.

Around us, other families burn counterfeit paper versions of things: iPhones, BMWs, mistresses. All the good, Western brand names.

Lu Xun was the one who said Chinese people worship spirits in a way that mocks power. There is always something slightly tongue in cheek about Chinese ancestor worship, whether it's the ridiculous idea that your ancestors from long ago will require an iPhone in the afterlife when your living grandparents don't even know what the internet is (are the dead going to download WeChat and give you a call? What would you do if that happened?) or the placing of chickens next to their graves when their physical bodies, and appetites with them, have become one with the earth. And why do Chinese people burn fake paper for their dead? Why do we burn fake, paper versions of Western commodities, prestigious brands that reek of colonial power, for our ancestors?

Lu Xun says that given the way Chinese people worship spirits, we must either be mocking them or tricking them. No, we could not truly mean it when we place an image of the *nian* demon at our door so he will be scared away by himself. We could not be truly serious when we think our ancestors are satisfied when we give them paper bills that cost $2 for an entire stack of Ben Franklins or red Maos. If we burn mistresses for our grandfathers, we could not be serious without offending our grandmothers.

Our gods are a bureaucratic order of politicians scheming for power that represents the living government of the land. Our relationships to our patriarchs are supposed to reflect our relationships to our party officials and chairmen. We mock our leaders when we imagine our celestial rulers as easily deceived and outwitted. We treat the gods as idiots who can be bought.

Confucius said this about our relationship to the dead:

In dealing with the dead, if we treat them as if they were entirely dead, that would show a want of humanity and should not be done; or, if we

treat them as if they were entirely alive, that would show a want of
wisdom and should not be done. This is why they should be provided
with vessels of bamboo that are not fit for actual use, earthenware vessels
that cannot be used to wash in; wooden implements that are left unfin-
ished; lutes that are strong, but not evenly made; mouth organs that are
complete but not in tune; bells and musical scores that have no stands.
They are called numinous objects (mingqi) because they are used to treat
the dead as ancestral spirits.

In other words, we give the spirits fake things because we can neither deny nor accept them. Acts of worship, for us, are acts of grief that resemble fits of laughter.

Chinese fakes are not real fakes but the liberation of a logo—an advertisement or a brand—from its material existence. The vegetable seller uses Supreme awnings. Grandma's Mike belt has an orange swoosh. The neighbor's Chamel bed sheets are hung out to dry. None of these people have heard of the real Supreme, Nike, or Chanel. Chinese fakery treats all signs as fundamentally owned by fans. If you like it, you can go ahead and define it on your own terms. Because China is both the manufacturer and the market of the world, where products begin and where they go to die a postironic death, it is only in the middle of a commodity's journey, through the West, where it can take the form of the original. In its beginning and at its end, it assumes the role of the copy.

The proletariat is not just the producer from whom time and energy is extracted. The proletariat is also the consumer who must refine an object by consuming it. Rather than living in reality, the proletariat creates their own culture. Only the bourgeois middleman is allowed to be original or real. And that's how white power hid itself—by mediating the raw commodities that the plantation worker produced through the ever-expanding Asian market, held hostage by a consuming addiction. By mediating the relationships that the proletariat is able to develop with themselves, the middleman extracts all value by creating reality.

Truth and realness are fickle feelings. Before and after a thing becomes real, whether that thing is a coin or a worker, it must become a copy first. Fake it until you make it. The original relies on the copy just as much as the copy relies on the original. The value of Louis Vuitton handbags and Supreme hats are bolstered, not inhibited, by the proliferation of their fakes.

To trade only in fakes, as we do with the spirits, in excess displays of abundance—piles of counterfeit cash stacked on top of one another—is the language of a public that trades with itself. Fake money is an oxymoron because money is already the liberated sign.

Money Magic

In the documentary *The Great Hack,* it is mentioned that data has surpassed oil as the world's most valuable commodity. This is a false statement because data itself has already replaced money as capital. Since capital cannot be a commodity with any value because it is the measure by which all other commodities are measured, it can't be said that data has any value. The value of data is also speculative, meaning that it trades on babies who aren't even born yet and seeds that haven't been sown. Data has no value.

Data also has no value because it is debt. Debt is empty of value but full of power. However, neoliberalism is not a power that lives above us but the power that lives within us. It disciplines us not through rigidity but through personal empowerment.

Astrology's doctrine is: as above, so below. So below, as above. Accompanying this maxim is the idea that, because culture is a consensus, we are all players in negotiating our mutual orientation to the world. However, capitalism has taken away the idea of magic as an encompassing cosmological order and reduced magic to the trick—the subtle sleight of hand of a stage magician or shopkeeper.

Money magic means that there is a cosmological order to the ways that value, authority, abundance, and scarcity show up in our world. We do have magical customs—of gift giving in times of scarcity to create abundance and trading in times of abundance to create scarcity—that create fortune. Money magic is not a trick, not a singular ritual that will give you the Midas touch. It is the balancing act otherwise known as community accountability. Community accountability is a love language that turns expected cruelty into tenderness.

Marx once said that capital is a social relation. However, capital is more than a social relation; it is a psychic relation. This means neoliberalism is not only defined in outer mechanisms of a hard economy but also in inner mechanisms of an imagined reality. If capital is really located in the cold, unfeeling light of a computer screen and in loosely connected strings of data that represent their loosely connected human counterparts—if capital is really the magic that pretends to be rational—then the magic of community accountability is the best resistance to neoliberalism.

Magic is an agreement between actors of nature. All we hear about nature is the relationships of competitive species, but that's just the projects that are able to receive funding, because believers in game theory think that there is something to be gained. In nature, there are just as many stories of mutualism, diversification, altruism . . . the list goes on. Practitioners of magic create their own cosmological order.

Capitalism is bad luck. It is bad luck to believe that capital can increase itself and that the world will be reborn on an anticipated doomsday. What money magic means is: create your own Fortune. Create your own alignments between body and land. Work on the relationships that you have, not the ones you dream for.

Creativity Is a Destroyer

One of the ways neoliberalism has changed production is by redefining reproduction as creativity. Creativity is associated with neoliberal values such as entrepreneurship, personal and market freedom, competitiveness, and free land or space. Reproduction, on the other hand . . . not so much.

Joseph Shumpeter describes what he calls creative destruction, which is such an oxymoronic term if you think about it, as an inherent flaw within capitalism. Because capitalism always tries to find the new, the avant-garde, the new frontier, the cutting edge, it leaves behind a trail of old trash. Creativity that destroys. This is the creativity of the pioneers—the creativity of the doctrine of discovery.

And it's not that values of freedom, creativity, and experimentation are bad values. Neoliberal values are often feel-good values. However, neoliberalism is not only the values that it claims to possess. Neoliberalism is an apparatus that negotiates the relationships we are able to develop with ourselves, our friends, our lovers, and our publics. It is a system that mediates intimacy, primarily by extorting the players of its game, whether human beings or public institutions, through debt.

In my book *Astrology and Storytelling,* I talk about the hypocrisy of using the word "karma" if you do not support reparations or decolonization. If karma is your debt, then it is the debt you inherit from your ancestors. Before industrialization, debts were canceled or cleared during certain moons because the habit of owning through owing is an unfortunate one.

We've mentioned before that the first banks were temples in which reserves of gold were held to be used in the event of collective emergencies. Because money was a sacred object, banks themselves were holy places. The right to forgive debt was God's mercy. The ability of the collective to survive Saturn's whims and the Moon's changing nature, or the changing appetites of the land and the eventual failing of the body, depended upon the temple-bank.

Today, what banks export more than resources is debt. This model began in Holland, when Venetian investors granted their emerging commercial classes the seed capital needed for political autonomy from the Hapsburgs. Eventually, as Holland's trading industry diminished and other countries became more competitive, it became the financial center of Europe. In the eighteenth century, Holland created an industry around lending its huge reserves of capital to England. In turn, England copied this model and created a national bank that not only lent money to the government for social services but also to the public itself, by minting bank notes. England exported this model to the United States and lent its former colony capital by the millions. By the end of the eighteenth century, the United States had a national debt of over $75 million.

Marx, in the next century, writes that the wealthiest countries are the ones with the most debt. Alexander Hamilton agreed in theory but not in principle and worked to control American debt, because he understood that power comes from debt. By arguing the case for a national bank and the benefits of a national debt, he and the other Federalists sought to consolidate financial power within the national government. The legacy of Hamilton is the legacy of American debt. To this day, the notes, or dollar bills, that we receive from the Federal Reserve are notes representing the debt that the American public owes the financial sector. Only the Federal Reserve has the authority to create new currency. Since most of our money today is not represented by metals or even paper bills but segments of data, the Federal Reserve controls debt by managing the algorithm of money.

One of the forces that impoverishes third-world countries today is the huge amounts of debt that CIA-installed former puppet dictators took on during moments of neoliberal revolution. These loans were given by the International Monetary Fund at high interest rates with the intention of stripping a country of its assets. Most countries that took out these loans paid off the premiums long ago by depriving their people of much-needed social services, but they are still stuck paying off interest in a never-ending loop.

It turns out that it is possible for wealthy countries to have a lot of debt and that it is also possible for poor countries to have a lot of debt. It turns out that debt is a social relationship unexempt from basic social forces, such as who likes whom, who is related to whom, and who was formerly in love with whom. It turns out that, because debt is a social relationship subject to the whims of a feeling economy, it is fundamentally unpayable.

Renaissance monk François Rabelais laments that, without debt, the astrological and symbolic alliances of the cosmos would simply fall apart:

"A universe sans debts! Amongst the heavenly bodies there would be no regular course whatsoever: all would be in disarray. Jupiter, reckoning that he owed no debt to Saturn, would dispossess him of his sphere, and with his Homeric chain hold in suspension all the Intelligences, gods, heavens, daemons, geniuses, heros, devils, earth, sea and all the elements . . . the Moon would remain dark and bloody; why would the Sun share his light with her? He is under no obligation. The Sun would never shine on their Earth; the heavenly bodies would pour in good influences down upon it."

What Rabelais may have missed is that, in the stories, Jupiter did in fact reckon that he owed Saturn no debts. This impetuousness was the origin of political power.

In the etymology of Saturn we already noted that the authority of government is located not within some external structure but in a consensus of the people who are ruled. Value, too, is not *their* stuff but *our* stuff. When we read the Moon and Saturn together, we find that authority and value are created when there are fortunate alignments of body and land. If the Federal Reserve is the only institution allowed to create *currency,* then the laborer is the only person allowed to create *value.* This is what the origin of Saturn and the Moon, that sickle and crescent, symbolize. Labor produces, and what it produces is *ours.* On the other hand, debt creates currency. Much of the debt owed in today's world is not *our* debt but our actions, decisions, and behaviors reinforce existing debts.

But it's not enough that we, the people as organisms subject to nature, are the real sources of both authority and value. Neoliberalism has never been a system that controls from above. Neoliberalism has always been a from-the-bottom-up system, one that is made from below and by individual economic players. This is what Foucault meant when he described the present as a biopolitical system of control. Neoliberal strategies don't work because someone higher than you in a hierarchy tells you what's what and you must obey or face physical punishment. They work because they provide for you the vocabulary that you use when you seek a relationship with your own body.

If you really want to work on your debts, then work on your relationships.

The oppositional relationship between the Moon and Saturn, rulers of the solstice signs, are about debt. Cancer and Capricorn are signs that are about owing and owning. The oppositional relationship between the Sun and Saturn, however, is about death.

Russell Means once said: "My culture, the Lakota culture, has an oral tradition, so I ordinarily reject writing. So what you read here is not what is written. It's what I've said and someone else has written down. I will allow this because it seems that the only way to communicate with the white world is through the dead, dry leaves of a book."

The only way to communicate with the white world is through the dead, dry leaves of a book.

The only way to communicate with the white world is through the dead.

The Sun is a capital. Capitals distribute death outwardly. Saturn is Arcadia—land of the ancestors. Saturn is dead people. Saturn is people who will not die.

Jodi Byrd writes that "the story of the new world is horror, the story of America is a crime."

Alejandro Murguía writes that American settlers "hungered for gold with a sickness":

> *They would do anything for it. They left families, homes, everything behind; they sailed for eight months abroad leaky, smelly ships to reach California; others, captains and sailors, jumped ship at San Francisco, leaving a fleet of abandoned brigs, barks, and schooners to rot by the piers. They slaughtered all the game they could find and so muddied the rivers and creeks with silt that the once plentiful salmon couldn't survive. The herds of elk and deer, the food source for Native Americans, were practically wiped out in one summer. The miners cheated and killed each other in the goldfields.*

California is a utopia carved out by the craze for gold. In her essay "A Non-Euclidean View of California as a Cold Place to Be," Ursula le Guin writes that:

> *I was told as a child, and like to believe, that California was named "The Golden State" not just for the stuff Sutter found but for the wild poppies on its hills and the wild oats of summer. To the Spanish and Mexicans I gather it was the boondocks; but to the Anglos it has been a true utopia: the Golden Age made accessible by willpower, the wild paradise to be tamed by reason; the place where you go free of the old bonds and cramps, leaving behind your farm and your galoshes, casting aside your rheumatism and your inhibitions, taking up a new "life style" in a not-here-not-now where everybody gets rich quick in the movies or finds the meaning of life or anyhow gets a good tan hang-gliding. And the wild oats and poppies still come up pure gold in cracks in the cement that we have poured over utopia.*

Le Guin also writes that "in 'assuming the role of creator,' we seek what Lao Tzu calls 'the profit of what is not,' rather than participating in what is. To reconstruct the world, to rebuild or rationalize it, is to run the risk of losing or destroying what in fact is."

For Western utopianists, creativity is destruction. When we assume the role of a creator, we see ourselves as capable of reconfiguring the world. Western creatives don't want to deal with the world as it is but with what the world can be. Le Guin also notes that "what the whites perceived as a wilderness to be 'tamed' was in fact better known to human beings than it has ever been since: known and named." When we look at the world and only see what it can become, we neglect what it is.

Saturn is not about should-bes or could-bes. Saturn is about the world as it is.

The luminaries, on the other hand, have often been theatrical. The Sun has to do with the spectacular images that began with monarchy and continue to the stock market. The Moon has to do with carnival and race as a theater that is controlled, performed, and judged by whiteness.

A lot of the time, the conversation around cultural appropriation borrows from the vocabulary of cultural ownership. In these conversations, it is up to the person who feels as if their culture is being taken from them to prove their cultural ownership. These conversations frame culture as something that can be owned. The reason why cultural ownership is borrowed is because property is the only thing that white culture knows how to respect. However, the issue with cultural appropriation is not that a culture owned by one party is stolen by another party. The issue is that, when white people treat cultures of people whom they have enacted violence against as peopleless fashions or mannerisms, they are entertaining the possibility that those cultures can exist without the people behind them. When people see simulations of our own identities and cultures on white bodies, we see people who have tried to kill us wear our clothes as if simulations of us could live while we die. When our cultures are celebrated but not our people, we understand this as white society's comfort with our disappearance. One "Red Man" wrote about the genocide of Indigenous Americans as if he were looking forward to the day when Indigeneity would become a memory that is archived and celebrated by killers. Race as a theater that white people control, perform, and judge among themselves is a theater that anticipates death.

When we imagine and create new worlds, it is also important that we do not adopt the logic of the killer. Western creativity is a killer's creativity. Killers see the act of destroying and the act of creating as the same act. Killers love a blank slate upon which they can start anew. Killers love new identities, and they love to wear other people's clothes. A lot of Western creatives like to be seen as a little bad, a little mischievous, and a little uncontrollable. The American hero is an antihero. The creative antihero is not truly a response to institutional morality but a character who developed out of the horror of America's origin story, which is a story that tries to romance and to mine goodness out of murderers. These antiheroes show up in American fables—the Joker, Jack Kerouac, Huckleberry Finn, Columbus. They are nihilists, hippies, counterculturalists, boys, and conquistadors. For the Western antihero, the world is a bad place that must be conquered. The world is often evoked through femmes, elders, Indigenous people, foreigner Others, and nature as metaphor.

A creativity that works against the Western antihero is a creativity that grows from the world as it is. We create in resistance to the Western antihero when we create with people and with accountability. Living creativities resist destructive creativities. This creativity must reside in resilient community.

CONTRACT WITH SELF AND COMMUNITY

I will never be afraid of precarity because I know you will be there for me. You will never fear precarity because you know I will be there for you.

I refuse to profit from the exploitation of your body and refuse to allow you to profit from the exploitation of mine.

I will never treat a debt/loan to my mother, father, auntie, uncle, sister, brother, friend, or lover the same as a debt/loan to a bank, government, or other institution.

I will never let you treat a debt/loan to your mother, father, auntie, uncle, sister, brother, friend, or lover the same as a debt/loan to a bank, government, or other institution.

_____

_____

5

ETYMOLOGY OF VENUS

Inanna's Ruin and Descent

The ways in which the Romans understood Venus came primarily to Rome from the Near East. Ishtar or Inanna, who was the same goddess worshipped in different nation-states, was the most expansive goddess. This one figure was actually an assimilation of older, local goddesses whose images represented everything from fertility to sexual attraction to forests to sovereignty. Within Venus, one of the oldest archetypes, hides a multitude of meanings.

Venus is the most important planet, after the luminaries, and shines the brightest. When it is at its brightest, it also happens to be in its crescent shape. When Sumerians drew the most important stars, they drew a divine trinity of the Sun, the Moon, and Venus. While the most important astrological text in Babylon and Assyria, the *Enuma Anu Enlil*, barely mentions any other planet except for the Sun and Moon, it is devoted to Venus. The priestesses of Ishtar were not only employed by the king but were also considered to be part of the royal family.

Almost every single civilization implicated in the production of Western astrology, from the Americans to the Chinese to the

Babylonians, distinguishes Venus in its morning phase from its evening phase. As astrologer Robert Hand writes:

> *There are two distinctly different Venuses. All astrological traditions except the modern Western one, and to some extent the Hindu one, recognize this. There is a warrior Venus and a love goddess Venus. They're both female. But one of them is more like Athena. The warrior goddess Venus is Venus as a Morning Star. Phosphorus Lucifer, although it should be 'Lucifera.' There's nothing satanic about it. It's just a warrior goddess. And the evening one is the soft, squishy love goddess. They actually have different names. In Mesopotamia it was Ishtar Akkad and Ishtar Uruk. One was a Morning Star, the other the Evening Star Venus.*

Venus is visible as an evening star in the west for about eight months before it retrogrades, crosses the Sun by inferior conjunction and disappears behind its rays, before becoming visible again but this time as a morning star. There, now visible in the eastern part of the sky, Venus is at its brightest for about another eight months before it, going direct now, disappears behind the Sun again by superior conjunction. When Venus is close to the Sun, it is always invisible unless there is an eclipse, during which it is seen as a speck in the vast body of the Sun. When this happened in the past, it was seen as a very bad omen. The entire cycle takes about 584 days or two years.

Because Venus has a dual presence as a morning and evening star, it has two sides or personalities. Early Greek civilization actually thought that Venus as the morning star and evening star were two separate planets and named them Phosphorous and Hesperus. Only later did they accept the Babylonian view that Phosphorous and Hesperus were the same planet and adopted Ishtar (eastern star) through the goddess Aphrodite.

Inanna/Ishtar's "Descent into the Underworld" is one of the most famous stories about the Babylonian goddess. However, there's another story that complements this one—that of Inanna's rape. In this story, Inanna is sleeping beneath a poplar tree when a gardener, Shukaletuda, strips her of her divine garments and rapes her in her sleep. When Inanna wakes and realizes what happened, she is angry and looks for Shukaletuda to enact her revenge. Three times Inanna looks for him in the mountains; three times Shukaletuda asks his father for advice, and his father says to hide in the city; and, three times, Inanna enacts plagues on the land when she does not find him. Finally, Inanna visits Enki and asks him to allow her justice. When he agrees, Inanna finally finds Shukaletuda and kills him.

Inanna's "Descent into the Underworld," the more famous story, in contrast, tells how Inanna begins her journey to the Underworld dressed lavishly. However, at each of the seven gates of hell, she must take off one article of clothing. As in the story of her rape, Venus is stripped down. By the time Inanna enters hell, she is completely naked and, unprotected, is hung from a hook and unable to escape. In this story, Enki is again the one who rises to the occasion and rescues Inanna. Because of the rules of the Underworld, for Inanna to escape, there must be a replacement for her body in hell. Enki offers three people, and this time, Inanna shows mercy. With her own body at stake, she refuses to subject her servant, her beautician, or her son to hell because she sees that all three have mourned for her. Finally, when she finds her husband has not mourned her one bit and is relaxing under a tree, well-dressed and cheating on her, she chooses him as the one who will replace her in hell and sentences him to eternal damnation.

Both of these stories are about divine justice. Inanna's rape (or, as it would have been called in ancient times, her ruin) is compared with her descent. In the first story, Inanna tries three times to enact justice and, in the second story, she gives three pardons or acts of mercy. In both stories, she is stripped of her divine garments in the same way that Venus, the planet, loses its light twice when it gets too close to the sun. While Enki, the creator of life, plays a part in both stories, justice is ultimately Inanna's decision. She is the one to kill her rapist and choose her husband for her own tribute. Venus is a distributor of justice.

Venus, which spends about an equal amount of time as both a morning and an evening star, is symbolized by the scales—that symbol of law, justice, and legislation. Back and forth, Venus swings from morning to evening appearance like scales weighing what is just and unjust. The oldest and deepest stories about Venus have always related Venus to law. The two stories about Inanna are about how acts of vengeance and mercy balance one another.

In the story of Inanna's rape, it is Shukaletuda's violation of her body that makes him fit for sentencing. It is his act of violence, his rape of her, that creates the injustice that must be corrected. In the second story, it is Inanna's husband's breaking of his marital vows and his inability to mourn her death that makes him a creator of injustice. She comes back like a ghost to haunt and kill him. From these two stories we can see that the law works through both negativity (being passive and deciding to not do anything) and positivity (being active and deciding to do something). It is unlawful both to do something you're not supposed to do *and* to not do something you're supposed to do. Inanna's myths describe what you're not supposed to do (rape) and what you're supposed to do (grieve your wife when she gets sent to the Underworld).

Inanna plays the role of a legislator not only by condemning lawbreakers to death but also by forgiving those who uphold the law. The three plagues of Inanna are a mirror image of her three mercies. The legislator doesn't only discipline but also shows forgiveness. Venus's scales and her appearance as morning and evening star represent the duality of the legislator as both the punisher and the redeemer. The punisher acquires her identity through ruin, and the redeemer acquires her identity through descent. The ability to legislate is the authority to forgive and punish.

The two stories in which we see Inanna's dual sides as punisher and redeemer show up in Christianity in the Old and New Testaments. When Moses leads the Israelites out of Egypt in the myth of Exodus (and it is a myth, as ancient Egypt was never a slave economy—it had a surplus of labor), the plagues that God unleashes upon the people of Egypt, turning water into blood and releasing storms, are similar to the three plagues that Inanna sends upon her land. The story of Jesus, who saves the world from sin through his blood by descending into hell and staying there for three days, is based on Inanna's descent into the Underworld. These stories about divine justice and retribution again define the lawmaker as both vengeful and merciful. It impresses upon the population that receives these myths of the dual purpose of the prime legislator—to both condemn and forgive.

Venus Victrix

Venus was the favorite planet of famous conqueror Julius Caesar. He wore her image on his ring, stamped her name on coins, and dedicated his biggest temple to her. In fact, he said his family line was a direct descendent of Venus.

In Rome, Venus is a *war* goddess. In contemporary astrology, Venus gets attached to peace and abundance. However, in the Roman understanding, peace is never the absence of war but rather is always symbolized by the presence of material abundance. This material abundance, symbolized by feasts and open land, coexisted with a war economy and the acquisition of new resources through conquest. Venus's benefic or positive qualities were always the result of Roman imperialism. If peace has anything to do with Venus, it is the peace of an empire that absorbs wealth through martial conquest.

Roman society spread its empire by normalizing Romanization within its colonies. The decisive factor in the Romanization of colonies was the adoption of Roman law and civil administration to administer said laws. The adoption of Roman laws was not only the adoption by the colonies of Roman ideas of what is property, who is a citizen, and what a work contract entails but also the creation of administrative bodies (assemblies, senates, and consuls) modeled after Roman bureaucracies. The cultural elites already existing in a conquered region would adopt Roman ways of dress, conform to Roman institutions, and perpetuate Roman ideas of what is good and bad. From there, discrepancies between local cultural practices and Roman ones would be joined together after local elites assimilated into the Roman upper classes, keeping the existing class structure intact. Finally, the colonies would be granted citizenship as their formerly enslaved peoples became citizens by joining the military. Then, because Rome was a slave economy that always needed a constant influx of new enslaved bodies, new territories would be conquered again.

As David Graeber observes, ancient empires such as Rome were induced to conquer new territories and enslave new peoples over and over again because, while their economies were slavery based, the military became a path toward citizenship. After a generation or two, the majority of foreign-born slaves in Rome would have become Roman, and new territories would be needed in order to provide new exploitable forms of labor. In antiquity, empire was a cycle.

In this context, Venus is no longer the justice principle. Rather, Venus becomes one and the same as civilization—the type of civilization that distinguishes itself from the barbaric outside. Rome depicted Venus as a war goddess with a civilizing influence. The Roman army was considered to be a social equalizer because any slave could become a citizen, and make his offspring Roman citizens, by joining the military. The Roman version of Venus, Libertas, always wore a cap called the *pileus*. The *pileus* symbolized a specific type of liberty, which was the type of liberty that a slave could hope to achieve through military means. As the Roman Persius writes, "Among the Romans the cap of felt was the emblem of liberty. When a slave obtained his freedom he had his head shaved, and wore instead of his hair an undyed *pileus.*"

Thus, Rome's Venus is not just a legislative principle. Law, for the Romans, is primarily associated with the state and with Roman identity. The Roman Venus, or Libertas, is a form of cultural assimilation and civilization. It is a civilization that assimilates the foreign and enslaved through military means. Roman liberty and freedom is predicated on martial power. Roman depictions of peace do not show any absence of war; rather, they depict domesticity. War occurs on the borders of an empire, and peace is the rich inside. Liberty is the path that leads from the outside toward the inside. What Caesar liked in Venus was her effigy Venus Victrix. Venus Victrix always wins. Venus never represented defeat. She always represented victory and, with victory, the perpetual engine that powers the martial cycle that expands Rome outward. The Venus Victrix was not only the victory of one battle fought well and won but the type of society that builds itself on reproducing victory repetitively. The repetition of military victory builds the bureaucratic and civil state.

When Foucault writes about social norms and the disciplinary society, he writes that power is able to work invisibly precisely because it is power. Instead of seeing power as oppressive acts on an unwilling people through coercive and violent acts by a sovereign power, Foucault describes power as a dispersed set of scripts that everyone perpetuates about what is understood to be normal and good. What Foucault was describing was not a power that was in the process of struggling to be dominant but a power that has already asserted its dominance, like the Roman Empire, and must erase its origins in the present. It keeps its power not by forcing its subjects to obey but by enforcing ideas about what is good and normal. Venus, the planet of power that has already asserted itself, has to do with making social norms. This is why Venus is primarily concerned with describing positive values such as peace, civilization, and liberty. These values all reinforced the Roman martial state in highly specific ways—peace as the promise of richness within an empire, civilization as the Roman social political life that citizens have access to, and liberty as the path that all foreign-born slaves could take to turn themselves into Roman citizens.

If Venus is almost always associated with positive values in Roman culture, the Romans also linked Venus with the public benefactor. Both of the astrological benefics, Venus and Jupiter, are related to the social role that public benefactors played in Rome. Chris Brennan describes the benefactor as "a wealthy private citizen who paid for . . . civic amenities out of their own pocket." These civic amenities included arenas for public discourse, such as the gymnasium and theater; areas for state administration, such as the buildings in which senators met; and the military itself. These civic amenities are distributed to the public by the upper class but also enforce the Roman social order. Public virtues were paid for and controlled by its wealthy citizens. Thus, Venus is associated with both the civil state and wealth—the civil state because civilization resides in the interior of Rome's empire, and wealth because civilization is distributed to a benefiting public by powerful individuals.

If the Babylonian Venus describes justice, then the Roman Venus describes morality. As a moral benefic, Venus focuses on images of goodness. Goodness is peace, which is described in civil administration and material abundance. Venus is a benefic because the Romen upper class controls both the civil state and material resources. As a civilizing goddess, this Venus, despite being a feminine goddess, behaves in a patriarchal manner, as Robert Hand also points out, and looks very much like Athena, who stages a trial to impose Zeus's patriarchal law against the matriarchal vengeance of the Furies. Athena, like Venus and like the Romans, conceals her rule by brute force with rule by decrees and legislation. The type of social relation that a Venus relationship describes is never one understood to be between equals but, instead, establishes a civil society built on hierarchy. The Roman Venus turned justice into law; the civil state and the military that creates the civil state are its institutions. Thus, Venus is the civil state that is often *contrasted with* the military but also *relies on* the military for its material and political means. While the Roman Venus represents herself with a feminine goddess imagery, her de facto form is that of the powerful, wealthy, and patriarchal Roman legislator. The values associated with Venus, despite her feminine mask, represent the interests of powerful men.

Venus, the Highest and Lowest of All High Femmes Both Beautiful and Ugly

Trigger warning: this section contains historical examples of hypersexualization.

The duality of Venus changed when Roman ideas were resurrected during the Renaissance. This resurrection of Roman ideology, which was also a resurrection of astrology, meant Roman ideas were not brought back intact but were recreated to suit Enlightenment ideology. The Renaissance is the first time we begin to see Venus described as a love goddess—specifically, a love goddess who is typically described through the eyes of a male suitor. As Venus, still named with her Roman name, reemerged, she reemerged with a gendered image that emphasized Enlightenment sensibilities.

No longer was Venus's duality associated with discipline and mercy or the administration of morality by a civil state. Her duality now emerged from hypersexualized feelings around morality. The Renaissance version of Venus was either the divine goddess, chaste and pure, who represented divine innocence; or she was the debauched goddess, fertile and wanton, who represented the eternal whore. As Anthony Aveni writes in his book *Conversing with the Planets,* Venus's "extreme swings of position between evening and morning star made her capable of the lowest, most reprehensible debauchery as well as the highest form of pure love."

The Greco-Roman depictions of the beautiful human body celebrated the male, athletic body. For Socrates, the beauty of the wrestler and the runner came from the activation of their bodies on the fields, in competition, and in sports. Greco-Roman ideas about bodies, purpose, and utility were centered around the gymnasium, and they looked for beauty through the real, living, moving bodies of men and boys. The judges of beauty, who were also men, looked for beauty in bodies that they could project themselves into. If the Roman Venus was a feminine symbol, it wasn't because of her associations with sexuality. It was because women in Rome were relegated to the private sphere. Venus represented the patriarchal values that also defined the private spheres of domestic affairs and private wealth.

When the nude body was depicted in Renaissance-era art, however, it typically was the female, unathletic body. This body was usually seen reclining and receptive to a male viewer. These paintings of beautiful women didn't celebrate the nobility of athleticism even if they, like the Greeks and Romans, followed the formula of symmetry and harmony as beauty. These paintings of women depicted their bodies as flesh, tempting men away from the true, divine, and ideal beauty that cannot exist in the living world with all of its imperfections.

Botticelli's *Primavera,* which he painted in 1478, shows the Renaissance-era duality of Venus. Venus's figure splits the canvas in two. On one side are the three figures of Juvenescence, Splendor, and Abundant Pleasure; on the other are Chastity, Pulchritude, and Voluptuousness. Aveni describes the first side as "the carnal-terrestrial aspect," the second as "love of the more ethereal kind," and the painting in its entirety as an elaboration on "the paired aspects that constituted the nature of love in Babylonian Ishtar's morning and evening star duality." He writes, "Renaissance philosophers recast celestial Venus in these two aspects in a rather complex history of love. One is contemplative, divine, and immaterial, the kind we still call platonic and to which only prophets and saints can aspire. The other Venus is tangible and terrestrial; she tempts the male imagination through visual, tactile sensation, ultimately into debauchery."

Botticelli's other painting of Venus, *The Birth of Venus,* follows the *Primavera* compositionally and puts Venus at the center of the painting. However, this time she is depicted fully nude with her hands covering her genitals and breasts. On one side is the Hora of spring (perhaps representing Taurus) about to cover her with a cloak, and on the other is Zephyr (the west wind, perhaps representing Libra) about to take her into his arms. This painting summarizes the male reaction to the feminine body in the Renaissance era. On one hand, the Hora's clock and Venus's hands illustrate the patriarchal urge to instruct women to cover parts of their body before anyone violates them. On the other side of the painting, the incoming Zephyr heading toward the naked body of Venus creates the feeling that she is something ready to be taken away and conquered. From both sides, *The Birth of Venus* illustrates the vulnerability of Venus. If Renaissance-era painters are concerned with Venus's vulnerability, then what does Venus represent that makes it so pertinent for her to be felt as vulnerable?

In Titian's *Sacred and Profane Love,* the celestial Venus is seen nude, reclining before a background of trees and wildlife, while the terrestrial Venus is clothed and ready for a wedding. Behind her is a castle—a marker of civilization. Titian paints sacred love as a nude woman sitting in nature and profane love as a clothed woman constrained by society. The dichotomy that Titian references in this painting is the Neoplatonic relation between the sacred and the profane. While the sacred expresses a unity of nature and the ability to live naked and innocent, the profane expresses mundane, worldly affairs that distract man from the divine. The nude figure of Venus, in Titian's painting, is meant to depict the lost purity of naked truth. Titian's Venuses are a dichotomy between civilization and nature, referencing the lost innocence of paradise.

The nude Venus, who is also the sacred Venus, is unashamed of her nakedness, as if she does not know or understand the sexual power of her own body. This is important because it references a relationship with the body that existed before Adam and Eve left Eden. While the sexualized female figure is made into a fetish, she is also more pure, closer to nature, and in a state of perfection that is no longer attainable. While the clothed and marriage-seeking female figure is chaste, she is also considered worldly and less divine. She clothes herself because she is aware of good and evil, of sexuality and things that should not be known. The splitting of the canvas into sections represents the Christian splitting of the universe into different moral dimensions: hell, paradise, and the worldly realm.

The hypersexualized imagery around the Renaissance Venus is not only a gendered relation but a fundamental relation between nature and civilization. The anxieties that the hypersexual images of Venus express—vulnerability, temptation, and excess—may be expressed through gendered aesthetics, but they emerge from the patriarchal relation between nature and state. The Renaissance was a historical period in which wealthy merchants began to establish financial and banking centers of power within cities such as Florence and Venice. The Italian arts paid for by these wealthy patrons centered culture around wealth. Subversively, both Botticelli and Titian used the nude female body to represent the pure arts and truth as oppositional to a civilization that depended more and more on the financial power of the banks.

While the dichotomy between nature and civilization shows up through a gendered presentation, gender hides its economic intention. The natural side of Venus describes Italy's link to its natural landscape, while the civilized side describes an urban life controlled by wealth. Botticelli's and Titian's moral anxieties concerning the natural and sacred or the civilized and profane are anxieties about the state: What is the state as an identity? Is cultural inheritance the fortune of powerful families such as the Medicis and the Albizzis, or does culture reveal itself through the cultivated Italian landscape? If the civil state promises peace to its citizens, and that peace must also provide material abundance, then where does that material abundance come from? The cities or the land?

In the 1800s, an African woman named Saartjie Baartman was exhibited by Scottish "handlers" in London under the name of the "Venus Hottentot." Though Baartman never allowed herself to be seen nude, almost all drawn images of her show nudity. Her exhibitors claimed that "she would make the fortune of any person who shewed her in London" and that "people came to see her because they saw her not as a person but as a pure example of this one part of the natural world." Around the same time, an archeological craze had taken over Europe. Figurines of nude female figures found in Austria, Germany, and Siberia were named Venus. While the Venus figurines were always found in Europe, Baartman was compared to these archeological findings. Though the Africa that Baartman came from was, in fact, located in modernity, Europeans of the 1800s equated contemporary Africa to a prehistoric Europe. As a Black woman, Baartman's body represented to Londoners a long-lost sacred and primordial sexuality. What Baartman's exhibitors meant when they said she was a "pure example" of "the natural world" is that, as a Venus archetype, Baartman was trapped within a European complex around civilization, nature, and sexuality.

The display of Baartman's person was accompanied by a small leaflet that gave her a backstory for Londoners who came to see her. On the leaflet, it claimed that "Her Country is situated not less than 600 Miles from the Cape, the Inhabitants of which are rich in Cattle and sell them by barter for a mere trifle. A Bottle of Brandy, or small roll of Tobacco will purchase several Sheep." The Africa that this leaflet represents is not only rich but full of inhabitants who are all too willing to exchange their natural resources for a "mere trifle."

The type of Venus that Baartman represented to the European imagination, which converges at the intersections of purity, sexuality, civilization, and nature, has everything to do with the Venus that represents the civil state. Whether Venus represents friendship or beauty or sex or love, the relationship it represents is never equal because Venus always represents wealth. Wealth is always a power relation. While Venus's power in Rome was related to the civil state, the Renaissance Venus represents an anxiety around wealth and power, and the colonial Venus represents the promise of the colonies as sites where wealth was accessible for European conquest. The colonial Venus redeems God's realm by imagining the purity of a paradise that was lost and must be regained. Europe seeks to save the colonized world through the Christian God because it perceives the colonies as a place of unprincipled wealth. If Rome's Venus provided a path toward civilization for its foreign-born slave—a path toward the interior from the exterior—then the colonial Venus seeks to conquer what is culturally alien. It redeems the interior through a power relation to the exterior.

The feminized body, as a site of reproduction, symbolically represents abundance to a patriarchal society. If the Roman Venus celebrated wealth, then it also celebrated subjugation. The Renaissance Venus depicts subjugation as a sexual fetish in order to illustrate an innocent and profane world turning away from emerging financial power. The colonial Venus celebrates subjugation and rejoices in Europe's position as a moral and redemptive purchaser of power. Venus is the question of who is civilized and who is savage— a question resolved through subjugation to power. The question of who is civilized and who is not is also a question of who is able to be innocent and who is not. The psychosexual impulses of Enlightenment-era men were preoccupied with the innocence or profanity of the feminine body. This anxiety, which was always the anxiety around the innocence or profanity of the state, became a preoccupation with the innocence and profanity of the colonized lands from which the state derived its wealth and power.

Stars, Hearts, Flowers, Pentacles, and Snakes

Deception and gender have a long and entwined history. Nudity, as in the paintings of Titian and Botticelli, is a metaphor for truth and artistic freedom. However, as the female body became displayed publicly more and more, the faces of the female figures in paintings also became more inaccessible and mysterious. Femininity became thought of as the deceptive gender.

For the Greeks and Romans, beauty was truth, and truth was what happened when the utility of an object aligned with its purpose. Socrates is recorded to have said that an object can be beautiful and ugly, just as a thing can be true to one person and false to another. Likening beauty to goodness and ugliness to badness, Socrates said, "What is good for hunger may be bad for fever, and what is good for fever bad for hunger; or again, what is good for a wrestler is often bad for a runner. . . . If, therefore, a thing is well suited to its purpose, with respect to this it is beautiful and good; and, should the contrary be the case, then it is bad and ugly."

The fabricating arts—which included painting, because it created an illusory and manipulated field of perception—were only imitations of the truthful beauty that might remain in nature. Beauty within nature was truthful and beauty within art was fabricated. As Plato writes in *The Republic:* "The imitator, I said, is a long way off the truth, and can do all things because he lightly touches on a small part of them, and that part is an image. . . . The imitative art is an inferior who marries an inferior, and has inferior offspring." Human imitative art was a gradual and inevitable decay of natural beauty.

In Greek and Roman art, just as in all ancient art, human figures were not depicted naturalistically but stylistically. They were depicted according to formulas of representation that followed religious principles. Greco-Roman art imitated Egyptian formulas, calculating exactly how tall a torso and leg could be drawn in proportion to a head. While the Greeks and Romans had their own unique formulas for the proper depiction of bodies, their stylistic choices reflected the fact that their art was a continuation of an ancient Near Eastern aesthetic tradition that synthesized a variety of bodies—whether male or female, old or young, animal or human—into a mathematical ideal. The heads of old men sat on young bodies, breasts hovered above phalluses, and the heads of animals formed chimeras with human arms and legs. These ideals were not spiritual ideations. They were imaginative mixtures of elements found in nature. Greco-Roman artists placed themselves within the context of Near Eastern art, drawing and painting and sculpting the body not as accurate depictions of nature but as ideograms.

Renaissance-era interpretations of Greek and Roman beauty ideals, however, were vastly different from how those ideals actually operated within the ancient Near East. In the Middle Ages, artists ceased depicting human bodies in a beautiful way. Instead, they looked for beauty in spiritual and formless dimensions. When Greco-Roman forms were resurrected in the Renaissance era, their formulaic stylistic choices were understood outside the context of continuing a Near Eastern tradition and were instead seen as the cooperation of forms within a designed world created by a Christian God. Vitruvius, whose works would inspire Renaissance-era architectural visions of geometry and harmony, writes that "symmetry is a proper agreement between the members of the work itself, and the metric correspondence between the separate parts and the scheme as a whole." Galen, writing in the second century AD, writes that "beauty does not lie in the individual elements, but in the harmonious proportion of the parts, in the proportion of one finger in relation to another, of all the fingers to the whole hand, of the rest of the hand to the wrist, of this last to the forearm, of the forearm to the whole arm, and finally of all the parts to all the others."

What changed between the Greco-Roman era and the Renaissance period was that beauty (and truth) ceased to be something that could be found in the physical realm and became something that existed in the spiritual realm, unattainable by man due to his original sin. Beauty was uplifted from its historical materiality. Symmetry and harmony referenced a lost Eden of perfect and cooperating forms. For Renaissance-era philosophers, artists, and architects, sacred geometry merged Christian and Gnostic ideas of God, perfection, and spiritual purity with artifacts from Greek and Roman antiquity, which tended to follow strict formulas of representation. While Greco-Romans saw their aesthetic formulas as continuities of the Near Eastern styles, Renaissance-era artists used their rules of representation to create an exclusively Western and universal canon. Artistic forms that deviated from these rules of representation were seen as ugly and primitive. Beauty was no longer only objects that were well-suited for their intended purpose, as it was for Socrates, but objects that were well-formed and well-proportioned according to the divine design of the universe. Through a mixture of Christianity and a longing for antiquity, Renaissance philosophers yearned for a beauty that was objective, ideal, and universal.

Because Venus has a regular cycle, it represents the symmetry and divine ordering of the cosmos. When the conjunctions of Venus to the sun are plotted along a circular zodiac wheel, five evenly spaced points emerge, upon which a five-pointed star can be drawn. Over the course of several cycles, Venus's synodic cycles represent a perfectly symmetrical flower. If Venus's alignments and intersections with the Earth are plotted within a circle, they form a sacred heart shape.

True beauty, for Renaissance philosophers, left the realm of aesthetics and entered the realm of mathematics. Because mathematics was a rational and spiritual practice without the sin of depicting worldly forms, it became synonymous with godly wisdom. As symbols of mathematical Venus, the symmetrical heart, flower, and star were not aesthetic inventions but discoveries within the field of mathematics about the divine world. These symbols do not try to depict a human heart, any actual species of flower, or what stars look like to the eye accurately; they are abstract renderings of principles that seem to organize the universe through symbolic cooperation and harmony. Instead of finding beauty in the natural world, which includes the messiness of bodies and animals and plants, Renaissance philosophers found beauty in clean geometric shapes. The heart, the flower, and the star are symbols of Venus not because they attempt to depict elements of physical beauty but because they depict examples of mathematical beauty. While parts of the natural world could become beautiful when they conformed to sacred geometric shapes, their lack of perfection revealed their fleshly and sinful nature that could only be redeemed by God, the prime legislator.

However, again, Venus, along with all astrological symbols, always has a dual image. If Venus is sometimes perfect, beautiful, and good, then Venus is also flawed, ugly, and evil. Around the same time that Venus reemerged as a femme figure, Venus also emerged as a masculine figure: Lucifer. If Venus is sometimes the moral perfection of God, then Venus is also the bankruptcy of Satan.

In Christian folklore, as Rob Hand mentioned, bright Venus eventually became attached to Lucifer as the light bearer. Venus's five-pointed star, referencing Venus's symmetrical and perfect conjunctions of the Sun, become the Satanic pentacle when inverted. Like Inanna, Lucifer is a figure who is defined by his descent. Lucifer, who used to be God's favorite angel, rebelled against him. In doing so, he defiled himself against all that is holy and became the personification of baseness. Before his fall, according to Hildegard von Bingen, Lucifer was "adorned with gems that sparkled like a starry sky, so that the countless flittering beams that shone out from the splendor of all his ornaments flooded the world with light." Dante writes about Lucifer during his fall from grace: "If once he was as beautiful as he is ugly now, / And lifted up his brows against his Maker, / Well may all sorrow proceed from him."

Lucifer's fall from grace was described in aesthetic terms. Grace, as a concept, was similar to how late-Renaissance philosophers understood beauty. When Lucifer fell from grace, he didn't just become evil. He also became ugly. For Renaissance philosophers, good was represented by grace and beauty. Ugliness personified evil.

In the Roman Empire and Middle Ages, concepts of ugliness and monstrosity didn't exist in the same form they assumed in the Renaissance and later. While Pliny the Elder's chronicles of the world, *Natural History,* described all sorts of impossible beings, such as people who had eyes in the middle of their heads and odd numbers of limbs, the existence of these beings was not portrayed as demonic or evil. Instead, they were described as extraordinary, curious, and part of divine Creation. Only after the Renaissance, when beauty was allied with impossible divinity, did deformation and ugliness also become synonymous with evil.

However, Lucifer is not always described as ugly. There is an equally long tradition of describing the prince of darkness as beautiful. John Milton, who lived and wrote in the seventeenth century, described Satan in *Paradise Lost* as a being who was once the most beautiful angel of them all but, because of his hubris, descended and became ugly. In the following passage, Satan is a metaphor for Venus's descent in the heavens:

> *He above the rest*
> *In shape and gesture proudly eminent*
> *Stood like a tower. His form had yet not lost*
> *All her original brightness, nor appeared*
> *Less than archangel ruined, and th' excess*
> *Of glory obscured: as when the sun new-risen*

Looks through the horizontal misty air
Shorn of his beams, or from behind the moon
In dim eclipse disastrous twilight sheds
On half the nations, and with fear of change
Perplexes monarchs. Darkened so, yet shone
Above them all th' archangel; but his face
Deep scars of thunder had intrenched, and care
Sat on his faded cheek, but under brows
Of dauntless courage, and considerate pride
Waiting revenge. Cruel his eye, but cast
Signs of remorse and passion to behold
The fellows of his crime, the followers rather
(Far other once beheld in bliss), condemned
Forever now to have their lot in pain.

The appearance of Lucifer is compared to the "original bright-ness" of Venus. Only later in the verse is the archangel Lucifer "ruined," "darkened," and his "glory obscured." However, even then, the faded Lucifer is "of dauntless courage," "considerate pride," and full of "remorse and passions." Though Lucifer falls from divine grace and beauty, Milton doesn't describe him as deformed or physically ugly. In fact, Lucifer, the masculine version of Venus, was a sexual temptation. Statues depicting Lucifer were frequently deemed too sexy for church, such as Guillaume Geefs's 1848 sculp-ture *The Genius of Evil* and his younger brother Joseph Geek's *The Angel of Evil.*

Later on in *Paradise Lost,* Milton describes the snake in the garden of Eden, the one who convinced Eve to eat the apple, as Lucifer in disguise. In the Bible, deception was not always seen as evil or even a sin. There have been multiple instances in which God himself deceives his followers. In Milton's version of events, how-ever, Lucifer as the snake becomes a symbol of deceit, cunning, and guile. Falsehood becomes the embodiment of evil. In *Paradise Lost,* original sin was not an informed choice for Adam and Eve but one that resulted from Satan's original deception.

Whereas truth is often conflated with masculine beauty, feminine beauty is often conflated with deception. Decorative pieces of clothing and jewelry, or makeup that conceals, represented a type of beauty that deceived other people into attraction. As Baldassare Castiglione writes in *The Courtier:*

> *Haven't you noticed how much prettier a woman is if, when she makes up, she does so with so little that those who see her cannot tell whether she is made up or not. But others are so bedaubed that it looks like they're wearing a mask and dare not laugh because they fear that it will crack. Such women never change colour except when they dress in the morning, and must spend the rest of the day like motionless wooden images, showing themselves only by torchlight or, as crafty merchants do when they show their cloth, in dimly lit places. How much nicer it is to see a woman, a good-looking one I mean, who obviously has nothing on her face, neither white nor red but just her natural color, which may be pale or sometimes slightly tinged with a blush caused by embarrassment or the like, maybe with her hair tousled and whose gestures are simple and natural, without working at being beautiful?*

As further evidence of this cultural norm, Sophie Volpp observes in "The Discourse of Male Marriage: Li Yu's 'A Male Mencius's Mother'" that male sex workers in the seventeenth century were seen as less artificial than female sex workers. One of the buyers is quoted as saying, "If a boy's unattractive, he looks it; if he's perfect, he also looks it. There's absolutely no artifice about him; he's natural from head to toe. With a pretty boy, what you see is what you get; with a pretty woman, you never know." Feminine beauty, done up by makeup and costuming and learned charms, is deceptive; only male beauty is the real thing. Within Western gender norms, femininity is adopted by putting on decor, while masculinity is adopted by simplifying the wardrobe and removing decor. Artifice is put on to express femininity, and it is removed to express masculinity.

Likewise, the fall of Lucifer from grace took place because he had become vain, which occurred because he was beautiful. Vanity is a particular type of hubris that is almost always feminine in representation. Vanity is also a sin of being overly civilized, being too self-aware about your appearance, and attempting to define God's gift of beauty to you as your own property. In the relation between nature and civilization, vanity is the attempt to overcivilize nature.

If nude female figures represent the experience of femininity when it appears outside the rules of civilization, femininity that predates civilization, and femininity that has yet to be conquered, then Lucifer's vanity represents the pitfalls of overcivilization. While Venus painted as a nude goddess becomes the male artist's subversive alienation from society and his attachment to sublime artistic truth, Lucifer fell because he identified too strongly with the civil state. Beauty disappears when it becomes self-aware. It is unable to describe itself and relies on its gazer's eyes to tell it who it is. In other words, beauty is attached to innocence because it does not seek to define itself. Since the innocence of unaware beauty can only be depicted by male artists who paint seemingly unaware female subjects, divine truth is only available to male authors.

The Decadent Garden

Venus entered popular imagination in the 1800s through venereal disease. The root of the word "venereal" is, in fact, Venus. In the 1800s, almost all politicians, artists, and other public figures suffered from syphilis. While the symbolic decay that the bourgeois was concerned about was coded as cultural and racial, the bourgeois also suffered the biological symptoms of syphilis. The symptoms of syphilis—mood swings, loss of memory, and a change in taste—became compared with a narcissistic aristocratic culture that young members of the bourgeoisie sought to emulate, even as they critiqued their old rulers.

Novels such as Huysmans's *À Rebours (Against Nature)*, the public appetite for the otherworldly sensations produced by absinthe, and the paintings of Klimt reproduced the aesthetic quality of the aristo-crats for the new bourgeois elite through the Decadent movement. In *À Rebours,* a lone man suffering from syphilis isolates himself from society and seeks to indulge himself only in aesthetic things. He sur-rounds himself with orange because it is the most garish color, and he feasts on a banquet of black foods—some fresh, such as plums and caviar, and others rotten. Klimt represents nudity not as ide-alized figures, as in the classical tradition, but as undulating and frequently masturbating nihilistic figures. Part of the myth around Klimt was that he kept a cast of nude women and cats around his home and encouraged the women to masturbate openly. The Dec-adent movement that Huysmans and Klimt were involved in saw art—artificial, humanistic, and impulsive—as a disease. Instead, Decadent art was, like venereal disease, a result of overcivilization and overpopulation—the alienation of modern man not only from God but also against nature.

The Vienna of the Decadent movement chose Athena as the protector of their city. Athena, for bourgeois Austrians, represented a new culture of rationality, science, and progress that would take over both the rotten aristocracy and the irrational masses. Athena's wisdom exemplified the bourgeois values and sought to unify all social classes in a well-coordinated dance, cultivating the mind through the arts and public education. These values were captured in the motto of the Austrian bourgeois elite: *Wissen macht Frei* or "knowledge creates freedom."

In this era, public executions disappeared from the city center, and the penal state became an institution of prisons and schools. Rather than punishing the body in executions during which the public often perceived the executed as a folk hero and the execu-tioner as a criminal, the bourgeoisie hid the incarcerated away in prisons and sought to reform the mind. Art became secular. The new bourgeois class redefined culture away from religious morals and as a secular tool through which decayed minds could become redeemed and renewed. This cultural renewal was necessary in what the bourgeoisie saw as a decaying world ruled over by the values of an isolated aristocratic class that cared only about its own affairs.

Roman ideals, such as Venus, lived new lives inside that great bourgeois project, the modern metropolis. On an urn that was given to Georg Ritter von Schönerer—an anti-Semitic Austrian politician who succeeded in organizing nationalists into a powerful force— Minerva, the Roman version of Athena, was presented as a goddess who stood for civil engineering, while Mercury became administration. The Vienna of the 1800s did not just want to revive culture through Roman antiquity; they wanted to use its rhetoric to create a new, modern project. They remade modernity and its patron saint, Venus. Within the metropolis, Venus as civilization and Venus as power were firmly established through new architectural forms.

From medieval times to the modern era, the garden occupies a special position within Europe's literary and artistic traditions. The garden represents Venus. The garden correlates points along the dichotomies between nature and civilization, God and man, and paradise and the world. In Christian folklore, the garden of Eden represents the primordial site where humans were created in perfect harmony with nature. In industrial times, the garden ceased to be a representation of perfect nature and became a representation of cultivated nature. Nature, in the industrialized metropolis, was found in the predesigned parks that became arenas for public discourse. These parks were not made to represent nature but culture. Architects saw the private garden as an extension of the house and the public park as an extension of the metropolis. As William Morris writes: "Large or small, the garden should look well-ordered and rich; it should be closed off from the outer world; it should in no way imitate the purposes or accidents of nature, but rather look like something which one could see nowhere else but in a human dwelling."

While land use in the Renaissance era was still mostly common to those who worked the land, though protected by feudal lords, modernity embraced private industry. A vital part of industrialization was the claiming of public land by private interests. Before the 1600s, most of Europe's landscape was farmed as common land reserved for communal use by peasants. By the 1800s, all farmable land had become privatized, and the only common lands that remained were in the rough mountainous regions or the lowlands. If, before industrialization, the walled garden represented the contrast between nature and civilization, then after industrialization the urban garden represented the contract between the public and the private—between common and corporate. The public parks inside industrial Europe's cities reinforced bourgeois values regarding privacy as a continuation of comfort and grew with the private sector. As an extension of the house and of private property, the garden within industrial Europe was a private space and not a public space. The metropolis itself, as an urban garden, was designed to protect privacy and bourgeois comfort.

The Ringstrasse, a pentagonal road, encircles Vienna's city center and buffers institutions of the liberal bourgeois—parliaments, libraries, museums, and buildings of civil administration—against the city's proletarian outskirts. As Carl Schorske writes in *Fin-de-Siècle Vienna: Politics and Culture,* the old city enclosed by the Ringstrasse became "museum-like," while the road itself served as a "sociological isolation belt." It provided a buffer zone, inside which institutions that protected private industry formed a rich center and outside which the proletariat lived and worked in the more polluted factories. As Otto Wagner put it, "the metropolis is where modern luxury resides." Hitler, especially, believed that the architecture inside the Ringstrasse of Vienna reflected his own cultural values: "From morning until late at night, I ran from one object of interest to another, but it was always the buildings that held my primary interest. For hours I could stand in front of the Opera, for hours I could gaze at the Parliament; the whole Ring Boulevard seemed to me like an enchantment out of the 'Thousand-and-One Nights.'" This walled garden that enchanted Hitler was a protected zone that made the metropolis seem to harmonize with nature. The bourgeoisie metropolis was an urban garden.

The garden is a Venus symbol because it is a place in which gendered relations are heightened, made violent, and hypersexualized. The walled garden offers chastity and the protection of sacred desire from worldly decay, while the original garden of Eden is the site of original female sin. In early modernity, female figures in paintings began to represent a social force responsible for the healing and redemption of a degenerating masculinity. In Oskar Kokoschka's play *Murderer, Hope of Women,* there are two main characters: Man and Woman. While Woman first rejects Man's advances, he is wounded but, eventually, Woman nurtures Man back to health. Once Man has recovered, he is able to become fully redeemed when he kills Woman. In this play, Woman is the figure who must be sacrificed to redeem Man. This psychosexual drama imagines femininity as a temptress who must be killed. In short, the death of Woman, in Kokoschka's play, represents both Man's alienation from the natural world and his alienation from the artificial world. The sexual fetish of Woman shocks Man into action, but only by murdering his sexual fetish can Man redeem his morality. Through violence, Man sacrifices Woman and regains paradise. The metropolis, as garden, is an arena where gendered aesthetics are staged. In the garden as stage, femininity is sacrificed and masculinity is redeemed.

Joseph Banks, a wealthy explorer who traveled to Tahiti in the 1700s, became interested in the island because the journals of earlier explorers had called it paradise. Once there, he set up camp at what he called Fort Venus and wrote extensively about how innocent, clean, and sexually liberal the Indigenous people were, especially the young girls. In a colonial context, the literary trope

of paradise became projected upon real lands. For Banks, Tahitian girls represented the sacred, natural love that Titian idealized
and contrasted against profane or civilized love. He saw Tahitian
people as more pure, sexually free—as if they had never left the
garden of Eden. Like the paradise that Man seeks in Kokoschka's
play, the colonialist seeks redemption through the colonies; is spiritually awakened by his sexual desire for its young, feminine inhabitants; and redeems himself by killing the object of his desire. As in
Kokoschka's play, Europe kills the primitive Venus of the colonized
world to revive itself.

In the Renaissance, Venus represented a moral complex.
In modernity, Venus is often imagined as a garden. This garden
sometimes takes the form of the metropolis and, other times, takes
the place of the countryside or island. Venus's domain is not a
real place but a bordered, or walled place, that is constructed to
stage morality. The bordered garden is a bourgeois invention that
negotiates morality. Because Venus is always imagined to be constructed or artificial, bourgeois morality is also imagined as protection (from outside forces) and anxiety (over overcivilization and
overprotection).

Venus, as moral complex, is about the border. For Venus, borders protect and domesticate. Borders protect both the profane
and sacred gardens of the European metropolis and the idealized
sites where colonizers imagine paradise. This border, however, is
not a neutral construction but a power relation. In the same way
that Man fears the temptation that is Woman and redeems his
own morality by killing her, Europe, fearing its own decay, seeks
spiritual redemption in Paradise. As in *Murderer, Hope of Women,*
the redemption is ultimately both tragic and violent. Venus is the
social performance of gender and gender is never neutral. Rather,
gendered is a set of staged aesthetics that are defined within bordered relations. Civil society and sexuality emerges from processes
of colonization that organize people, plants, and animals into these

bordered relations—the masculine/feminine, the public/private, the natural/cultural, and the sacred/profane. The social performance of gender that Venus enacts does not describe individual experience but is poised to organize large social bodies in relation to one another.

The Mass Social Body

Schoenberg's three-act opera, *Moses und Aron,* provides context for how modern Europe thought about the mass populace. In this work, Moses receives unfathomable knowledge from God. However, he is unable to communicate this message to the Israelites in terms they will understand. Aaron agrees to be Moses's spokesperson and to translate the message. However, the more that Aaron tries to communicate Moses's message, the more glib it becomes. While Moses seeks to illustrate God's abstract truth in metaphorical terms, turning his staff into a snake to demonstrate God's flexibility, the people he leads only care about how God will crush the Egyptians. When Moses disappears for a long period of time to receive God's commandments, the people become impatient and start to lose hope. When Moses smashes the tablets, the people are confused. Aaron, as Moses's translator, tells the people of a promised land full of milk and honey, allows them to worship idols such as the golden calf, and creates an image of a pillar to lead them forward. While Moses stands for absolute truth that is impossible to comprehend save for a select few, Aaron represents the deliverance of a partially falsified truth to the masses.

The enclosure policies that built modernity—the processes through which the bourgeoisie stole proletarian land by privatizing common land—was a displacement process. As industrialization forced peasants away from farms and into the cities, the bourgeois elite began to describe the populace as a great, big moving mass in which individuals are not distinct from one another but move mindlessly as a collective. Foucault found that, while sovereigns during feudalism orchestrated power by distributing death, liberal governments exercised power by preventing death. One of the fundamental arguments between the aristocrats and the middle class was around the question of how many poor people should be allowed to exist. The aristocrats feared a large poor population, since the presence of more poor people made a successful rebellion more likely. Feudal lords tended to live in relative isolation, surrounded by their peasants. The new bourgeoisie, however, needed to keep a large population of poor people around so they could control the market of labor power. Because industrialists lived in cities where poor people were workers and not farmers, they needed a large number of workers to compete with one another to drive wages down.

Descriptions of the mass, which were really descriptions of the proletariat, were incredibly gendered and resembled bourgeois ideas about femininity. Le Bon, in his book *The Crowd,* claims that crowds are "little adapted to reasoning," anarchist, and "barbarian." The mass was described as irrational, fickle, and overly pragmatic or materialistic. They devoted far too much time to thinking about when the next meal would be coming and too little time to acquiring the knowledge necessary for class ascension. Members of the proletariat were part of this undistinguished collective mass until they received the proper education that led them to establish private industry and rise in the social hierarchy—a process through which they left their identity as a part of the mass and became individuals. The ways in which the proletariat were blamed for their own condition (a lack of education, dirtiness, and spending too much money on knickknacks) were similar to the ways in which feminine people are blamed for the oppressions of their own existence (wantonness, frivolity, irrationality). Since femininity as a gender must inherently resist being self-aware—or risk adopting a masculine gaze, since only men can see women for what they are—likewise, poor people are represented as being without knowledge, unable to reason, and lacking class consciousness. Being poor was also a process of becoming feminized. Both conditions reflect a sense of not knowing, naïveté, and worldly innocence. In bourgeois literature, both femininity and poverty are rhetorical devices that hint at some lost edenic innocence that more cosmopolitan types lack and must try to regain.

The language used to describe the population referenced the human body, or more specifically, the feminized human body. Men were described in terms of the activity of thoughts and decisions, while women were described in terms of the passive "mass" of their bodies. The mass referred not to the thinking mind, which possessed many abstract talents unrooted in material reality, but to the physical body which was unthinking and had to undergo discipline to tame its many appetites. The mind is the master, and the body is the slave. The language around the great proletarian mass, which was highly statistical (the number of hands available at a factory, within a metropolis, or in a tenement building), begins and ends in the prison. As Donna Haraway writes:

> While we can trace population thinking back to Malthus in the eighteenth century, the managerial sense of population—as a quantity problem fixed by adjustable birth and death rates—is a twentieth-century formulation. Population, in the twentieth century, became a calculative concept used to govern the stock of people in the nation-state for the sake of economic productivity. In nineteenth-century Britain, the term designated the working class as an undifferentiated mass, and in mid-twentieth-century United States, the word named the totality of people in a prison. Population, as an artifact of a particular way of counting, bundles of bodies into a single tally, creating distance and abstraction for a managerial gaze that is then poised to ask, "What should be done about them?" It is a formulation that allows the anonymization of lives into deletable data points.

The archetype of the vast majority as an unthinking proletarian mass had psychoanalytical and political dimensions. Freud's theories of the id and ego flourished in this era because they tended to reinforce existing perceptions of social order and cooperation. Like the managerial bourgeoisie, the ego controlled and disciplined the id, which was malleable and didn't know what was best for itself. While the ego is self-aware and critical, the mass is unaware and susceptible to unconscious and emotional manipulations. The mass must be instructed and controlled because it lives in an endless stream of projections and delusions. As Theodor Herzl describes a socialist rally he witnessed: "Their murmuring swells, it becomes a dark and ominous *[dumpfe]* flood in this still darkened hall. It runs through me like a physical premonition of their power. Indistinguishable from one another as individuals, together they are like a great beast beginning to stretch its limbs, *still only half conscious of its power.* Many hundreds of hard heads and twice as many fists.... That is only one district in one city in France" (italics my own). Herzl's emotional response to the mass, from his position as a member of the bourgeoisie, was a feeling of anxiety about its perceived power. Only later in his career, when he learns to speak to the mass, does Herzl's attitude toward it change. "The mass was his lover and his mirror," writes Carl Shorske about Herzl, after he begins his career as the founder of Zionism, building his own career speaking to the populist mass but receiving funds from the elite class.

In modern Europe, it is assumed that adding members to a group automatically makes that group dumber. It is better to go on your own, but to go far, it is better to go together. The assumption that bigger groups of people are always dumber than smaller groups of people or individuals arises from the highly specific way in which images of feminine people were first appropriated to frame moral questions about civilization. This appropriation occurred before femininity itself became conflated with artificiality and self-deception, and then the sexual anxieties around femininity developed into social anxieties around the proletariat. The assumption that big crowds are dumb doesn't make sense. A larger number of people equals more heads, more experiences, and more knowledge. In the same way that Venus images in Rome and the Renaissance were images of femmes that represented patriarchal motives, the idea that the proletariat is a big, dumb mass reflects bourgeois motives. The invention of the mass is also the invention of another figure: the fascist. Fascist figures, like Herzl, loved the mass as a lover and mirror, projecting themselves and inseminating their ideology into the group. These figures always emerged from the bourgeoisie and relied on bourgeois money to fund their rallies and speeches. Venus's form is no longer located in the singular, fertile, female body but in the multitudes and in the crowds—the social body rather than the individual's body.

Let's return to Inanna. The mass is a Venus symbol not only because it is a gendered image, with feminine traits such as irrationality, volatility, and irritability attributed to it; nor only because of its fertility, as the value of the modern economy derives its power from the labor power of the working mass; but also because it is *retributive*. The mass is almost always described in terms of socialism and, more specifically, in terms of the bourgeois fear of socialist revolution. Inanna is the goddess who kills either her rapist or her husband. She unleashes three plagues but also grants three mercies to her friends and child. While the Renaissance and modern image of Venus framed rape through the experience of the rapist by celebrating sexual desire and violence, the story of Inanna speaks justice from the perspective of someone who is raped.

When the Greco-Roman version of Venus, Athena, imposed Zeus's patriarchal law onto the matriarchal Furies, she was not just saying that people who have been raped should not take revenge into their own hands; she was also taking away the retributive power of the people and giving it to the state. In the same way that the state has always reflected patriarchal values, it also always reflects elite values. Thus, since Venus is such a moral planet, ideas around what is good and moral also reflect patriarchal and bourgeois values when Venus is imagined by white men. These values instruct us that the social mass is unable to plan or organize itself, that it is a big, dumb thing that must be led by another. In patriarchy, the mass social body has no truth and believes only falsified versions of the truth.

Community is not a great social mass built of unthinking reactions to an existing violence that is only capable of retribution. Community is a complicated and negotiated thing that continually transforms itself by enacting justice. Unlike the sacred garden, community does not need protection in order to strengthen itself. It is capable of protecting itself. It is not dumb and it is not unaware. Social bodies are intelligent bodies full of people who think together. Large groups of people are capable of dreaming together and organizing together.

Venus is about justice. When we imagine large groups of people to be dumb, we imagine that we need justice to be a process that is distributed to people from the top, the head, the leadership, or the state. State distributed justice, like the patriarchal God's justice, is something that sacrifices the disempowered to redeem the already empowered. Representational justice exploits issues of injustice to distribute the people's power toward the top. Patriarchal justice is not justice but a perpetuate conquering that protects private gardens and private interests.

In order to imagine that large groups of people are capable of negotiating justice and community transformation together, we must first imagine that large groups of people can hear one another without the necessity of false truths and figureheads. We must imagine that we are or can become people who are whole enough to comprehend the existing violence of the state. We must imagine that we are capable of believing each other and that we are capable of saying things that mean something.

6

ETYMOLOGY OF MARS

Trigger warning: this chapter discusses rape culture, immigration, and prisons.

The Losers of the Zodiac: Ares and Eris

Mars is a malefic. When attempting to understand just who Ares was as a god and what he represented, it's important to note that everyone universally hated him. When Ares is wounded in battle and begs his own father, Zeus, for help, Zeus calls him a "two-faced liar" and the "most hateful of all the gods on Mount Olympus." His sister, Athena, says he is "evil-wrought" and a "double-faced liar." His mother, Hera, is angry at him when he betrays her for the Trojans and "wishes him ill," while the whole mess of the Trojan War itself started when his twin, Eris, was left out of a party that she wanted to go to so she could prank Ares.

Eris, Ares's twin sister, is also described as despicable. In *Works and Days,* Hesiod describes her as "cruel" and says "no man will love her." In *Theogony,* Hesiod lists the names of her children: Hardship, Forgetfulness, Starvation, Pains, Battles, Wars, Murders, Manslaughters, Quarrels, Lies, Stories, Disputes, Anarchy, Ruin, and Oath.

Although the hatefulness of Ares and Eris is attributed to their association with war, they were by no means the only gods linked to war. As we saw before, Venus was also primarily a war goddess. All gods participated in war to some extent, and the principles they represent all have some kind of wartime function. However, only Ares and Eris were despicable in their association with war. Neither enjoyed any temples of their own and were not worshipped but feared. In contrast, Venus was almost always celebrated and enjoyed several temples celebrating her military power. Unlike Venus, who was the goddess who blessed Greek and Roman armies with victory, or Jupiter, whose *fulmen* lightning sigil was worn by Roman soldiers, Mars was a war god who represented foreign armies instead of Greek or Roman ones. Mars did not originate in Greece or Mesopotamia but in Thrace (current-day Turkey). As David McCann writes, "Homer showed that he considered Mars to be a foreigner by making him fight for the Trojans, along with other immigrant gods."

Ares and Eris, then, are not only war gods but war gods who represent the foreign enemy. As a representation of the foreigner, Mars is often seen as envious or up to no good.

Eris means "strife," and she is the goddess of discord. Her function in myth is that of the one who always stirs up trouble. When Hera is jealous of a couple who proclaims that their love is stronger than the love between Hera and Zeus, she sends Eris to stir up unhappiness and discord between the couple. When Eris isn't invited to the party that started the Trojan War, she throws into the festivities an apple of discord that induces Hera, Athena, and Aphrodite to compete among each other. In the *Iliad* Homer describes Eris as "only a little thing at first, but thereafter grows until she strides on the earth with her head striking heaven."

Ares, on the other hand, has a name related to the Greek word *are*, which means "bane" or "ruin." It's not that Ares is only a military god; it's that his very name and presence in war is about the demoralizing and ruinous aspects of war. When Ares fights, he fights not on the victorious side like Venus, but on the losing side. Thus, Ares represents loss and defeat. In the *Iliad*, Ares switches to the Trojan side exactly at the moment when the hero Diomedes enters the war, allying himself with the side fighting against Athena, who already stood for military victory. If we consider Ares switching sides to be symbolic, we could say that when Diomedes entered the war, ruin and defeat entered the Trojan ranks. Both Eris and Ares are gods whom the Greeks wish to give to their enemies, not gods whom they wish to preserve for themselves.

Likewise, in matters of love, while Eris is simply said to be someone whom no man will ever love, Ares's love affairs are never described as successful or legal consummations; instead, they almost always have to do with cuckoldry. Ares's most famous love affair was with Aphrodite, who cheated on her husband Hephaistos with Ares for the entire duration of their marriage. When Hephaistos catches on to them, he builds a net, pretends to leave, and uses the trap to capture their bodies for all to see. Ares is not only humiliated in war but also in love.

This triad—the wife, the husband, and the sexual threat—shows up again and again in ancient texts on war. Ancient sources often used rape as a metaphor for seige warfare, comparing the breaking of the city wall with forcible penetration. Brad E. Kelle and Frank Richtel write, "Not only do prophetic texts *describe* city destruction with language of physical and sexual violence, but a survey of references to women within the prophetic texts indicates that cities are personified as females exclusively in contexts of destruction." In these texts, city-states are again and again described as wives, brides, mothers, and whores. Cities were feminized when they were perceived to be under threat, and the foreigners who represented the threat became hypermasculine. In this way, sympathy with the foreigners—which was very possible, since the newly integrated pieces of the empire may have been more sympathetic to their

neighbors than to their Greek or Roman conquerors—were mor-
alized when compared to a wife (the city-state) who cheats on her
husband (the empire). Venus, the feminine war goddess, also provided the means of feminizing hypermasculine foreign enemies. At
the altar of Venus, defeated enemies were feminized. If Mars is a
stranger, then Mars is also a foreigner who threatens to rape the
feminized city.

Thus, when the Greeks talk about Ares as the god of destruction, they're not only talking about war in general as a destructive
force; they're also using Ares as a motif that symbolizes racial and
sexual invasion. Eris and Ares were not just wartime planets but
also something that emerges through war: they represent the foreign enemy. As we will see, this threat of foreign invasion does not
always come from outside the empire, as epic poems on war seem
to suggest. It can also arise within the empire. As foreigners and as
enemies, Ares's and Eris's antics are never legitimate political struggles but always signs of discord seeking only to corrode institutions
meaninglessly. Their presence signifies not blessings but losses or
the destruction of cohesive identity, and their love is not legitimate
but a threat to the institution of love itself.

Although many of the elements that show up in myths surrounding Eris and Ares—including ruin, sex, and war—also show
up in myths around Venus, ruin, sex, and war are narrated in such
a way that they support institutions instead of corroding them.
Inanna gets her justice, while Hephaistos never does. Since Venus
supports institutions, Venus represents the civilized world. On
the other hand, Mars represents the barbaric world. In the Greco-
Roman imagination, Venus was the military goddess who *conquered,*
while Mars was the god who *had to be conquered.* Thus, the reason
everyone hated Ares was not that he was violent. Violence was not
the issue. All the gods and goddesses were violent. They hated Ares
because he represented to them the ultimate *loser* as a god who was
fundamentally not Greek, not Roman, and not civilized. Ares was

the despicable god because he was the foreign god—the god who was a stranger.

Ruin

The root of Ares, *are,* meaning "ruin," is not only associated with the ruins of a city after it has been conquered by another army but is also associated with *phthoras gunaikōn,* which Joelle-Frederique Bara and Robert Schmitt translate as "ruination," "corruption," and "seduction"—all of a sexual variety. According to Chris Brennan and Roger Beck, ruination means rape in this context. Brennan notes that, apparently, this association between Mars and rape is made explicit by the Roman astrologer Valens when he describes a rape committed by the owner of an example chart against a servant during his Mars profection year. The association between Mars and rape also comes from rape as a metaphor for war.

While depictions of rape were typically used to produce masculinities and femininities that cohered subjects toward one another in ancient texts from Greece and Rome, depictions of rape in modernity produce masculinities and femininities that are socially alienated from one another. For the antiheroes of European modernity, who saw themselves as compelled to fly against the world, modern society is not a place where they are able to construct masculinity but a place in which they are robbed of masculinity by capitalistic alienation and moral crisis. The antiheroes of James Joyce, Ernest Hemingway, and Samuel Beckett are cuckolded, emasculated, and paralyzed by the world. Their women give them orders and cheat on them. For these fictional masculine archetypes, the loss of masculinity is always paralleled by the promiscuity of important women in their lives. In *Ulysses,* Molly, the wife of the main protagonist, is sleeping with his best friend and has a list of twenty-five past lovers. In *The Sun Also Rises,* Lady Brett Ashley is presented as a promiscuous divorcée who has not only married twice but has had numerous love affairs.

For these antihero survivors of World War I, war and violence has stolen the masculinity they are entitled to. They redeem their heroism by reasserting their masculine vitality through sexual acts with promiscuous lovers. The emasculated hero's counterpart is always the debauched woman, from whom he earns his vigor through sexual acts, consensual or not.

Mars, in this context, is a cycle of trauma that is initiated through the humiliating rituals that create and recreate masculinity, which then enacts violence on characters who are judged to be immoral or decadent in their sexual styles, which is itself a humiliating experience and creates the conditions necessary to inspire the revolt and birth of masculinity all over again. While the characters who are framed as promiscuous—and thus seen as deserving of sexual violence—in the fictional worlds of *Ulysses* and *The Sun Also Rises* are gendered as female, this cycle of violence is not limited to heteronormative relations in which men rape women. In some settings, men experience sexual assault at the same rates as women or at even higher rates, while trans people experience sexual violence at higher rates than cisgendered men and women. The rituals of humiliation that create conditions needed for the assertion of masculinity do not only affect cis men or cis boys. Rather, people of all gender expressions can recreate masculinity as protection when they experience humiliation. As Lionel Trilling writes in his essay "Art and Neurosis," Western civilization holds a "pervasive and deeply rooted . . . notion that power may be gained by suffering." Masculinity is produced by suffering and is also the evidence of past humiliation.

Ares is always described in acts that feature humiliation as a central emotion—defeat in battle or cuckoldry in love. David Keen writes in *Complex Emergencies* that "one of the most important roots of violence is a sense of having been *humiliated*. Combatants have frequently harbored some sense of humiliation, whether arising from wartime or peacetime, and this can feed into their own violence." For Hitler, the feeling of humiliation was one of his strongest motivators and justifications for dictatorship. In a 1939 speech to the Reichstag, he said: "During the time of my struggle for power it was in the first instance the Jewish race which only received my prophecies with laughter when I said that I would take over the leadership of the state."

Mars, as a symbol, is closely associated with masculinity, just as Venus is closely associated with femininity. However, there are far more male planetary symbols than there are female planetary symbols. Mars does not have to represent masculinity in its totality but, rather, a specific type of masculinity. While Saturn may have represented the masculinity of a melancholic patriarch and the Sun the masculinity of the sovereign, Mars represents protest masculinity. This type of masculinity arises from the institutions that house the foreigner: the prison and the military.

In interviews with incarcerated members of the American public, James Gilligan found that humiliation was the strongest motivator of violent crimes, more so than self-preservation. He found that those he interviewed were willing to engage in self-destructive behavior if it meant eliminating a source of shame. Within the military, humiliation is not just the consequence of being defeated in formal battle but also a prerequisite of initiation and training. For Russian soldiers in World War II, hundreds of young soldiers died every year in violent initiation rituals, while older soldiers practiced sexual violence on younger ones. Historian Seburo Ienaga describes military training as a humiliation ritual that made recruits capable of the violence expected of them: "Individuals whose own dignity and manhood had been so cruelly violated would hardly restrain from doing the same to defenseless persons under their control." For American soldiers in Vietnam, "the training officer treats the trainee in the same way that he wants the soldier to treat the enemy in battle. To escape the low and painful status of victim and target of aggression, the mantle of the aggressor is assumed with more or less guilt."

The making of a soldier—a militant form of masculinity—
through rituals designed to induce humiliation, shame, and trauma
are not exceptional cases of creating masculinity limited to the
military but are normative to civilian life as well. Often, masculinity is not a prescribed mode of behavior that is taught in schools
and absorbed by students; rather, it emerges through an internal
conflict that is often thought of as being produced by an individual against the society that they live in. As R. W. Connell writes in
Masculinities, "School authority served as a foil *against* which the
boys constructed an oppositional masculinity." Sources of school
authority are often enwrapped with the overwhelmingly female
workforce that works in primary education. Although masculinity is a social script as much as any other gender expression, it is
often framed as the rebellion of mischievous boys who cannot be
constrained by the rules and regulations of a normal society. Alfred
Alder calls this "protest masculinity" and describes it as "arising
from the childhood experience of powerlessness, and resulting in
an exaggerated claim to the potency that European culture attaches
to masculinity."

The protest masculinity that Mars symbolizes is also a young
masculinity. Young protest masculinity is quickly integrated into
state power. In his book *Teenage,* Jon Savage chronicles the invention of the teenager as a unique age group between the two world
wars and found that the teenager emerges from the institutions of
the prison and military. Teenage rituals, which have become conventions today, such as the playing of ritual team sports designed
to emulate war, are predesigned mechanisms that attempt to civilize the young into the machine of imperialist power. Although the
teenager was invented in Britain and the United States, the figure
was quickly appropriated by the Germans. As German lieutenant
colonel Baron Colmar von der Goltz writes, "The strength of a
nation lies in its youth." Marx notes that national socialism was a
movement in which the youth pledged to save their culture from

their elders. The protest masculinity that we associate with youth is not spontaneous and natural but also engineered and institutional. They are part of a larger social military technology that integrates rebellious youthful masculinity into the military or the prison.

Protest masculinity represents the world as a whole against which a singular man struggles. This cultural trope of one man fighting against the world—a world that seems to seek to humiliate the masculine person—is metaphorized as the struggle between a head against its body. Western military strategy, in works such as *On War* by Carl von Clausewitz, recommended that military officers strike at the head (or headquarters) of an army, which Clausewitz called the "center of gravity" that all communication lines led toward. The head is where the brain and the rational processes are located. It is where strategies, tactics, and logistics are deliberated. Like the head of a human, the head of an army was to be protected. This head held the important generals of the gentry class, while the rank and file (the body of the army) constituted its battering arm. The military segmentation of a larger social body into a head and body carried over into civilian life, where the elite classes were often the gatekeepers of rationality.

Ideas about the irrationality of mass society, and the rationality of certain "men of genius" who refused to "swim with the stream," influenced everything from psychology to economic theory. The work of Edward Bernays birthed a propaganda movement that sought to control the irrational masses through subconscious manipulation according to the agendas of a rational elite. In the field of psychology, Freud's theories of an id ruled by an ego resembled the structure of a hierarchical army. Leo Tolstoy differentiated between a free, individual life and a "swarm-life," which is an "unconscious instrument" that lays down laws for the individual. As Gustave Le Bon writes in *The Crowd: A Study of a Popular Mind,* "An individual in a crowd is a grain of sand amid other grains of sand, which the wind stirs up at will."

This brand of protest masculinity, of man against the world, first became hegemonic during the Spanish colonization of the Aztec empire and originated in the figure of the conquistador. The conquistador, according to Connell, was "the first group to become defined as a masculine cultural type in the modern sense." He "was a figure displaced from the customary social relationship, often extremely violent in the search for land, gold, and converts, and difficult for the imperial state to control." Because the conquistador, as a masculine icon, represented a break with the normal laws of the state and existed beyond the control of the state, he was able to commit violent acts that the sanctioned state was unable to prevent while expanding the state's territories. Likewise, pirates, who were romanticized for their rebellious and pioneering courage, were used by the colonial powers as early slave traders. The conquistador, as a modern Mars figure, is at once able to stage a rupture from normal conventions and to exist as a tool of the state. Like the soldier, who uses violence in times of exception outside of civilian life, the conquistador is allowed to be violent because he works in a space of exception. While the soldier works to exclude others and punish those who threaten those who are included, the conquistador steals resources from those who are excluded for the benefit of those who are included.

The type of masculinity that Mars represents is not present in all social spaces but only in those social spaces that are also perceived as borders. The conquistador and the soldier both work on the border. The borders where Mars works do not, however, function in the same way that the Moon's borders function. While the Moon normalizes the border through the market, Mars pathologizes the border as an exceptional place where the normal laws of the civilized world no longer work. These borders are exceptional places. Mars masculinity is also an exceptional type of masculinity in which actions and behaviors that would normally be condemned can happen.

Public Enemy #1

The Romans had two words related to fighting: *tumultus* (tumult) and *bellum* (war). While war was fought on the borders against the enemies of those within the great expanse of empire, which can have the effect of uniting the empire against a common enemy, tumult is related to the word "tumor," which means an abnormal swelling or internal disturbance. Unlike formal warfare, tumult is not the fighting of a known external enemy but the fighting of different factions within the state itself. It is a state of special disorder, internal unrest, or civil war. Eris, goddess of discord, represented social unrest or tumult.

In the event of tumult, Roman law allowed for a special type of exception called the *iustitium,* which translates to "standstill" or "suspension of law." When the state was under threat by powers that sought to disturb it, the law would be abandoned, and the Senate released all magistrates from any restrictions of lawmaking. During an *iustitium,* the Senate was allowed to do whatever it took to preserve the structure of the state, even activities that were illegal. In other words, when threatened by either external or internal forces, ancient Rome went into an extralegal state in which the normal laws of the land were suspended, and might became right. Roman law and norms of conduct were only valid during times of peace. When under threat, Rome entered a dictatorship, and an elected military commander, the *auctorias principis,* had full power. Under an *iustitium,* an *auctorias principis* was able to commit acts that were normally illegal.

The Italian philosopher Giorgio Agamben calls the emergency suspension of law a "state of exception," and he points out that the state of exception is an inherent contradiction of the law. Agamben describes the state of exception as a structure where the rule of law does not exist—a structure into which the enemies and the threat (perceived or real) are contained so that outside of the structure, law can go on as normal. He writes that because the protection of the law also means the abandonment of the law, the law is not founded upon its own effectiveness, moral certainty, or even its ability to protect itself. The law is justified on the basis of an extralegal state in which all violence is allowed and no law exists. Agamben argues that the state of exception, which is a state without law, "seems, for some reason, to be so essential to the juridical order that it must seek in every way to assure itself a relation to it, as if in order to ground itself the juridical order necessarily had to maintain itself in relation with an anomie." Lawlessness is embedded into Roman law.

Agamben writes that the state of exception is integral to law. When law becomes that which is abandoned when it's not obeyed, it becomes a thing that is enforced only through extralegal violence. Because the law (violence is not okay) must be abandoned to be enforced (violence is okay), its very existence is exceptional and contradictory. Roman law treats obedience as the normal state and violation of the law as the exceptional state. Thus, it is able to provide a different legal process for those who violate the law and are considered enemies of the state than for those who are seen as being protected by law. Because of this dual process, the law is able to function as one thing to the law-abiding Roman citizen and another to the law-violating barbaric outsider. It is able to function as nonviolent civil authority on the inside while maintaining the border. This border maintains a space of violence. Legal authority, then, is not only the authority to define a threat but also the ability to differentiate between those on the outside and those on the inside.

The state of exception, or *iustitium,* also includes the right of self-defense for individual citizens. Although acts like killing are not excusable in the normal state of affairs, citizens living in a state that honors *iustitium* are allowed to kill without penalization when under perceived danger. In the same way that the state has the right to use what violence it deems necessary to preserve itself from immediate danger, an individual under threat has the right to use violence in order to counteract the future threat of violence. This also means that the taboo against killing only matters in circumstances when there is no perceived threat to either civil society or state-protected individuals. In other words, you're not allowed to kill anyone until you really have to kill someone. This is the contradiction of the state of exception.

While states of exception are assumed to be brief or contained, history shows that exception occurs often and spreads pervasively. World War I, from the British islands to Continental Europe, was a state of emergency that lasted from 1914 to 1919. Afterward, for the Germans, the Weimar Republic continued as a state of emergency due to the economic stipulations caused by Germany's loss. When Hitler took power as dictator, he was able to do so because the country had already been in a state of exception for some years. For dictators such as Hitler or Mussolini, the offices of the *Duce* or the *Führer* were continuations of the Roman tradition of the *auctorias principis,* who ruled during those states of exception and emergency. The *Duce* and *Führer* maintained emergency with self-created and almost mythological threats—the degeneration of Aryan blood by foreign influences, the destruction of an antiquated nobility by the modern free market, the British and American forces that were remaking the world economy on their own terms. The concentration camp, as a place where the normal laws of the state do not exist and extreme conditions are created, is a place of exception.

Inside the camp, enemies of the state would be contained and isolated, subject to state violence otherwise prohibited by normal affairs. As the Nazi philosopher Carl Schmitt writes, the camp is a place where "the state continues to exist, while law recedes." For such an extralegal place to exist, the nation must be under a constant threat. Without naming a national enemy upon whom violence could be enacted, the national spirit of Nazi Germany could not have defined itself as a fascist state. Fascism, then, is a state that is always under threat—a state that is always in a state of exception, emergency, and crisis.

The concentration camp was not only an apparatus special to the German state of the 1930s but also an apparatus of German law as a resurrection of Roman ideals. The other Western empire that bases itself on Roman law is the United States. As in Nazi Germany, American law defines itself differently in exceptional states from the way it defines itself in normal states. For example, the use of full military power is contradictory for a liberal democracy because the very ethos of liberalism strives to limit government. However, as Abigail Thorn says, liberalism is an ideology that does not define itself fundamentally but, rather, in its tendency toward the making of exceptions. While American liberalism seeks to grant universal suffrage, for example, at the time of its founding, it made an exception for Black people and women, and it continues to make exceptions for Black people by making exceptions for the incarcerated. While liberalism encourages commercial freedom and national sovereignty, it makes an exception when countries resist American-dominated global capitalism. While liberalism protects individual sovereignty, it makes exceptions for those who are seen as too foreign or too strange. In other words, while normal citizens live in a normal state of affairs, strangers and foreigners live in an exceptional state of affairs.

Sherene H. Razack, in her article "The Camp: A Place Where Law Has Declared That the Rule of Law Does Not Operate," writes that "bodies become camps when they are cast into a state of indeterminacy that is simultaneously inside and outside the law. For such bodies, judicial protection no longer applies as the law itself determines that they are deprived of fundamental rights." This "anomalous legal zone" that bodies as camps find themselves within are created when "race, immigration, and security combine to form a legal and social black hole from which there is no exit." Terrorists, who are defined as the state enemy of the current age, are put into concentration camps because their form of violence, according to Nisha Kapoor in *Deport, Deprive, Extradite,* "are automatically disqualified from discussion . . . because they are simply 'evil.'" As Michael Walzer puts it in *Arguing about War,* terrorism is considered "extra-normal" because it violates "the norms regulating disputes, protest, and dissent." Therefore, one does not negotiate with terrorists, because to negotiate with terrorists means they were never terrorists to begin with, as beings capable of rational thought and civil discourse. Because terrorists are "simply evil," they belong to a subset of violence that is outside normal violence and must be contained with extralegal concentration camps.

In normal states, the United States does not torture, probable cause must be found for the court to prosecute an individual for a perceived crime, and killing is illegal. Abu Ghraib would be an example of an exceptional state, since the United States does, in practice, torture. The one-hundred-mile paramilitary enforcement zone along land and sea borders declared by Immigration and Customs Enforcement—a zone that includes 60 percent of the US population—would also be a state of exception, because individuals within the zone who are perceived to be immigrants must prove they have not violated immigration laws to ICE officials who do not need to provide probable cause for arrest. The area just outside George Zimmerman's house the day Trayvon Martin was shot would also be a state of exception, since Zimmerman was not penalized for a murder that would normally be prosecuted in a normal state.

If Mars represented the foreign enemy who seeks to ruin the feminized city-state for the Greek and Romans, then the neoliberal Mars also represents a perceived threat to normal society. Mars figures, such as prisoners or terrorists or Black kids, are hypermasculinized. Moreover, while the exceptional borders where Mars figures are assumed to be located are often thought of as infrequently occurring, sparsely scattered, or isolated, exceptional borders are not contained to land and sea borders, detention centers outside normal jurisdiction, or rare moments of emergency. Rather, Mars figures *themselves* embody the perceived threats that construct the state of exception. The incarcerated, foreigners, and Black kids who represent perceived threats do not live in a normal state where normal law is enforced but in an exceptional state in which exceptional laws are enforced *all the time.* The state of exception is not fixed nor separate from society but is a social space that hangs around Mars figures. Borders do not exist between countries but are felt and perceived in schools, hospitals, and shopping malls, and on the street. As Nisha Kapoor writes: "This expansion of securitization means that the border is rather explicitly encroaching into everyday life such that responsibility for border control is not limited to officials working at the border but filtered down and made the duty of professionals—doctors, landlords, driving instructors, employers, teachers, administrators—and the public at large."

Police killings, concentration camps in Texas, and the surveillance state are perceived to be incidents that are necessary to the preservation of the nation. However, these events do not function as incidental, and they can no longer be described as events. Instead, they are institutions. In a neoliberal (or new liberal) state, war no longer has to be declared. Emergency powers of the state—exemplified in such agencies as the Department of Homeland Security, which was founded in 2002 by George W. Bush, or the FBI and CIA, founded within the last century to grant the federal branch of government unprecedented military power and information—have become normative institutions even during peacetime. Former institutions that emerged from the state of exception engineered by the plague, such as the quarantining of a city, the expansion of sovereign power, and the mandatory registration of all citizens, have not disappeared after the threat was over but remain.

While war is perceived to be a last resort and a reaction to countries that behave unreasonably, war has continued as a normal industry ever since the Cold War. Rosa Luxemburg writes that, because worker-consumers are paid less than the total value that their work generates, the total number of workers and consumers in a society cannot afford to buy all of the commodities that their labor produces. As a result, the capitalist must find ways to sell commodities or realize surplus value outside the market. In some cases, the state steps in as a client to realize surplus value. The military is no longer used for fighting, negotiation, or even the development of technology; rather, the military is only the instrument through which the state becomes a client and buys technology in order to sustain capitalism. As Clinton L. Rossiter writes in *Constitutional Dictatorship: Crisis Government in the Modern Democracies,* "The instruments of government depicted here as temporary 'crisis' arrangements have in some countries, and may eventually in all countries, become lasting peacetime institutions." The stickiness of states of exception after periods of crisis are over is not accidental. Rather, crisis is a normalized institution that develops technology for profit.

Rape, too, like prison and war, is perceived to be exceptional. In the cisnormative narrative around rape, rape is rare and operates outside of normal social relations. Sara Ahmed writes about a memory in which she and other classmates in a predominantly white private school were taught about "stranger danger." This lesson was really a lesson on the politics around rape. Ahmed recalls this experience as "an instruction into whiteness and not just femininity" and elaborates by writing that "it is a white female body that is assumed to be vulnerable and in need of protection from others." The white female body represents the state that is constantly under siege so that crisis states can continue to occur and the institutions that emerge from the crisis state can continue to function. In this cisnormative narrative of rape, it is the stranger who rapes. Strangers are Mars figures: hypermasculine, incarcerated, and dark.

However, rape, like prison and war, shows up as normal despite being perceived as exceptional. Strangers do not rape as often as family members, teachers, congregation members, and supervisors. Rape occurs most frequently in protected institutions, such as school, the family, or the church, and when it happens in places of exception, it happens *to* prisoners. While rape is often described as something that cultural outsiders commit against insiders, the ultimate insiders—those with power and status—commit rape the most. In the same way that military-technological institutions that emerge from states of exception stick around after the time of perceived threat is over and end up reproducing the conditions for continued crisis, police are perceived as protecting people from rape but are actually responsible for rape. Police rape the people of color they arrest because policing is a form of power and power creates the conditions for rape.

This cycle of abuse, in which abusers are created by abuse which is created by abusers who are also created by abuse and so on, does not corrode normal institutions as Mars tumults are thought to corrode civil society. Rather, normal institutions reproduce ideas around gender, vulnerability, and aggression in a way that reinforces the power dynamics around rape culture. In the military, which humiliates its recruits with the threat of rape, or the prison, which threatens its inmates with rape, rape provides the logic around gender relations necessary to contextualize the humiliation rituals that produce certain forms of masculinity.

Mars, whether through the prison, foreignness, or Blackness, is often conflated with men of color. Like Mars, men of color are thought to be hypermasculine sexual threats. Images of men of color as hypermasculine sexual threats reinforce institutional power so that white men can continue to have power and identify with the role of protecting white women. Sometimes these white men extend their generosity toward brown women, as Spivak notes when she writes that white men are always wanting to save brown women from brown men. However, rape happens when power allows it to happen, and historically, it is white men who have been in the positions where they have been able to rape white women, brown women, brown men, and others. The positions of power where white men put themselves are not perceived as exceptional but as normal. White men, too, are perceived to be normal. Their actions do not happen in exceptional border states and cannot be protected against with the law because white men are identified as agents who use the law to punish others.

Famine

Also according to Valens in *Anthologies,* Mars is associated not only with formal warfare but also with famines, wandering, and exile. While formal warfare is often thought of as a political event created by humans, famine is often associated with natural crises outside the control of any governmental power. Like rape and war, famine is often framed as a deviation from the usual way that things are done—as an exceptional state of trauma that exists outside of life itself. As a 1971 article on the effects of famine written for the Swedish Nutritional Association states, famine is a "breakdown of normal human relations and deviation from customs and mores." In literature, famine is normally used as a tool to show a deterioration of family and society. As a metaphor, it represents not only biological degeneration but also moral and social degeneration.

It's interesting that famine is one of the lenses through which we see the third world because, through other lenses, the third world is not characterized by scarcity but by overflowing natural resources. In fact, when seen through Venusian eyes, colonized places are not places of famine but of abundance—paradises ready to be taken. Because Venus and Mars represent two different needs of the imperialist state, colonized people live a contradictory existence. Colonies are at once abundant and famished.

Amrita Rangasami argues that famine is not actually the shortage of food and resources but of the *transfer* of food and resources from one region into another. Famines, according to Rangasami, do not usually occur naturally but are actually man-made. In addition, they are created with the intention of turning people into wanderers—of detaching people from the land to which they are attached. She argues that, although the language used to describe famine treats it as discontinuous from the normal state of affairs, famine is actually continuous with social and political processes normalized under colonization. Famines are engineered by colonizers who intend to steal land. While often framed as a natural degeneracy that imperialist power must save the third world from, famine is actually an instrument of colonization. Rangasami describes famine as a long process of poverty, one in which "starvation is imposed and accelerated." In her essay "The Study of Starvation and Famine," she lists three phases of famine:

> As famine worsens, the victims surrender all semblance of right to assets of land or labour for access to food. Arrangements such as becoming "famine pawns" have been known to be institutionalized in certain communities where famines tend to recur. Famine enters the final phase when it is no longer in the interest of the patron or "master" to provide even that moiety of protection necessary to sustain life. At that phase, the collapse is biological, economic, and social. The victims are uprooted, their families fragmented, their villages abandoned. They then become vagrants, the celebrated "wanderers" of famine.

Under British rule, India suffered twenty-four great famines in just fifty years. Millions died. These famines were the result of British administrative planning aimed at dissolving the people's links to the land they lived on. Rakhi Chakraborty writes in "The Bengal Famine: How the British Engineered the Worst Genocide in Human History for Profit" that the British purposely created famine conditions by increasing tributes from India to England while ordering Indian farmers to grow cash crops such as indigo and poppy instead of food. Far from being the result of natural disasters, famine is the natural end of the slow process of poverty. Poverty, as we know, is always orchestrated and is also always a normal, if not key, part of capitalism. Poverty dissolves the integrity of the colonized place by dissolving the relationships between colonial subjects and the land. Victims of poverty and famine become stateless.

Colonization could not have happened without dissolving the relationships between people and place. Colonization could not have happened without famine. Famine, then, is perceived as an exceptional state of affairs, but like war and rape, it is also integral to the normal functioning of the imperialist state. Famines, like wars, are meticulously planned. Colonized people are kept in a state of poverty so that, when the imperialist power orchestrates famine and cuts off resources, the people are forced to give up their labor and their land. When famine is understood only as a naturally produced phenomenon rather than a socially, politically, or economically produced one, when we regard famine as an accidental or exceptional state of affairs, we accept the normalcy of violence within colonization. When we understand famine as the outcome of a strategy, similar to war, we understand that borders and boundaries against the barbaric forces of natural disasters are politically engineered, disaster is always manufactured, and emergencies are planned.

Famine, like war, is an exceptional state of affairs. Famine is exceptional not because it is abnormal or rare but because it is simply something that does not happen to white people.

If Mars rules over states of exception, based on the Roman association between Mars and tumults, then Mars also rules over concentration camps, police violence, war, and famine. All of these phenomena have one thing in common: they're tactics that cultural centers of power use to create the conditions necessary to stage their own reproduction. By engineering the places outside the rule of power as both unstable and violent, those on the inside create the need to normalize the exception. By normalizing crises, the military-technological-industrial complex shapes itself as a perpetual institution. The states of exception described by Mars are scarce in natural resources, violent, and full of struggle not because they naturally are but because they have been made this way. Moreover, the states of exception from which Mars emerges are not contained by borders. Rather, they exist inside borders, at borders, and outside of borders. The border, then, is a technology that *controls Mars by both constraining it and extending it.*

Iron and Blood Sacrifice

The association of Mars with iron and blood seems to come from Mars's status as a god of war. However, in ancient societies before Rome, iron was not directly associated with war, or at least no more so than bronze. By Roman times, bronze and iron were both used in military artifacts, from armor to warheads. Iron was always cheaper and more crude than bronze. The making of bronze required copper, which was a precious metal whose status was elevated to use in currency and jewelry. Iron was more associated with the peasant classes and those who labored in the fields than it was with war. Like Saturn, which ruled the literal soil, Mars and iron were associated with toil, labor, and the social classes who had to toil and labor. Like Saturn, Mars was associated with farming. The difference is that, while Saturn is the earth itself, Mars is the iron instrument that manipulates the earth. If Saturn is the great outside, then Mars is the instrument that controls and works the great outside. Iron, within modernity, is associated with the heaviness and bluntness of a manufacturing economy that flourishes under the early days of capitalism. If Saturn is the soil, then Mars, as iron, is the blood that shapes the soil.

American rural masculinity asserted itself very differently from European cosmopolitan masculinity. While the masculinities of the cities was a narrative that saw thinking men as pitted against an unthinking world, rural masculinity in the early years of the United States empire was related to the gentry class. Gentry masculinity was based on landownership, did not assert itself through rationality, and was not individualistic in its expression but was related to the family as a social unit. More explicitly, gentry masculinity was related to the heritage or lineage of the gentleman in question. It described a new, landowning aristocracy, blue-blooded and noble. The concept of the blue blood referred not only to a person who was white but a person who was so white, with blood so pure, that the blood appears blue through skin that was perfectly translucent. It described the Anglo-Saxon—the perfect American citizen. Gentry masculinity was a unique masculinity that described itself almost wholly in terms of bloodlines. Pureness of blood was linked to excesses of virility. Emerson, who shared ideas around whiteness with Thomas Jefferson, praises the Norsemen, Saxons, and Anglo-Saxons for what he called their "beastly ferocity." He, like other thinkers of the time, had an obsession with Germany and Anglo-Saxon purity. Blood was really a metaphor for race, and it was responsible for everything from physical prowess to intelligence to matters of will and courage. Enemies of the state were described in terms of conditions of blood.

The word "eugenics" comes from the Greek word for "good birth." The founder of eugenics, who was actually Darwin's half cousin, Francis Galton, described his new field of thought, aimed at the improvement of society through biology, in Darwinian terms: "What Nature does blindly, slowly, and ruthlessly, man may do providently, quickly, and kindly." Unlike the race ideologies that existed before the invention of eugenics, the race science of the 1900s made the study and qualification of race an exacting and statistical venture. For romantics like Emerson or Jefferson, blood was merely a poetic symbol used to denote cultural and physical differences between what became known as the social realities of race. For eugenicists such as Galton, on the other hand, blood became a biological reality and race its cultural consequence. Standards of measuring race, such as the one-drop rule, are inherently contradictory because they attempted to collapse the romantic sensibilities of the early Americans with the scientific objectivism of the 1900s. Race treats blood as both symbolic and realistic.

The French linguist Lacan theorizes that we are only able to know the world around us through a symbolic order, which wraps around reality like a thin film and separates matter into objects we are able to describe through words. When we deal with an object such as a chair, it is impossible for us to access the object without making use of a symbolic order. If we see the chair as a commodity, we call it a chair. If we see the chair through the symbolic order of manufacture, we see it as wood and nails and glue. If we see it through the symbolic order of science, we see it as a mass of atoms. Reality that exists outside of any symbolic order is unaccessible. In her book *Powers of Horror,* Julia Kristeva writes that experiences with substances that come from the body, like blood, feces, or spittle, disrupt symbolic order. She compares excrement and blood with pollution and says they both provoke feelings of horror and disgust because they threaten to break down the symbolic orders of identity and language. There is something about blood that resists the symbolic. Language breaks down in the face of blood because subjectivity is violated when skin is broken. Kristeva then compares the pollution of order implied by experiences with excrement or blood with threats on the border, "supreme danger," or "absolute evil." Horrific things, like blood or absolute evil, break down the symbolic order. They exist beyond the symbolic order and cannot be integrated into identity.

Romans did ritual sacrifice before wars to send defeat to the opposition's side. This sacrifice was called Lustratio, or purification. During Lustratio, animals would be slain to purify the army for the acts of violence it was preparing to commit. Although it may seem counterintuitive to absolve oneself of the violence one is planning to commit in the future by committing more violence in the present, Byung-Chul Han writes in *Topology of Violence* that sacrifices were necessary in archaic culture because "violence represented an important medium for religious communication. Accordingly, one communicated with the god of violence *in the medium* of violence." He also writes that, for the West, sacrifice is "a deliberate act of collective substitution performed at the expense of the victim and absorbing all the internal tensions, feuds, and rivalries pent up within the community. . . . The purpose of the sacrifice is to restore harmony to the community, to reinforce the social fabric."

While the animal that would be sacrificed to bring about this reinforcement of the social fabric through violence was usually an animal such as a ram or pig in archaic cultures, the beings who are scapegoated in modern society are cultural Others. These cultural Others, who are outside the limits of civil or normal society due to their membership in a non-normative race or culture, are not considered fully human in the usual Western sense of the word. The West frequently sacrifices racially coded Others to reinforce the consensus of a normative, white society. The German preoccupation with the contamination of blood due to Jewish people was intensified, not placated, by Jewish assimilation into German society. Nazi anxieties around degeneracy were not caused by the cultural differences of Jewish people within Germany. Rather, it was because some Jews had assimilated so well into German society and had become culturally invisible that Nazi anxieties around the contamination of blood increased. The national borders of a country become threatened when faced with "supreme dangers" or "absolute evils" "coming from the outside." These "supreme dangers" or "absolute evils" "coming from the outside" are symbolized by blood, since blood breaks down social consensus and boundaries.

Blood is a metaphor for race. Those who are seen as having blood that contaminates others come from the outside. Blood is also a metaphor for violence. Racialized people are seen to exist as *already having violence* and as *already bloody*.

Though Kristeva writes that blood is antisymbolic, blood also works symbolically. Like Mars, blood is seen to be a breaker of the symbolic order and social consensus. However, blood and Mars are also symbols. Blood works symbolically because race is described through blood lineage. Mars, the exceptional state that cannot be understood through normal laws or rules, also works symbolically. The exception is a symbol that protects the normal from being treated exceptionally. Mars is the cultural scapegoat and the sacrifice zone. Scapegoats and sacrifice zones are perceived as threats because they disturb normal relations.

As David Keen writes in *Complex Emergencies,* "Genocides have frequently been pursued in the name of genocidal prevention: that is, the prevention of the genocide allegedly being plotted by the victim group." This cycle of blood sacrifice and national exorcism of the racial other through genocide closely imitates the cycle of trauma that creates masculinity, in which people avoid feeling like a victim by victimizing others. The state of exception from which Mars emerges is not marked by real borders or state lines; rather, it is marked by the biological and fictive element of blood. Blood is at once everywhere and something that must be contained. Since blood is not visible unless something is broken, states of exception are also invisible until something breaks. The state of exception is constantly being revealed, even when its job is to remain invisible and concealed, since it works both organically and symbolically. It must be revealed in order to stay hidden.

Iron Curtain and Iron Bars

The Cold War is commonly described as a feud between the opposing political ideologies of capitalism and communism. However, it is better described as an age in which war becomes technology. Communism and capitalism agree on the following: growths in production are good, declines in production are bad, and people are brought together when they have a common enemy. Rather than seeing the Cold War as a war that was fought between the United States and the Soviet Union, Noam Chomsky describes the Cold War as an alliance between the empires of the United States and the Soviet Union against third-world nationalism.

War, during and after the Cold War era, is something that is never declared but also never ends. Since the invention of the atomic bomb, war has become less of an act of physically harming your enemy and more of a constant process of gathering information. The atomic bomb brought to military sciences the vocabulary of game theory, which postulates that in uncertain situations, intelligent strategies can be worked out through computation. Game theory had a big influence on the nuclear strategy of deterrence. It was generally understood through game theory that when two superpowers are both equipped with nuclear weapons that can blow the world up, that they share an interest in world peace, just as two prisoners interrogated in separate rooms have a shared interest in not informing on each other. Thus, the "new world order" was one that strove for "universal peace," a term coined by George Bush Sr. Bush's universal peace is a deterrence strategy. In the new world order of universal peace, the only countries allowed to develop nuclear weapons would be the countries that already have nuclear weapons, the military became an informational and technological sector, and the countries that have nuclear weapons and an informational-technological sector would be responsible for enforcing universal peace. War could not exist in the new world order because the only country able to declare war would be the United States, and the United States is not a threat to the new world order since it is the new world order.

Chomsky describes how most of the battles fought during the Cold War were not fought against the Soviet Union but against small third-world countries that wanted national independence. Guerrilla warfare, another symptom of war in the nuclear age, is usually fought between opponents of vastly unequal military strength. First conceived by Friedrich Engels when strategizing revolutionary class action, guerrilla warfare was conceptualized as how a proletariat force might fight a capitalist class that controls the state and military. Guerrilla warfare happens when the United States gets involved in another country militarily. On one side we usually see the force of the United States, whose military actions are described as "stabilizing" for the region. On the other side, we see the Indigenous forces, who are usually called "insurgents" and whose actions are usually described as "destabilizing" for the region. These Indigenous insurgents are perceived as foreign enemies, even when they fight the United States on their own land, since the United States is not considered an enemy of a globalized world that it controls. The American is never a foreigner because the American extends her sense of belonging outward. Indigenous people become foreigners when they become enemies of the new world order.

In this chapter, we've already talked about Mars's relationship with hypermasculinity and how this extremity of gender is created through a cycle of violence. What is unique about Mars masculinity is that it typically references a type of masculinity that comes from powerlessness—a masculinity born out of emasculation. Although the glyph of Mars is the symbol for masculinity itself, Al Ma'shar writes in *The Abbreviation of the Introduction on Astrology* that typical rules about sect don't apply to Mars, despite it being a masculine planet, because it is also *effeminate*. The hypermasculinity of Mars, which is not patriarchal like Saturn but youthful and in protest against authoritarian structures, often isn't the masculinity of men who are already accepted as men but instead the masculinity of people who must prove themselves to be men. Mars masculinity, because it is the enemy of the sexual, hegemonic, ideological order, is also a *racialized and third-world* masculinity. Mars is the enemy of the liberal bourgeois state today—the terrorist, who is always turbaned, always brown, and always incomprehensible. Mars masculinity doesn't just describe criminalized cishet men. It is often projected onto anyone who becomes criminalized.

Mars, then, is related to the special outsider masculinity of "enemy combatants" or "insurgents" of a region that the United States seeks to control. They've been called everything from supervillains to delinquents—they're bad guys. As Ed Halter writes in *From Sun Tzu to Xbox: War and Video Games*, "*Bad guys* could be Al Qaeda terrorists, Iraqi insurgents, urban looters, Taliban warlords, or the resisting elements of wherever else US troops get dropped." The inherent criminality, the lack of belonging, and the barbarity ascribed to masculine figures of color makes them into outcasts, unacceptable to civil society. Nisha Kapoor writes that everyone knows that the enemy of the twenty-first century is the terrorist, and everyone knows that the terrorist is brown. Byun-Chul Han writes that the racial dimension of Mars's exceptional brand of masculinity finds itself revealed in the fact that Muslim is the "slang term for prisoners of a concentration camp who are completely enfeebled, emaciated, and apathetic." The Muslim, the cultural scapegoat who must be sacrificed to revive the social order of the West, lives within the concentration camp and beyond the border. The Martian enemy can only exist within a state of total exception from the law.

Martian enemies are sometimes actually Martians. While science fiction portrayals of the moon depict it as a potential colony or another home, science fiction portrays Martians as invaders and enemy combatants. Anxieties about the outsider are played out in movies about aliens. Science fiction is really an extension of the Western genre, replacing cowboys with astronauts and Indigenous people with aliens. Aliens, as Chomsky also notes, are almost always masculine. There are aliens, like Clark Gable or some of the *Men in Black* aliens, who assimilate into our society in the way that liberals seek to assimilate "good" immigrants. However, every story about a good alien is also a story about a bad alien. The MIB, which is a fictional stand-in for ICE, may treat good aliens like scum, pulling them aside and demanding to see their papers or shooting them in the head when they know they'll grow another one back in order to confirm their alien status; but the agency's main purpose is to exterminate the bad aliens that cannot be assimilated into human society. The alien is the ultimate outsider. As George Edgar Slusser writes in *Aliens: The Anthropology of Science Fiction,* "The alien is the creation of a need—man's need to designate something that is genuinely outside himself, something that is truly nonman, that has no initial relation to man except for the fact that it has no relation."

The alien is always superior to humankind in intelligence and technologically more developed. Stories of alien contact always begin in centers of military or economic power, such as Washington, DC, or New York City. In *Cloverfield,* even though the aliens themselves are not revealed until the end of the movie, they are evidenced through the presence of the tanks, security checkpoints, and soldiers we see on the streets of Manhattan. Slusser writes that the alien is undocumentable because it is by nature on the outside: "Thus, to speak of the alien is always to redeploy the problem of the border and to reopen the complexities of documentation. We cannot settle the score of the alien, even with the formidable help of the economy of anthropological truth, not because the alien is simply beyond anthropocentric documentation—this is little more than another 'truth' of anthropology—but because in naming the name of the alien, we document the parasitic illegality that is both the essence and destabilization of documentation itself." The notion of the documented alien is an oxymoron because the world of imagination surrounding the alien resists documentation altogether.

In *Do Metaphors Dream of Literal Sleep? A Science Fictional Theory of Representation,* Seo-Young Chu writes that science fiction descriptions of alien beings segment alien bodies into parts and relies on metaphor to describe these parts. In literature, aliens are described through metaphor. They are never pieced together into one coherent image because writers must construct the alien as an unfamiliar and unrecognizable entity rather than any known form. In contrast, human features are described with shorter sentences and holistically, relying on the reader's familiarity with human faces and bodies to allow them to draw their own conclusion about what the character looks like. Human faces are immediately recognizable, but alien faces can never be recognized. *Cloverfield* avoids giving us an image of its aliens. To look at an alien is to turn it into a nonalien; it begins to look like a roach, a worm, or some other familiar domestic creature. This may also be why images of prisoners and immigrants disappear once they become incarcerated. The alien must remain invisible. Once the alien is visible, it is no longer an alien. Although aliens are hypervisible because national boundaries are often justified using the figure of the alien, to be alien is to pull off a perpetual disappearing act.

Chu continues her analysis of aliens to find that veterans are often drawn to Cold War–era science fiction because fictional aliens describe the alienation of returning to one's home after a war. She quotes Bruce Franklin, who writes that US veterans experience two types of alienation: "first as alien invaders of a foreign land, then as aliens returning to what no longer seems to be their own society." US veterans become "extraterrestrial invaders of alien planets and exiles in time and space from planet Earth." Chu compares the fragmentary nature of the alien, which can never be seen or understood in its entirety, with trauma. Trauma escapes memory in the same way that aliens, being foreign and unfamiliar, escape history. It appears that trauma produces aliens.

Mars is both symbolic and unimaginable because Mars is the alien that cannot be imagined. This alien resembles the state of trauma because aliens, being foreigners, are created through trauma. Foreignness is not only a state of not belonging to a country but also a state of not belonging to a world order in which

American interests are global interests. Foreigners are not created through immigration or displacement but by an American hegemony that constructs trauma. In the case of US veterans, alienation is produced by enacting American hegemony, but alienation is also produced in the third world, which is alienated from the new world order due to colonialism. The third world is an alien place because it is a place that has been produced by trauma.

7

POWER: VENUS AND MARS

normative/exceptional

victory/humiliation

conqueror/victim

protector/scapegoat

femininity/masculinity

domestic/martial

good/bad

fertility/famine

id/ego

body/mind

heart/blood

the mass/the enemy

avenging rape/cycle of abuse

law and order/ *iustitium*

interior/exterior

proletariat/alien

It was a while before we came to realize that our place was the very house of difference rather [than] the security of any one particular difference.

—AUDRE LORDE

Power

Whereas Venus symbols tend to talk about what is on the inside—the ways we authorize ourselves from the bottom up, our judicial decisions, and the governed body—Mars symbols tend to talk about what is on the outside: the ways we defend ourselves against intruders, our martial laws, and the threatened body. Venus rules the internal and domestic spheres, and Mars rules the external areas outside the state, which are dealt with using the military. Venus rules normal power, and Mars reinforces this power by implying that chaos lies just beyond the outskirts of civil society. As Byung-Chul Han writes, "Power always possesses a constructive core. Power *works*. It organizes and develops its area of influence by producing norms, structures, and institutions, inscribing itself within a symbolic order. Unlike power, violence does not *work*. Organization and management are not its traits. Thus it is de-structive. . . . Power is a *relationship* that connects the self and the other. Power functions symbolically, relating and consolidating. . . . Violence, on the other hand, is not a symbolic medium. Its essence is diabolic, that is divisive."

In this context, Venus is power and Mars is violence. While power works by developing and influencing norms within society, violence divides by defining the self as distinct from the other. While Venus always feels artificial or constructed, violence dissolves any symbolic frameworks and creates the feeling of looking at reality with all of its rawness. Venus constructs while Mars destructs. Power and violence are not antagonistic. Rather, they are cooperative.

Love Stories/Roman-ce

The root of "romance" is "Roman." This isn't a coincidence. The great love affair, a narrative trope that shows up in everything from popular music to rom-coms to bourgeois novels, is a revival of Roman idealisms and aesthetics. The great love affair is a work of drama that involves two main characters: Venus and Mars. Romance stories center Rome, both subliminally and self-consciously. They are about the integrating violence of power and the redemptive power of violence. Because Venus and Mars principles are expressed through the ways in which we perceive, participate in, and reproduce gender, romance stories are often more about gender than about love, which can come in many forms and offers several types of devotion. When we think of romantic love (or Roman love), we tend to think about a heteropatriarchal type of love that plays with classical sentiments regarding beauty and truth, violence and power.

The greatest pop love story of my generation is the *Twilight* narrative, which eventually matured into the *Fifty Shades of Grey* narrative. These two stories offer redemption in the form of desire. In *Twilight* and *Fifty Shades,* both Bella and Anastasia are described as being exceedingly average, while Edward and Christian are described as being exceedingly exceptional. Both Bella and Anastasia hear about and know their male objects of desire before ever meeting them. Edward and Christian are status symbols that make Bella and Anastasia exceptional by association. Edward and Christian are monstrously wealthy and have monstrous traits that must be domesticated by their female partners (the folklore of vampirism was originally a metaphor for the aristocracy, which fed upon the peasant classes). Edward and Christian do not desire Bella and Anastasia because they are status symbols. Rather, their desires are depicted as raw, uncontrollable, and frightening. Edward's desire for Bella literally strips her down to what she is inside, since

Edward desires Bella for her blood. Male desire is represented as base, while female desire is represented as superficial.

If Venus represents the socially normal, then Bella and Anastasia must domesticate their monstrous men. If Mars represents the border, Edward and Christian must continually protect their partners to define their love. Edward protects Bella against everything from humans to cars to other vampires. He says to her, "I am very protective over you," and "it's my job to protect you." Christian protects Anastasia against workplace rivals, a creepy boss, his own exes, and those he perceives as sexual rivals. Similar to the way that violent actions that are normally unacceptable become permissible during periods of martial law, behaviors such as stalking (the security state), using excessive violence (military violence), and forbidding contact with friends or family (border control) become legitimate when they protect our female protagonists against a perceived threat. When Edward and Christian overreact to perceived threats, they construct the vulnerability of the white female body. When agents such as Customs and Border Patrol or ICE overreact to perceived threats, they construct the vulnerability of the domestic body.

While the female characters in *Twilight* and *Fifty Shades* seem to move in resistance to male desire and the male characters in resistance to female expectations, the genders within these two narratives are actually collaborative. Edward and Christian's base desires authenticate Bella and Anastasia so that they are able to accept lavish gifts and resources without being perceived as inauthentic. Bella and Anastasia's perceived vulnerability validates Edward and Christian's obsessive overprotectiveness. Within these two narratives, gender emerges as a mechanism that serves both defensive and economic needs. The antagonism between the two binary genders of male and female is obfuscated when they are perceived to be working together in collaboration against outside elements.

Since 1945, when the atomic bomb was first used on Hiroshima and Nagasaki, both sides of the nuclear standoff have continued to invest in military society at the expense of civil society. This is what Virilio means when he calls the state of total war we find ourselves in—a pure war that requires no fighting to exist, only the existence of weapons of mass destruction—"a relative pauperization of civilian society in favor of military society." This means that the manufacture of weapons is really the funneling of public resources into the private sphere through weapons manufacture. The continual innovation of weapons, creating hydrogen bombs that can blow the world up eight times over and sonic weapons that can wreck the intestines of anyone standing within range, aren't made to be used. They're innovated on so that they can be invested in, taking tax dollars and putting them into the hands of arms dealers. War is an industry first and a government agency that supports industry second. As Virilio states, in ancient societies the army's job was the protection of borders; today the army's role is mostly to "exact the funds necessary" for the "infinite development of their weaponry." Virilio calls this process "endocolonization"—the process of underdeveloping civilian society and overdeveloping military society.

The military-industrial complex is more of a conflict between the military and civilians than a conflict between the state and the foreigner. Military technology is developed at the expense of civil society. Chomsky talks about how the inflated budgets of Pentagon spending, which are appropriated from tax dollars without any civilian authorization or even notification, take away money that could be spent on public goods such as infrastructure, education, or libraries. The military-industrial complex depicts political struggle as a conflict between nations in order to mask the political struggle between civilians and the military. Under this mask, the military functions mostly as a way for public money to enter the private hands of weapons manufacturers, private detention centers, and other technological specialists. This expansion of the military-industrial complex represents a collision between Venus and Mars—between civil institutions and military ones. In the same way that wealth does not simply appear in the hands of men but is acquired from the rest of society through normalized violence, wealth does not simply appear in the technological and informational industries that frame the military; it moves there through class violence.

When war is perceived as a struggle between the state and the foreigner, it becomes impossible to analyze it in terms of class struggle. Like Bella and Anastasia, who excuse Edward and Christian's violent actions because they believe such actions are appropriate to emergency scenarios even when they're not appropriate to daily life, we excuse war because war is perceived to happen outside of civilian life. The class differences between Bella and Edward or between Anastasia and Christian are concealed when Edward and Christian act as though they are on Bella or Anastasia's side. Gender is evoked by the military and conceals class conflict.

The rhetoric of war—which informs a binary of what or who is worthy of protection versus who or what we are protecting against—reinforces bourgeois ideas about what is precious or valuable. Bella and Anastasia's ability to derive pleasure from the security state that masculine figures like Edward or Christian create around them speaks to their own ethics of how they understand their own preservation. Bella and Anastasia are worthy of being protected not just because they are women but also because they are white women who play by the rules. Edward and Christian are capable of protection because they are white men willing to break the rules. In the same way that the military-industrial complex is closely related to luxury (military aesthetics often *are* luxury aesthetics), Edward and Christian cannot exist without Bella and Anastasia, because gender does not exist in isolation but always through contrast. The illusion of the romance story is in its ability to make us believe it is showing *conflict,* when in fact all gendered players are really in *coordination.* These coordinated stories, being *Roman*-ce stories, are about justice, protection, worthiness, and what is normal. *Roman*-ce stories are not really stories about love. They are stories about war.

Colonial gender was never an institution that sought to describe personal experience or work for personal expression. Rather, colonial gender emerges from war, describes national identities, and engineers national threats. These gender norms also describe identities that obfuscate class. As Paul Virilio writes, "The original war-machine is a man and a woman. The couple is not only good for making babies. Marriage is in reality a war-machine, not a machine of production." What he means is that gender, in the heteropatriarchal sense, is really a weapon. The illusion of heteropatriarchal gender derives from its ability to *contrast* the male and female genders as if they function completely separately, when this contrast is actually highly coordinated. Heteronormativity is uncomfortable not just because it wasn't made to express bodies but because it was made to expand imperialism. When we express heteronormativity, we also expand empire while concealing class struggle.

Wounding

Feminist scholars Wendy Brown, Lauren Berlant, and Sara Ahmed write that identity originates in the wound. For Ahmed, "Wound culture takes the injury of the individual as the grounds not only for an appeal . . . but as an identity claim, such that 'reaction' against the injury forms the very basis of politics." Identity begins in wounds. These wounds are not apolitical or historical. Rather, wounds reflect vulnerabilities that are already understood and reflect the imagining of pain. Wounding takes place at the site of the perceived border, where vulnerability is imagined. To wound is to ruin. The white female body anticipates being ruined by the foreigner. Wound culture conceals histories of pain, as do all origin stories. Ahmed writes that fetishizing the wound only conceals history; Kathryn Yusoff writes that all origin stories work to conceal history. Wounds exist on the boundaries between the internal and the external, between the domestic and the insurgent. Wounds exist between Venus and Mars. Venus, because it seeks to represent femininity, is the domestic and the internal. Venusian environments are interior environments. Mars represents exteriority and the social outsider. Mars is the wild planet that can never be civilized. Both Venus and Mars imagines victimization—Venus through sexual vulnerability and Mars through social oppression.

Since Venus has a gendered logic and Mars a racial one, women of color are often represented through interiority and exteriority at the same time. In Franz Fanon's essay "The Woman of Color and the White Man," he recounts the experiences of Mayotte Capécia in her semiautobiographical novel *Je suis Martiniquaise.* When Capécia dates a white man and goes with him to a social function, she experiences her exteriority as an outsider, stating that "I was barred from this society because I was a woman of color" and that "I felt that I was wearing too much makeup, that I was not properly dressed, that I was not doing André credit, perhaps simply because of the color of my skin." However, Fanon does not accept Capécia's exteriority and outsider status; he writes, "I have the feeling, however, that Mayotte Capécia is laying it on."

Fanon sees Capécia as a collaborator in whiteness because she dates a white man and seeks to demonstrate her insider status by telling us how she tries to bleach, "lactify," or otherwise whiten her own existence by working for white people as a laundress and dating white men. Fanon sees this desire to become white by loving white people not as an isolated case but as normal for women of color, describing these women as "frantic," "in quest of white men," and left waiting. He writes that women of color refuse to love men of color and instead work hard to earn the approval of whiteness. In contrast, Fanon describes the man of color as a victim in his relationships with women. When men of color internalize racial constructs of inferiority, Fanon characterizes them as victims of social, economic, and political processes. Fanon does not characterize men of color who choose to love white women as double agents or insiders but rather as perpetual outsiders who are victimized by cultural insiders.

Rey Chow evaluates the pervasive assumption that women tend to collaborate in their own oppression. Gender dynamics cast women as social insiders and men as undomesticated and naïve, especially in terms of mores relating to sexuality. Chow writes that "as portrayed by Freud, the little boy is an innocent victim of his cultural environment, whereas the little girl is an active agent in her grasp of the politics of sexuality." Women of color are seen as knowledgeable not only about sexual knowledge but also about racial knowledge; women of color are not only active sexual agents but also active racial agents who use sexuality to collaborate against their own race and with whiteness. "Similarly, in Fanon's portrayals, we sense that the Black man is viewed as a helpless victim of his cultural environment," Chow writes, "whereas the woman of color is viewed as a knowledgeable, calculating perpetrator of interracial sexual intercourses." When she chooses white men, Fanon calls her a traitor. Fanon sees Capécia as more accessible for and closer to whiteness due to white men's attraction for her; thus, she is an oppressive social force. Chow writes that, for Fanon, "the woman of color is either a Black traitor (when she chooses the white man) or a white woman (when she chooses a Black man)."

Because the woman of color is not interior or exterior but struggles to hold onto interiority and exteriority at once, her origin wound does not seem to exist. Because the woman of color that Fanon describes wishes to be on the inside but is read as a social outsider by white society, any sexual desire she has rips her open. Chow writes: "Fanon portrays women's sexuality in the main as characterized by an active, sadomasochistic desire—to be raped, to rape herself, to rip herself open." Because interiority and exteriority can not coexist, love is inherently destructive and rips the woman of color open. This ripping open of the woman of color is not seen as painful or as a wounding, however, since it doesn't expose the woman of color's vulnerability. Rather, women of color seem to be collaborators in their own ruining or wounding. These wounds are not political but masochistic—they are not shared and collective but self-inflicted and perverse. They do not form the basis of any social identity because they do not express any boundary between interiority and exteriority. The woman of color's wound is not a political struggle between self and other but a masochistic struggle within herself. When she rips herself open, she is not seen as suffering, because she is her own aggressor and victim. For Fanon, the woman of color is masochistic and self-victimizing.

If wounding is what forms identity, then women of color do not have their own origin wound from which their political identity is formed. Since origin wounds reflect the politics of imagining pain, and these politics conceal certain histories of pain, the wounds of women of color are always masochistic. Women of color are the caretakers of the wounds of others. They take on white female wounds when they take on feminist issues that frame feminist struggles as domestic protection, and they take on the wounds of men of color when men of color frame racial struggle through sexual ownership or conquest. Because women of color do not own their wounds and must take on the wounds of others when forming political identity, they must struggle against themselves in political struggle. Their struggles are not perceived to have political coherency because women of color take on wounds that conceal their own histories of pain. The narrative of the white female victim and the racialized male aggressor conceal the real histories of rape, in which white men overwhelmingly rape women of color.

Innocence

Trigger warning: this section discusses rape culture and anti-Blackness, and it mentions the murders of Trayvon Martin and Isaiah Simmons.

Merriam-Webster defines innocence as: 1) freedom from legal guilt of a particular crime or offense, 2) lack of knowledge, ignorance, and 3) a synonym for chastity. Kimberlé Crenshaw writes that chastity has often been defined as property. Once chastity as property has been either devalued or taken away, it can no longer be stolen again. Only white women are seen to possess the virtue of chastity. Women of color, being associated with sexual deviance, do not seem to possess chastity as property. Thus, rape cases become spectacles when they are committed against white women. A white woman who has been raped must work quickly to establish her innocence. Establishing innocence takes the form of establishing the white woman as white, as not being a sex worker, and as not straying from any buffered white zones. Cases of rape against sex workers, and especially sex workers of color, are not considered to be assault. For example, police in California commonly filed all cases of assaults against sex workers, gang members, and addicts with the acronym "NHI," or "No Human Involved."

Knowledge is an implicit part of innocence. As *Merriam-Webster* defines it, innocence is also a state of ignorance—a state of *not knowing*. Establishing one's own innocence after having experienced sexual assault is also establishing *ignorance*. Innocent rape survivors must not only prove they communicated to their assailant that they knew they were being raped in the moment of the assault (saying "no" so the lack of consent is clearly communicated to the assailant); they must also prove that until the moment of assault took place, they were ignorant of their rapeability (proving that they were tricked into the situation, that the rape surprised them, that they had no way of knowing). Within innocence discourse, knowledge must be distributed for the benefit of the rapist.

In "Against Innocence: Race, Gender, and the Politics of Safety," Jackie Wang writes that "using 'innocence' as the foundation to address anti-Black violence is an appeal to the white imaginary, though these arguments are certainly made by people of color as well." She finds that, while the death of Trayvon Martin galvanized a national movement and public outcries, the death of Isaiah Simmons—a Black boy who was suffocated to death by several counselors at a juvenile detention facility—was ignored by the public. Media outlets repeatedly referred to Simmons as a "juvenile offender," and reactions to his death responded to this identity as a criminal. In contrast, the public cried out against Martin's death because he was a child who was killed in a suburban area.

For Fanon, white women are ignorant of racial knowledge, while men of color are ignorant of sexual knowledge. For him, women of color are never innocent because they are knowledgable about both gender and race. Thus, Fanon sees the woman of color as using her sexual knowledge to collaborate with white men against her own race. Because women of color have knowledge, are *"knowing,"* they are never innocent.

What would a politics without innocence look like?

A politics of innocence assumes that rape victims must not know that they could be raped, and that their assailant is a rapist, when they get in the same room as him. A politics of innocence assumes that murder victims must not know that their assailant wants to kill them when entering spaces where police can kill. A politics of innocence assumes that those who suffer racist attacks within some institution do not have prior knowledge of histories of racial violence happening within that same institution beforehand. A politics of innocence demands that when we are violated and killed, we are always prepared but surprised. A politics of innocence assumes that because we know but don't know what could happen, we take on the personal responsibility of preventing our own violations and murders. It assumes that everyone has the agency to stay away from institutions where violence occurs.

Politics of innocence don't make sense. All people of color know about racism from a very young age. All femmes know and experience rape culture from a very young age. Often, people choose to enter institutions where there is a real threat of violence because these same institutions have resources needed for our survival. Often, people enter institutions (prisons, detention centers, jails) when they know nonconsensual violations are likely to happen in these institutions. Often, people know they are going to be raped before they are. Often, people are raped again and again, knowing what will happen each time it happens, without the ability to clearly communicate their lack of consent to their rapist. Often, people don't know they are raped and do not have the ability to say no. Often, people are criminalized for their own rapeability.

A politics against innocence must understand all of these things. It must understand that asylum seekers often carry contraceptives with them when they cross borders because they know they are likely to be raped when they make their journeys, but they choose to make their journeys anyway. A politics against innocence must understand that an asylum seeker's choice to cross that border with knowledge of the threat of assault does not invalidate her assault. It must understand that most rape victims know their rapists and are often unable to walk away because they are incarcerated or detained. A politics against innocence must understand that people often choose to be in situations where power relations are stacked against them, not because they choose their own victimhood but because power relations are stacked against them everywhere all the time. It must understand that a person of color who works in a white workplace often chooses that workplace not because they want to choose a *white* workplace but because work exists within a white capitalist patriarchy. A politics against innocence must understand that people who are disempowered often know they are disempowered; that they sometimes make choices anyway or that they sometimes cannot make choices; and that none of those choices or lack of choices take away from the validity of their experiences under a certain power relation. A politics against innocence must understand that, in the worst-case scenario, someone may choose to be in a situation that results in rape and that this choice does not count as consent when there are no other choices available.

Innocence is a privilege. Freedom from legal guilt and chastity is a privilege. *Ignorance* is a privilege. Fanon had an issue with women of color because he saw them as *knowing*. For him, women of color who date white men could not be proper victims, as men of color who date white women are, not just because they are knowing but also because they choose not to *communicate* that knowingness all the time. Fanon sees women of color as dishonest. For the woman of color to be a double agent, in Fanon's terms, she must hide her knowingness.

Venus and Mars are about deciding who is "us" and who is "them." In the 1980s and 1990s, neoliberal politicians imposed harsher penalties on criminalized people. Wang writes that as a result of these policies, "Black convicts, initially a part of the 'we' articulated by civil rights groups, became 'them.'" Power works when it is divisive and also colluding. The choice to frame some people as "us" and others as "them" is *never* a personal choice but *always* an institutional one. Innocence discourse works hand in hand with liberal wound culture. It sees racism as isolated acts of violence that the state must protect and penalize against. Both innocence discourse and liberal wound culture need the "legitimate victim" to do the work of proving their own legitimacy and victimhood. Socially progressive innocence politics and liberal wound culture provide outpourings of support immediately after highly publicized rapes and murders of "legitimate victims," but they otherwise ignore everyday power relations that are violent. As Wang writes, "When we build politics around standards of legitimate victimhood that requires passive sacrifice, we will build a politics that requires a dead Black boy to make its point."

Both Venus and Mars have mythologies that began with sexual assault: Inanna's ruin and rape as a war metaphor. After examining these mythologies and histories, it is obvious that rape is not something that the state protects people from; it's something that the state institutionalizes and holds a monopoly on. The institution of rape not only creates victims and criminals but also cultures of victimhood and criminalization.

What would a politics against innocence look like?

A politics against innocence answers questions about the legitimacy of victims—questions asking whether a rape victim is a sex worker, whether they knew they were in a situation where they would be subjected to sex without consent, whether they were bribed or coerced into their own rape—with a resounding "YES, and—." "Was she a sex worker when she was assaulted?" "YES, and sex workers are not only highly vulnerable to assault; they are also often criminalized for their own assaults." "When the victim entered the room with the rapist, did she know he was going to rape her?" "YES, and the rapist had institutional power not only over her but also several other people." "Did the victim receive favors in exchange for coerced sex?" "YES, and she was in a situation where she was not able to receive necessary resources otherwise." "Was Isaiah Simmons considered a juvenile offender when he was killed?" "YES, and he was nonconsensually incarcerated in a center where he was unable to report his abuse or get away from his abusers." "Were protestors violent?" "YES, and not only are these actions a healthy expression of political anger; they are also a direct challenge to the state's monopoly on violence."

Innocence, just like whiteness, chastity, and ignorance, is a property. For those of us who were never owners of our innocence, chastity, or ignorance—those of us who "know"—those of us who are not "us" or "them" but come to realize, as Audre Lorde says, "that our place was the very house of difference rather [than] the security of any one particular difference"—see each other and hold each other when we refuse politics of innocence and liberal wound culture. When we answer "YES, and—," we see and *know* power and violence.

Without innocence, love becomes possible. Love is not innocent, and there are no victims in love. Love knows power, and
love survives power. Love acknowledges violence, but love doesn't
emerge from wounds. Love is everyday, but love is also exceptional.
There is no morality in love. Love can only be a thing that cuts very
deeply into patriarchal, racial capitalism. Any love that doesn't cut
into capitalism is not really love and will make you think you're
crazy with its inauthenticity. Fake love will make you feel unworthy
and uninnocent. Love that cuts into capitalism can make you whole
again. This love is also work. It takes an immensity out of you. It
moves you and it moves with you.

8

ETYMOLOGY OF MERCURY

Going Under

Like Venus, when Mercury retrogrades, it passes by the Sun and disappears for a short period. This period, called the cazimi phase, is when Mercury, like Inanna, descends into the Underworld only to reemerge some days later. However, unlike Venus, Mercury retrogrades often. It disappears behind the sun in retrograde about three or four times a year, while Venus appears to descend only once every two years. Mercury was Zeus's youngest and favorite child. He was allowed to go anywhere he pleased. Mercury was allowed to go to Mount Olympus, Earth—even the Underworld. Mercury was the only god who was allowed to go to the Underworld without the explicit permission of Hades.

A lot of the attributes we associate with Mercury today, such as being two-faced and glib, are actually traditionally associated with the Moon. Although the journey of Mercury's descent is more light-hearted than that of Venus, Mercury was not associated with the commercial sphere. In contrast, Mercury was strongly associated with the Underworld and mining. In the Greek and Roman cosmological world order, the Underworld was the source of all wealth, since agricultural plant life seemed to spring up from the richness of what lay below the dirt. Gold, too, was mined from its hiding places within the earth. Mercury was the messenger of the Underworld, and mercury, the chemical compound, was used to process gold ores taken from the ground. As a planet that appears to follow the Sun around, Mercury processes the solar metal.

In Homer's *Hymn to Hermes,* we follow Hermes/Mercury around on the very first day after his birth. We learn that he is the child of Zeus and Maia. In this telling, Zeus was the most famous of the gods, but Maia was a "shy goddess, for she avoided the company of the blessed gods, and lived within a deep, shady cave." We learn that Hermes is "of many shifts, blandly cunning, a robber, and cattle driver, a bringer of dreams, a watcher by night, a thief at the fates" and "one who was soon to show forth wonderful deeds among the deathless gods."

The first thing we see Hermes do is kill a turtle and invent a lyre from its shell. He says to the turtle, right before killing it: "Living, you shall be a spell against mischievous witchcraft; but if you die, then you shall make sweetest song." Later in his first day, Hermes steals Apollo's cattle by leading the cattle backward and "revers[ing] the marks of their hooves, making the front behind and the hind before" (just like a planet that appears to move backward in the sky three or four times a year). When his mother and Apollo confront him over his theft, Hermes replies that he can't be to blame because he's just a baby, saying he's "a feeble child" and a "fearful babe" who was "born yesterday." When Apollo takes Hermes to Zeus, Hermes gives the same story. He tells Zeus he was "born but yesterday" and says Zeus should believe his tale because he claims to be Hermes's own father. He tells Zeus that "you yourself know that I am not guilty: and I will swear a great oath upon it."

What's startling about Hermes's lies isn't just that they come so easily and convincingly, with him crying out like a baby to his mother even as he lies blatantly to her about the cattle that he stole only a moment ago. It's that no one in the story ever believes him even once. When Hermes cries to his mother for pity, she calls him a shameless rogue and says Apollo's going to come tie him up for what he did. When Hermes appeals to Apollo on account of his own weakness, Apollo starts laughing and says, "O rogue, deceiver, crafty in heart, you talk so innocently that I most surely believe that you have broken into many a well-built house and stripped more than one poor wretch bare this night." When Hermes tells Zeus he is innocent, Zeus does not for one second doubt that Hermes is guilty. Instead, he just asks Hermes to show him where he's hiding the cattle.

However, what is also crucial about the story is that Hermes is never punished for his crimes or deceit. While Inanna's descent was about divine punishment and retribution, the descent of Hermes is about thievery. When Apollo is about to punish Hermes for what he did to him, Hermes starts to play the lyre and sing praises to the gods despite obviously not respecting them earlier. Charmed by the lyre, Apollo accepts it as a gift, and because he's afraid that Hermes will steal back this gift of music, Apollo blesses him with three gold branches that protect him in every task. Then Apollo tells Hermes of three virgins who know how to divine the future but will only speak truth when they eat honey. After Hermes is blessed with these two gifts, Zeus appoints him messenger to Hades, who will give Hermes "no mean prize" because Hermes will take from him "no gift."

Thus, the three attributes granted to Hermes/Mercury by the gods are as follows: he is blessed and protected by the three branches; he is able to divine the future but he doesn't know whether his divinations are truth or lies; and he alone is able to go to the Underworld without permission, but only because he can never take anything from Hades (who in Greek mythology was the source of all wealth, as all living things grow from the earth upward). Before Hermes is granted these gifts, we see that he is a person who does mischievous things but never suffers for them because his charm protects him. We see that he is a person who can lie well but seems cursed because no one ever believes him. We see that he is a fantastic inventor but can only make things by killing others. Every blessing given to Hermes is also a curse. Hermes is seemingly able to evade the fate and hierarchical order that Zeus uses to control the rest of the world. Hermes is a puzzle—a liar who is never believed and the recipient of blessings that turn into curses. The cryptic Hermes says one thing and means another.

The word "cryptic" contains the word "crypt." Hermes's role as messenger of the gods to the Underworld is an important part of how Mercury functions in cosmology. The Hermetic arts, which rose in popularity along with other cults such as Christianity during Roman times, were the hidden or occult arts. Like Hermes, who entered and left the Underworld with ease, the Hermetics were interested in penetrating the surface of things and understanding how things operated truly down deep inside. The Hermetics did not believe that truth was common. The Hermetic arts and sciences have become synonymous with the occult and philosophies that portray themselves as hidden. Like Hermes, who could take nothing from the Underworld, the language of the Hermetics was frequently intentionally obscure and incomprehensible to the world at large.

The Homeland of Hermeticism

Traditionally, the study of astrology is said to be under the domain of Mercury. To understand what the relationship between the Hermetic arts and astrology was actually like, we must look not only at how Hermeticism developed but also how it developed out of Egypt's reputation within the Greek and Roman empires that subjugated it. The first Greek astrologers had a strange relationship with the older cultures that surrounded the new nation-state. Before Alexander the Great, Greeks felt culturally inferior in comparison to the richness of the Persian traditions that surrounded them. They compensated by mimicking the Persians in their religion, cosmology, and arts. It was customary for Greek philosophers to credit their theories to an ancient Persian source. As Roger Beck writes: "The Greeks were aware that compared with the cultures of the ancient Near East, theirs was a young culture much indebted to 'alien wisdom.'" Since the older the source, the more ancient and magical the speaker seemed, Greek quotations and translations of Persian and North African works tended to increase in number as time went on, going against the logic of historical decay. This means the Greeks made a lot of things up but said the things they made up came from Persia and North Africa.

Joanna Komorowska writes in "The Lure of Egypt, or How to Sound Like a Reliable Source" that "traveling to Egypt has a long tradition in Greek literature and even more importantly, in Greek science, with Herodotus and Plato constituting the standard examples of Greeks drawing from the Egyptian tradition." In her essay, she follows Valens in his pilgrimage to Egypt, where he writes in his *Anthologie* that "having traveled through sea and wilderness, I was finally considered worthy of attaining a safe harbor and most secure shelter." Later, he writes that he has seen many lands and people and that he's also gained knowledge through pain. Valens depicts himself as a serious student of astrology, traveling far to the ancient world to learn its technicalities and persevering even when confronted with Egyptian teachers who use astrology for commercial gain. Valens, looking for truth, only finds a false truth in the commercial-minded Egyptian teacher; but through his own spiritual purity, he remakes false truths into divine epiphanies. As Valens continues to study on his own and embarks upon an austere lifestyle, a divine daimon guides him toward Egyptian falsehood and into illumination.

The astrologer Thessalus treats us to a similar account of his own pilgrimage to Egypt. Thessalus describes himself on his journey as having the same obsessive drive for knowledge as Valens, convincing us that his intention to learn the esoteric arts comes from a spiritual place and not merely an intellectual one. In Alexandria, Thessalus finds a book by King Nechespo and is struck dumb. Later, Thessalus continues to travel in Egypt, but his quest for knowledge has become spiritual rather than philosophical. He declines the company of common philosophers from that point on and is only willing to talk to sacred priests. In these tales, Greek astrologers represented themselves as authentically curious, even obsessive in their need to understand the esoteric workings of the world. Traveling to Egypt to have an Egyptian experience was considered to be a sacred journey for spiritual men looking to elevate themselves above philosophers with political goals. Komorowska describes Egypt as the "homeland of Hermeticism." This is because, while Hermeticism as a doctrine developed out of the Greco-Roman traditions, it is only in reference to Egypt that it claims cultural validity. From Egypt, or from their image of Egypt, the Greeks and Romans were able to gain transcendence.

By the early 200s AD, the role Egypt played in the Greco-Roman imagination had become a common convention. The Neoplatonist Iamblichus actually fashioned for himself an Egyptian alter ego named Abammon, which he assumed to explain esoteric and erotic mysteries, although Iamblichus was actually Arab and not Egyptian. By convincing his audience of his Egyptian influence while keeping his daytime persona intact by relegating the Egyptian influences of his work to an alter ego, Iamblichus was following a Greco-Roman tradition of evoking Egyptian pseudo-ancestors. By claiming to have an Egyptian persona as well as an Arab-Roman one, Iamblichus made sure that those reading his works thought of him as akin to Porphyry, Plato, and Pythagoras, all of whom claimed to have received knowledge from the Egyptians. By claiming Egyptian influence, Iamblichus made himself seem more, nor less, Roman. Claiming an Egyptian influence had become a necessary rite of passage for anyone who wanted to become a respected philosopher within the Greco-Roman tradition.

For Greco-Roman thinkers, Egyptian and Persian sources were always magical but never institutional, always sacred but never authoritative. They were raw sources of knowledge that had to be reinterpreted by a Greco-Roman author before they were made into real theory. The Egyptians were characterized as a people who did not understand their own culture enough to know what to do with it. As Asclepius says of Nechespo, "though [he was] a wise man possessed of great magical powers . . . he had grasped the affinities of stones and plants with the stars, but he did not know the times of places where the plants must be gathered." Greeks and Romans sought Egyptian knowledge but saw themselves as authors capable of fine-tuning Egyptian ideas into spiritual truth.

Even in the classical era, which is precisely the period that Western philosophers constantly refer to over and over in their continual project of developing and revising the West, Mercury's occult qualities could not be distinguished from exoticism. Exoticism, in the Greco-Roman tradition, was not merely an intellectual school but one with religious and spiritual dimensions. Philosophers used Egypt as the homeland of the occult not only to impress upon their audience evidence of their sincerity in their pursuit of higher learning but also to establish themselves as thinkers motivated by spirituality more than material gain or intellectual ego. Esotericism seeks to describe the world in depth without being fooled by surface impressions, just as Mercury is able to transgress into the hidden realms without being completely captured by its neverending mysteries. Esotericists, modeling themselves after Mercury and calling themselves Hermetics, saw themselves as those possessed by a spirit that called them to make a pilgrimage to the homeland of the occult—Egypt—and save its religion-culture from its own inhabitants.

A Cult/Occult

Modernity brought to Europe cabinets of curiosities from faraway lands, from P. T. Barnum's traveling circus to Europe's obsession with inhaling powdered mummified remains from Egypt to the world fairs that showcased the colonial world as spectacle. Almost all notable thinkers from Europe's modern period had an Orientalist influence, from Aldous Huxley to T. S. Eliot to Friedrich Nietzsche. New schools of thought, such as abstraction and Jungian archetypal psychology, developed out of primitivism and Orientalism. These schools of exoticism, which influenced European culture from high to low, modernized Mercury's occult traditions.

Europeans didn't just see Asia and Africa as far away in terms of distance. Colonies were also described as being far away in terms of time. African or Asian societies that were contemporary with modern Europe were described as more ancient, less currently relevant, and unchanging. Europe saw humanity as a tree; itself as the fresh, impressionable branches; and Africans, Asians, and Indigenous Americans as the primitive roots—archaic races that only happened to still exist in the present but without the modern traits of reason and sentiment. Europe looked for a primordial sense of self in its colonies as it began to change rapidly with industrialization. In the same way that Egypt represented ancient authority to the Greeks and Romans, India represented primordial wisdom to the English. As Vyacheslav Ivanov writes in 1909, " Symbols ... are the experience of a lost and forgotten heritage of the people.... They have been deposited since time immemorial by the people in the souls of the bards as basic forms and categories in which alone a new vision can be framed.... The poet ... is the organ of collective awareness and collective recollection. Through him the people recalls its ancient soul."

In 1923, D. H. Lawrence writes in *Fantasia of the Unconscious* that "in the [previous] world a great science and cosmology were taught esoterically in all countries." He also writes that, "in that world men . . . were in one complete correspondence over all the earth" and that "Knowledge, science was universal" and as "cosmo-politan as" his contemporary society. Then, Lawrence writes, the "world flood" came and some societies "retained their innate life-perfection," including "the South Sea Islanders, Druids, Etruscans, Chaldeans, Amerindians or, Chinese" "refused to forget" and con-tinued to teach "the old wisdom" albeit "in half-forgotten symbolic forms." Lawrence finishes by adding, "And so, the intense potency of symbols is part at least of memory." Lawrence compares histor-ical categorizations of people (Druids, Etruscans, and Chaldeans) with races contemporary to his day (Amerindians and Chinese).

The symbols that Europe sought to use in exploring its subcon-scious, primordial self came directly from its colonies. As classical art and theory were revived within modernity, so were its conven-tions. The Near East, Africa, and Asia were quickly incorporated into a classical framework of looking outside, to spatially distant and temporally faraway places, for ancient wisdom to make one's own theories speculative or literally otherworldly. In Robert Musil's book *Young Torless,* one of the characters encounters a book of Indian philosophy. His experience with this book resembles the metaphys-ical associations that the Greco-Romans had with Egypt—other-worldly, mysterious, and exclusive to the spiritually pure: "In the . . . act of opening a book, he sought to enter . . . exquisite knowledge as if through a secret gate. They had to be books whose . . . possession was like the sign of a secret order and . . . the guarantee of super terrestrial revelations. . . . He found that . . . only in books of Indian philosophy, which he did not consider mere books, but revelations, reality-key works like medieval books of alchemy and magic."

Not only did the book of Indian philosophy within the story of *Young Torless* allude to a magical and secret order from a fantastical place outside of Europe, the book also stands in for more Indige-nous superstitions like "medieval books of alchemy and magic." The magical book isn't just a book. It is also a fetish object, captur-ing modern sentiments about geographical difference and a special type of authorship that could be gained through secrecy. The Indian book represents the archaic and magical knowledge that only a European could wrest from its colonial reaches. The Theosophical Society, hoping to create its own Indian books, stationed its head-quarters in colonial India.

While Europeans preferred to frame non-European cultures as existing outside modernity, the appropriation and reinterpretation of non-European cultural forms cultivated modern Europe. So-called religio-cultural backwash from Europe's colonies was what brought European culture into modernism. Modernist forms of art, such as color field theory and compositional abstraction, sought to infuse a sense of spirituality with brutal forms. Painters like Kandinsky and Picasso painted abstract shapes not only to make an aesthetic statement but as part of a larger spiritual claim. By breaking down the elements of a painting into simple, geometric shapes, Kandinsky and others were seeking to revitalize art by finding a sense of primitivism within stripped-down images of pure shape, line, and color. Cubists, like Picasso, looked to African sculpture to create a new vocabulary of art, which only discussed the fundamentals of form and color. As Bernard Smith writes, "A primitive mind . . . now lived in the basement of the rational European mind and revealed itself . . . in the art of children . . . the mentally ill, [and] naïve, untutored painters." Modernist painters, such as Kandinsky, emulated the aesthetic of primitivity to frame themselves as spiritually transcendent.

Astrologers such as Alan Leo and Dane Rudhyar also looked to India and China to build their own reputations as learned but enlightened men. For them, enlightenment was not merely a humanist endeavor but also a Buddhist one. Books like the book of Indian philosophy found in *Young Torless,* which imply that outside of Europe's current events lay a vast cartography of occult knowledge that has never been mapped by any rational observer, reproduced Hermeticism as modern exoticism. While the Greco-Romans found a sense of the hidden specifically within Egypt, modern Europe replaced Egypt with India, Syria, China, and Africa. Mercury, who was said to be allowed to journey to the Underworld and return unscathed, was really only ever allowed to journey to the colonies and return endowed with archaic and incomprehensible knowledge.

The occult was not incidental to modernity but foundational to it. Eventually, the occult rebranded its institutions as modern and scientific. Most of Europe's gentlemen scientists were also occultists. Ideas of atomic matter, magnetism, and Newtonian physics emerge directly from occult ideas about vibration, polarity, and causality. The book *The Kybalion: Hermetic Philosophy* was penned by an anonymous author who wrote under the pseudonym The Three Initiates and who claimed to write from the essence of Hermes Trigmegistus. *The Kybalion* discusses seven Hermetic principles that rule the universe: Mentalism, Correspondence, Vibration, Polarity, Rhythm, Cause and Effect, and Gender. These theories, working contrary to intuitive thinking while aligning with common ideologies, postulated that nothing in the universe is ever still, opposites attract, everything is connected, and binaries are inherently gendered. As Max Nordau writes in 1892 in his book *Degeneration,* "Ghost stories are very popular, but . . . in scientific guise, as hypnotism, telepathy, somnambulism . . . so are esoteric novels, in which the author hints that he could say a great deal about magic, Kabbala, fakirism, astrology and other white and black arts if he . . . chose" (the black arts being magical practices originating from Egypt and the white arts being Western interpretations of the black arts).

It is not just that the occultists of early modernity wrote in rhetoric that reflected the scientism of the times but also that all modern sciences come from an occult tradition. The tradition of the occult revitalized the modern sciences. Scientists styled themselves as alchemists and whiz kids or wizards. Newton, obsessed with alchemy in his youth, formulated his law of universal attraction when inspired by astrological principles of planetary influence. Tesla tried to communicate with extraterrestrials, and Edison built a device to help him talk to spirits. These scientists in early modernity, like their artist contemporaries, looked to the colonies for inspiration while also distinguishing themselves from the irrational world by way of their supposed technical skills and expertise. The shape and texture of modernity was occult.

Mathematical or empirical sciences especially relate to Mercury and the occult. It is not only that chemistry grew from alchemy or that astronomy grew from astrology but that the narrative of rationality, like Hermeticism, seeks to challenge preexisting and intuitive ways of gathering knowledge. Both modern science and occult studies are practices that seek to arrive at truth without needing to engage in the tiresome involvement of revising, reviving, and anticipating history, which the political, social, and even economic sciences must deal with. As Rebecca Goldstein writes: "The rigor and certainty of the mathematician is arrived at a priori, meaning that the mathematician neither resorts to any observations in arriving at his or her mathematical insights nor do these mathematical insights, in and of themselves, entail observations, so that nothing we experience can undermine the ground we have for knowing them." The modern mathematician is able to create theories at a younger age than any other scientist, armed with only a pencil and a pad of paper and liberated from the burdens of history and from observation. Mathematical theories, like occult ones, are meant to describe the world without observing the world.

The a priori nature of mathematics also shows up in modern art. The geometric shapes created by modern painters and sculptors, such as Kandinsky, stripped images down to pure line, shape, and color the same way a mathematician strips the world down to a series of formulas. Both modern art and modern mathematics sought to describe the world without observing the world. The language of modern art and science, being unintelligible to the layperson and disregarding the surface appearances of things, are not just credible but supercredible. Like modern science, which tries to push past assumptions to arrive at truth, modern art tries to push past observational images to arrive at visual truth. The word "credibility" implies that there is belief at play—that modern arts and sciences are languages that emerge from belief. However, artists and scientists of colonial Europe imagine themselves not as philosophers or spiritualists who encouraged their audiences to believe in their theories but as skeptical technicians who sought to liberate Europe from an older, belief-oriented worldview in favor of a new, rational level of discourse. The technicality and rationality of modern art and science are abstract. Abstractions are supercredible and create a sense of reality *more real than other forms of reality*. Because abstractions are technical, they do not seem to require belief.

It is not just that Europe became more rational or scientific when it also became colonialist; rather, Europe became technical. Europe's technicality was not confined to the sciences but also shows up in its arts and spiritualities. This technicality is also a sentiment—a feeling. These technical and rational feelings of Europe's institutions, parlors, and societies is a power relation between itself and the colonial world.

Anthropologist Graham M. Jones writes that magic occupied a special place in the colonizer's imagination. In his book *Magic's Reason: An Anthropology of Analogy,* Jones follows the journey of Robert Houdin, who was hired by the French colonial forces to disillusion Algerians who frequently staged revolutions inspired by marabouts, or Muslim holy men, using stage magic. Houdin, writing about his journey, says: "It was hoped, with reason that my performances would lead the Arabs to understand that the marabouts' trickery is naught but simply child's play and could not, given its crudeness, be the work of real heavenly emissaries. Naturally, this entailed demonstrating our superiority in everything and showing that, as far as sorcerers are concerned, there is no match for the French."

Jones observes that Houdin's description illustrates a tension: the goal of magic had the dual purpose of *disenchanting* Algerians from the influence of local religious authorities and of *enchanting* them to accept French domination. European humanists tended to view themselves as fully rational and evolved while seeing colonial subjects as children. Louis Rinn describes Arabs as "ignorant and credulous" and Muslim holy men as "jugglers and prestidigitators" and "mere exporters of human stupidity," explaining that their magic accomplishments had perfectly scientific explanations and "are simply phenomena of neurosis, hysteria, magnetism and hypnotism—all easily explainable." For Europeans of the time, metaphysical studies such as magnetism and hypnotism *were* considered perfectly acceptable scientific explanations for what could formerly only be explained through superstition and religion.

Max Dif conflates the ancients and Africans when he writes that "the reactions of Africans today [to magic] resemble those of people in the Middle Ages, antiquity, and certainly prehistory" and that Africans "remains in a vague middle ground between these two concepts" of trickery and real magic. It is difficult to tell from the passage where Dif himself draws the line between tricks and real magic and whether Europeans were able to faithfully distinguish between the two. In contrast, after Houdin's trip to Algiers, the Arabs give him a certificate thanking him for his popular magic show and comparing his technical accomplishments not to religious and magical figures, as naïve minds presumably would have done, but to intellectual and scholarly figures that the European humanists saw as their intellectual ancestors. Rather than accepting that Arab audiences seemed to view magic shows in the same way that European ones did, Houdin responded by continuing to propagate the idea that Arab audiences were enchanted by his illusions.

Jones writes that anthropology itself, as the study of culture through analogy, began as a humanist tradition seeking to study magic. "The 'irrationality' of native superstitions and practices was necessary to demonstrate the rationality of modern European institutions," Jones writes. Frenchness, Englishness, and other European identities were only able to become individualistic, rational, and enlightened through the colonial descriptions of Arabs, Africans, and Asians as biologically driven, irrational, and in the dark. What the myth of European rationality and colonial irrationality did was create a boundary. This boundary lay between dark magic and the white light of science, between the unknown world and the known, and between the feeling-impulses and the technical-rational.

Mercury is a trickster. Lewis Hyde, in his work on trickster archetypes, writes that the trickster is a "boundary-crosser" and that "there are also cases in which trickster *creates* a boundary, or brings to the surface a distinction previously hidden from sight." Modern abstract technicality not only tries to strip away observational biases that distort reality but also works in a distinctly Mercurial motion; it seeks to *uncover* a reality underneath reality the same way a messenger might uncover the Underworld. The Underworld uncovered by Mercurial modern technical abstraction was not a reality more real than the observable world but merely Europe's images of its own colonies. These images seem to be primordial and primitive in the context of European race supremacy. Modern arts and sciences can only be viewed as rational and technical when the assumptions that hold them in place—the assumption that the subaltern is the primordial and primitive basement of Europe's imagination—are assumed to be true.

In other words, modern art and science are only skeptical when their practitioners believe in the irrationality of the subaltern—when practitioners believe that the subaltern is ahistorical, prehistoric, primordial, and primitive. The supercredibility of the rational sciences, which include modern art, rely on images of the colonized world as magical, superstitious, and shamanistic. The boundary that Mercury the trickster creates, then, is the boundary between the irrational and magical world of the subaltern and the rational and scientist world of Europe. The supercredibility of the modern arts and sciences relies on the magical belief that this boundary between the subaltern and Europe exists. As Walter Mignolo writes, "Africans have experience; Europeans have philosophy; Native Americans have wisdom; Anglo-Saxons have science; the Third World has cultures; the First World has science and philosophy." For believers to believe in the boundary between experience and philosophy, between wisdom and science, and between culture and science, we have to believe in the cultural-biological distinction between the colonized and the colonizing.

Homo oeconomicus and the Mimic Man

Colonialism, like Mercury, is extractive. It is important to understand that colonizers do not build new structures or economies on top of land; instead, colonizers extract lands, labor, and economies. As J. Sakai writes in *Settlers,* imperialism is not "a process of creation" but "a process of extraction and transfer." Lands are extracted from common lands held by peasants and Indigenous people, labor is extracted from the enslaved and displaced underclass, and economies are extracted from communities and relationships that the underclass builds with one another. In settler societies such as the United States, no wealth exists outside what is created by colonial labor. Colonizers do not move from one place to another to create new societies but to annex land, extract labor, and appropriate economies.

When Hermes turns a turtle into a lyre, he says to the turtle: "Living, you shall be a spell against mischievous witchcraft; but if you die, then you shall make sweetest song." Hermes doesn't just kill the turtle but turns it into an *inanimate object*—Mercury turns living things not into dead things but into *nonliving* things. In *A Billion Black Anthropocenes or None,* Kathryn Yusoff writes that "historically, both slaves and gold have to be material and epistemically

made through the recognition and extraction of their human properties." In her analysis, Yusoff finds that slaves were accounted for
on the ships and plantations in the same way that inhuman materials such as timber or minerals were accounted for. "The movement
of energy between enslaved bodies in plantations, plants, long-dead
fossilized plants, and industrialized labor is a geochemical equa-
tion of extraction," Yusoff writes. "Slavery is driven by an indifferent
extractive geo-logic" that extracts "inhuman properties" and turns
them into surplus value, she says.

Sylvia Wynter finds, in her extensive work on the human, that
the politics of slavery is also the politics of the human and inhuman. She writes that the earliest definition of the human, which
she calls Man1, was religious—humans were those who were predestined to be saved by the Christian God (and Christianity was
synonymous with whiteness). The second iteration of the human,
Man2, is cultural. Humans are those who possess the right culture,
or the white culture, which Wynter calls "civic-humanist, rational self-conception." In order for Man2 to exist as a white subject,
whites had to institutionalize "Black Africans as the physics refer-
ent of the projected irrational/subrational Human Other." Thus,
Wynter writes, a slave was "transformed from the human subject of
his own culture into the inhuman object of the European culture."
Slavery is the institutionalization of the boundary between the
human and inhuman. Mercury doesn't just make boundaries—it
also turns living things inhuman.

In George Bernard Shaw's play *Back to Methuselah,* the scientist
Pygmalion creates automata with consciousness. He argues with
Martellus, the mystic, over whether these artificially intelligent
creatures can be considered human:

PYGMALION. *That is a very difficult question to answer, my dear. I
    confess I thought at first I had created living creatures; but Martellus
    declares they are only automata. But then Martellus is a mystic: I am*

a man of science. He draws a line between an automaton and a living
organism. I cannot draw that line to my own satisfaction.

MARTELLUS. Your artificial men have no self-control. They only respond
to stimuli from without.

PYGMALION. But they are conscious. I have taught them to talk and
read; and now they tell lies. That is so very lifelike.

MARTELLUS. Not at all. If they were alive they would tell the truth. You
can provoke them to tell any silly lie; and you can foresee exactly the
sort of lie they will tell. Give them a clip below the knee, and they will
jerk their foot forward. Give them a clip in their appetites or vanities
or any of their lusts and greeds, and they will boast and lie, and affirm
and deny, and hate and love without the slightest regard to the facts
that are staring them in the face, or to their own obvious limitations.
That proves that they are automata.

Mercury, as Hermes was, is the trickster. As a trickster, he lies.
Pygmalion's automata don't just lie with their words but lie with
their being—their reflexes that tell them to kick when clipped on
the knee just like a human, their programming that tells them to
become hungry after a certain amount of hours just like a human,
and their proclamations of hate and love as if they were human. The
more they act like a human, according to Martellus, the more they
become inhuman because they can only become humanlike through
deception. As Hyde writes, the role of the trickster is to confuse a
boundary while also articulating it. Like the Greco-Roman mystics
collecting scraps of the Persian prophets or the modern occultists
who turned their speculation on "Indian books" into an inscrutable
science, the automata that looks too human but isn't quite articulates the boundary between human and machine. The machine
articulates this boundary precisely when it attempts to cross it.

In "Of Mimicry and Man: The Ambivalence of Colonial Discourse," Homi Bhabha writes that the mimicking of imperialist

overseers by colonial subjects is not due to the subject simply copying the behaviors and cultural practices of their rulers. Rather, mimicry is really a double articulation, "a complex strategy of reform, regulation, and discipline, which 'appropriates' the Other as it visualizes power." In other words, colonial subjects do not mimic imperialists to become imperialist. Instead, colonial subjects, whose viewpoints are always marginal, subjective, and specific, attempt to visualize their own power struggle by seeing themselves from the outside in and, in doing so, mimic the universal, emancipatory, and rational viewpoints of their oppressors. As Chen Kuan-hsing writes in *Asia as Method:*

> The internal contradiction of colonial 'assimilation' is implied in its aggressive attack. It requires that you admit to the inferiority of your own culture. It forces you to abandon your existential dignity. It then wins over your active consent to learning and acquiring everything that belongs to the governing colonizers. To do this presupposes a painful process of self-negation. Once you have done that, you are told that your imitation is not quite right: you are still not like 'us'; you are, in essence, inferior. In this sense, assimilation has become the internal contradiction of colonialism. Paradoxically, the effect of assimilation was that it supplied a language of revolt.

Colonial subjects mimic objectivity so they can understand and articulate power. Albert Memmi writes that "the colonized fights in the name of the very values of the colonizer, uses his techniques of thought and his methods of combat. It must be added that this is the only action that the colonizer understands." The assimilationist pretends to act like a human, proclaiming declarations of hate and love as if they were human, but becomes more inhuman through humanlike deception. Since the process of dehumanization is also the process of alienating oneself from one's own cultural context, assimilationists dehumanize themselves when pursuing the human.

The very language of third-world revolt, the articulation of third-world identity, and the position of the third world must assimilate to the international order and prove itself through economic development, technological advancement, and national sovereignty. When Venezuelans established the First Venezuelan Republic, they saw no contradiction when borrowing rhetoric from the Constitution of the imperialist United States. In Taiwan, a political group called Club 51 sought Taiwanese independence by asking for Taiwan to join the United States as the fifty-first state. As Chen Kuan-hsing writes about this dilemma, "to become independent [from Japanese and Chinese imperialism], Taiwan must depend on the United States militarily, diplomatically, and economically, contrary to the very idea of independence."

In discussing what happens when we literalize our metaphors, Seo-Young Chu finds that "etymologically the word 'robot' comes from the Czech word *robota,* which means 'forced labor.'" She finds that when the science-fictional metaphor of the robot is literalized, the labor involved in creating the robot is revealed. The robot, literalized, becomes a forced laborer. Robots become the colonial subjects—primarily women of color—who assemble the mechanical world and the interface of the virtual world in sweatshops in the third world. Robots are often fantasized about as sex objects *(Ghost in the Shell, Blade Runner, The Stepford Wives, Her, Westworld, Ex Machina)* not because there is anything inherently sexy about a robot but because their makers are racialized and sexualized. Robots, as fantasy objects, look and act like women of color because robots are made by women of color. The sexualization of robots depicts the real power relation through which the robot is built. When we literalize the robot metaphor, we discover that metaphors do not stray very far from their productive (or reproductive) origins. Since women of color make our robots, then robots are also metaphors for women of color.

While the humanity described by European ideologies was religious and cultural in the past, Wynter writes in her conversation with Katherine McKittrick titled *Unparalleled Catastrophe for Our Species?* that contemporary humanity is no longer described in terms of religion or culture but in terms of economics, and she calls the contemporary human subject *Homo oeconomicus.* John Brewer, in *Pleasure of the Imagination,* writes that capitalism introduced a new border between the human and the inhuman: "Barbarism, which had long been equated with the absence of Christianity, was now defined by the absence of commercial society." While the religious human was Christian and white, and the cultural human was neoclassical and white, *Homo oeconomicus* is bourgeois and white. *Homo oeconomicus* lives in the first world, works a white-collar job, and consumes a diet rich in fruits and vegetables that are farmed in the third world and extracted into the first world. The human is no longer a religious or cultural ideology but an economic one. Whereas in the past whiteness evangelized and then taught, today it employs. Whiteness is an equal-opportunity employer.

Hermes-Aphrodite

Trigger warning: this section mentions the killing of Michael Brown.

When Mercury retrogrades, it appears to move backward in the sky past the Sun. Before the retrograde, Mercury is visible in the evening sky. After the retrograde, which is when Mercury passes the Sun by inferior conjunction, Mercury is only visible in the morning. Like Venus, Mercury's retrograde splits it into two phases, and Mercury the planet-symbol has a dual image. Hellenistic astrologers called Mercury the evening star Epimetheus, and they called Mercury the morning star Prometheus.

Mercury, through Prometheus, has a close relationship to technology. As James Bridle writes in *New Dark Age,* Epimetheus (whose name means "hindsight") was in charge of classifying all life forms the gods had created but runs out of virtues before he gets to humans. Prometheus (whose name means "foresight") takes pity on the humans and gives us technology, which he steals from the gods. Bridle writes, "Epimetheus is thus the god of big data ... of exclusion and erasure, and of overconfidence. Epimetheus's mistake is the original sin of big data, which taints it at the source. Prometheus ... [is] the white heat of scientific and technological discovery, and that desire for the oncoming rush of the future, the head-down drive of forward movement. It's resource extraction, fossil fuels, undersea cables, server farms, air conditioning, on-demand delivery, giant robots, and meat under pressure."

While Hellenistic astrology traditionally ascribed copper to the domain of Mercury, later astrologers attribute copper to be under the domain of Venus. By the 1500s, Jean-Baptise Morin confidently claims that copper is in the realm of Venus. Because copper is a precious metal and is similar to gold in hue, it was used as decor not only for the body as jewelry but also for interior design. The use of jewelry has been mostly gender neutral through most of history, but decoration itself and stylistic fabrication—which the Greco-Romans saw as inferior to the cultivating arts—was feminized, because men framed their pursuit of knowledge as more abstract and less materialistic than the pursuits of women. It's possible that copper became ruled by Venus in Renaissance-era astrology because it had become associated with decorative uses—decoration signaling femininity. Later on, aesthetic issues, once a symbol of aristocratic power that was employed by men as well as women, became a domestic (aka a middle-class white woman) concern.

In modernity, copper was valued due to its highly conductive nature, becoming used in electrical wires, particularly in communication technologies. The telephone and telegraph depended on copper's conductive nature (sending things by wire was really sending things by copper wire). As the world grew more connected, it also depended upon copper more and more. ARPANET, the precursor to the internet, was invented by a new class of American technologists working for the United States Department of Defense.

The Advanced Research Projects Agency (ARPA) was created by President Eisenhower during the Cold War to ensure the continued development of American technology and industry. The wide influence of the internet emerges from a military-industrial complex through which a developed country usually asserts its technological, informational, and economic power. In other words, the internet is a consequence of superpower. Most wars in a nuclear society are fought in a "cold" manner between economic partners who are both attempting to outdevelop the other. The internet is a weapon made for the nuclear age, able to influence the economic, informational, and technological spheres simultaneously. It is part of the military-industrial complex. Due to it being a military technology, the internet is Venusian. We cannot talk about the internet as a public space without also talking about it as a place of militaristic surveillance.

In addition, coding is Venusian when we consider it to be a type of architecture. The sacred geometry that Venusian symbols, such as the heart and pentacle, become ideal beauty when created by God—the divine designer. As Paul Virilio writes, "Architects are always close to the prince. Architecture is at the service of power. There is no such thing as a monarch without an architect, whether to erect his tomb, pyramids, or palaces; the architect's power is a major political power." Before cyberspace, the architecture of the metropolis described politics in spatial terms, as we saw with the Viennese Ringstrasse that insulated the bourgeoisie from the lower classes. Within cyberspace, code becomes architecture not only because it constructs the software of virtual spaces but also because we rely on algorithms to enforce law and political norms. Larry Lessig writes that "code is law," "code has supplanted law," and "code, not law, solves social problems."

However, the internet is also Mercurial because it is a technology in addition to it being a society. As a technology, the internet has occult roots. The wiring of the internet, including the complex code that describes its software or the circuitry that weaves its hardware, is Hermetic in origin. The binary system that all code is based on was a direct result of Leibniz's seventeenth-century fascination with the *I Ching* and Chinese divination. The yin and yang *yao,* which formalize the world in terms of broken and unbroken lines, was translated by Leibniz into os and is. From there, occultism became the numerous languages, incomprehensible to humans, that allow developers to speak to machines. Coding, with its absolute solutionism, takes the place of mathematics in an informational age. To write in Python, Ruby, C++, or Java is a technical feat that developers must cultivate after long periods of training. Developers are created through initiation rites just as the mystics of the Hermetic cults in Greece and Rome created themselves through initiation rites. Developers, in turn, style themselves as mystics. As Fred Turner writes in *From Counterculture to Cyberculture,* the connection between internet geniuses that inflated the dot-com bubble and Zen Buddhism was no mere coincidence. Early developers replaced journeys to Egypt or the Orient with acid trips, went heavy with the Orientalism, and came back to enlighten the rest of the world with their newly discovered but archaic knowledge. This means that developers branded themselves as Mercurial, often in resistance to the internet's Venusian (and military) formality and normativity.

It is not just that technology is Mercurial but that Mercury rules over technology that is made for the purpose of extracting land, resources, and labor from the third world into the first world. While Epimetheus classifies, labels, and defines, Prometheus extracts. This classifying, labeling, defining, and extracting are not the benign actions of human actors upon a neutral environment; they are the classification and extraction of the inhuman objects of the third world by human subjects of the first world. As Wendy Chun writes in her book *Control and Freedom:*

"Cyberspace is an odd name for a communications medium. Unlike newspaper (news+paper) or film, it does not comprise its content or its physical materials. Unlike movies, derived from 'moving pictures,' it does not explain its form; unlike cinema (short for cinematograph: Greek *kinhma, kinhmato* [motion]+graph [written]), it does not highlight its physical machinery. Further, unlike television (tele+vision; vision from afar), cyberspace does not explain the type of vision it enables, and unlike radio, it does not reference its means of transmission (radiation). Although all these names—newspaper, film, movies, cinema, television, and radio— erase sites of production, cyberspace erases all reference to content, apparatus, process, or form, offering instead a metaphor and a mirage, for cyberspace is not spatial."

As an extractive technology, cyberspace obfuscates its material basis by constructing itself as an abstract space. It hides how it is produced. Although cyberspace's gadgets and circuit boards are built by women of color in the developing world, cyberspace reads as neutral and without ethnic odor because it is perceived to be as a virtual reality rather than a material one. The internet promises to dissolve the boundaries of colonial relations. As Chun writes, "since race, gender, age, and infirmities are only skin deep (or so the logic goes), moving to a text-based medium makes them—and thus the discrimination that stems from them—disappear. . . . For those always already marked, the Internet supposedly relieves them of their problem, of their flesh that races, genders, ages, and handicaps them, of their body from which they usually cannot escape."

In Greco-Roman ideology, Mercury is transcendental. Ancient occultists, such as Valens, went to Egypt to prove that their spirituality transcended the political games that other philosophers were involved in. In modern Europe, Mercury became technical. Artists and scientists, such as Kandinsky and Jung, drew from the colonies to display their own technical expertise. In both of these examples, Mercury's extractive actions are religious and cultural. Since the human is the one who extracts and the inhuman is the one who is extracted from, humans extract religion and culture from the inhuman. However, we've already discussed how Wynter notes that the third stage of humanism frames the human not through religion or culture but through economics. The human is no longer only Christian or Western but also bourgeois. Mercury's extractive properties are not only religious or cultural but also economic. While Mercury seems to extract symbols, aesthetics, styles, and motifs from the colonies, cultural extractions are memorialized extractions. What these extractions hide is *the extraction of labor*. While Wynter's Man1 became human through the extraction of spirit, and Man2 became human through the extraction of cultural belonging, the *Homo oeconomicus* becomes human by extracting labor.

Cyberspace is esoteric. It is an extractive technology. However, the internet is also Venus: it is a coded and designed space. The internet is a surveillance machine and a place where identities are fundamentally deceptive because they are communicated immaterially. Chun writes that "the relationship between control and freedom in terms of fiber-optic networks is often experienced as sexuality or is mapped in terms of sexuality-paranoia." In the history of the internet, the most innovative spaces are often pornographic spaces. These innovations—the use of the internet as a social space, a commerce space, and as a feeling space—are appropriated by other industries before the pornographical spaces that created the technologies are censored and shut down.

The sexuality of robots is also the sexual projection of the first world onto third-world women. Robots are sexualized in the ways that women of color are sexualized; they are seen as use-objects, disposable, and detachable. Robots' body parts are optimized for pleasure, and their bodies are easily transformed by their users. However, robot skin is impermeable, and the robot itself is neither impressionable nor sentimental. Women of color, too, are seen as adaptable to white male pleasure. However, as Anne Anlin Cheng writes, colored female skin is seen as reflective and resistant.

Because the devices that provide the interface for the digital world are produced by women of color whose images, when seen in the West, are likened to mechanical robots, the internet exists as a power relation between first-world users and third-world producers. Hermes-Aphrodite is the integration of technology, which is extractive, and biopolitics, which creates power.

Chun writes that, for the first-world user, the internet relieves them of *"their flesh."* Hortense Spillers writes that the abstract entity of flesh is opposed to the liberal, self-possessed body. She finds that flesh is outside of civilization and relates it to "the concentration of ethnicity," writing that a person described as flesh has no gender, no temporality, and no rights. Flesh, for Spillers, exists to be "seared, divided, ripped apart" or "ruptured." Flesh is "the calculated work of iron, whips, chains, knives, the canine patrol, the bullet." Flesh is not a body but a state of inhumanity that exists to be extracted from. The person who is described in terms of flesh is also extracted from in terms of labor. Flesh cannot be white since to be white is to be self-posessed; flesh is not a body but exists unembodied and unself-possessed. When Chun compares the freedom promised by the internet to a liberalization from flesh, she is also writing that such freedom is a liberal freedom. For the internet user who is liberated from flesh, they are also liberated from the condition of being flesh—of being extracted from and of laboring. To use the internet without having to worry about flesh is also the liberal freedom of not having to worry about labor that constructs cyberspace.

Depictions of robots in pop culture frame any humanity of the robot as a consequence of design rather than production. The human qualities of robots come directly from their corporate designers. In *WALL-E*, WALL-E's job is to look for signs of life on a decaying Earth. This human desire for life is built into WALL-E's robot nature by the corporation Buy'n'Large. In the HBO series *Westworld,* Dolores Abernathy's human qualities are framed in terms of the liberal freedom of choice. Her humanity is also linked to her designer, Arnold Weber. Most wealthy-nation film and literary depictions of robots cut away scenes that might show the assemblage or production of the robot itself or show it in a way that cuts out workers. In *Ex Machina,* Ava is seen to assemble herself as if the production process is a sequence within her algorithm. *Westworld's* robots are seen as being assembled in the opening credits, but the plot of the show ignores the complications of robot as matter, preferring to speed up or make peripheral moments in which robots might need to be reassembled or sealed up. The premise of the show, in which robots are infinitely autoregenerating even as they break and suffer from the whims of the human guests, needs the obfuscation and abbreviation of the robot production process to be credible. If the robot healing process was too lengthy or expensive, questions around the disposability of the robot would be raised. In all of these examples, the human qualities of robots do not come from the producer but from the designer. Humanity lives in the software—not the hardware. Scenes of robot production can be cut away because it is assumed that production adds nothing to the creation act of the designer.

In the robot metaphor, the designers of robots are the *Homo oeconomicus.* Robot bodies, on the other hand, are assembled by inhuman workers—either by the robots themselves, other robots, or off-screen workers. When humanity is seen to come from design rather than production—from algorithm rather than machinery—corporations are seen as creator-agents more than workers are. In science-fictional universes, corporations are also more credibly human than workers. In the creative act of making a robot, corporations are seen as birth agents, while the identities of the workers who mold robot skin and weld robot bones are enveloped by the inhuman matter of the robot flesh.

A few years before the shooting of Michael Brown in 2014 in Ferguson, Missouri, police adopted new standards of surveillance because the city's bonds were predicted to sink to the level of junk by 2017. The new practices adopted by police were aimed at increasing the amount of fines that the city would be able to extract from its citizens through penalization. As Wang writes, the police are a state power whose sole purpose is "to serve the interests of finance at the expense of the public." The harsh discipline of a contemporary police state that serves the justice industry resembles Africa in the seventeenth and eighteenth centuries in which policies of over-policing created fissures within communities so that community members became vulnerable.

In the world governed by *Homo oeconomicus,* it is not just that people of color and particularly Black people are presented as inhuman objects rather than human subjects; it's also that the dehumanization of people of color also happens alongside the humanization of financial interests. Corporations are humanized when they are considered to be legal persons with protections that are not afforded to people of color. In the case of Michael Brown, Ferguson's city bonds are more cultivated and protected than the city's Black and brown residents. In the world surrounding the *Homo oeconomicus,* humanness is defined through an economic social position. White, bourgeois values, finances, and interests are treated as more human than people of color. The activist group Black Lives Matter circulated the popular meme "Black Lives > White Feelings." However, white capitalism is not just about white feelings. The human is not a feeling or sentimentality. The human is economic. Black Lives > White Feelings but also, Black Lives > White Economies.

ETYMOLOGY OF JUPITER

Dios

Zeus, who was also called Dios, was literally the sky. His name meant "bright one," and thunder was only one of the weapons in his arsenal, albeit the greatest at striking awe in those who beheld it. Zeus's domain was the entirety of the animated sky, which includes all the luminaries and stars. He was often described as clothed in blue and with a blue nimbus, representing the blue sky. If his brother, Hades, was god of what's down below and Poseidon was the god of what's distant, then Zeus is the god of what's hanging above. When his father, Chronos, swallowed all his children, Zeus was the son who defeated the titans of his father's generation to bring in a new, humanistic world. These humanistic gods symbolized the rational ordering of the world, and the primordial titans symbolized the natural forces of the earth itself. Zeus's throne was a mountain, and by delegating power to his brothers and sisters, he reigned supreme over the humanistic world that he constructed after the titans' fall. The mountain Olympus, where the earth stretched out to embrace the sky and where Zeus sat on his throne, represented transcendence, the pinnacle of knowledge, and the summit of integrity.

Zeus is the most famous of all the gods. For Greco-Romans, the divine patriarch of the sky was not the sun god but the storm god. All the gods who embodied Jupiter, including Zeus, Marduk, Thor, Thunor, and Bussumarus, were associated with lightning and storms.

Robert Eisler writes that Marduk was seen as "a personification of the spring sun during the soil after the inundation, restoring order from chaos, the slayer of dragons, the builder of the celestial house, and organizer of the world. He produces storms as his weapons in the fight against the primeval monster." Likewise, not only did Zeus escape the wrath of his father, Chronos; he also came to conquer the primordial world through an exchange with Moira, his mother. Moira, whose name means "share," was the goddess of the Fates. When Zeus threatened Moira with his lightning bolt, she gave him the power to distinguish right from wrong. As Zeus rejoiced in his newfound power—his judicial might—Moira told him she'd given him only the smallest portion of her own power.

From Marduk to Zeus, the gods of storms, thunder, and lightning are seen as antagonistic or at least complementary to the goddess of primordial wisdom or Fate. Storms were symbols of a war waged between the chaotic, natural world and the ordered, divine world. If the thunderstorms are the gods fighting again and again, thunder was the reassurance of the thunder god's victory over the whimsical fates and their ambivalence toward humanity.

Zeus's patriarchal, judicial power overcame matriarchal vengeance. Zeus's ability to legislate, to create human law, differs from natural law. Matriarchal vengeance was perceived as natural, reactionary, and emotional, while patriarchal justice was reasoned, litigated, and objective. In patriarchy's origin story, matriarchal might is monstrous, but patriarchal might is just.

The thing that Zeus was most jealous of, which he prohibited any other god from doing, was the power to divine the future. When Apollo introduces Hermes to the three bee maidens, symbolized by dice, who tell both lies and truths about the future, he tells Hermes that although Zeus is jealous of the power to divine future events, Zeus allows the bee maidens to exist only because they do not always tell the truth. The bee maidens are actually recharacterizations of the three Fates, which are sometimes called Moira when referred to as a singular unit. In this reading, it is possible that Zeus received his own divinatory power from the bee maidens from the beginning. Zeus received his judicial power from divinatory power. But how is the ability to distinguish between right and wrong the same as the power to tell of future events?

The Greeks and Romans saw the world as a battle between chaotic, matriarchal, and retributive elements on the one hand, and ordered, patriarchal, and judicial elements on the other. As we saw with Venus, who murders her rapist, matriarchal vengeance is seen as brutal, reacting to events as they happen, and it symbolizes the exposure of humanity to indifferent natural forces. In contrast, Zeus's judicial order was instructive rather than instinctive. Rather than reacting to events happening in the moment, Zeus's judicial power was the regulation of anticipated events in the future. If Venus's vengeance is brutal because it exposes humanity to nature, then Zeus's justice is civil and protects humanity from nature. Zeus's judicial power, his ability to tell right from wrong, was not only his right to order events in the future but also his right to *craft* them as he sees fit. Judicial power is a future-*making* power because it is also a civilizing power.

The astrological Jupiter, which inherits its meaning from Zeus, is called the greater benefic. In contrast to Venus, whose beneficial qualities were related to benefactors who supported public institutions and achieved power through their wealth, Jupiter's beneficial qualities are related to power through divinity. To divine means to wield the power needed to predict and craft the future.

Jupiter's brand of justice is often framed in direct opposition to matriarchal rule. Marduk, the Babylonian ancestor of Jupiter, is the son of Tiamat, the ocean goddess. When Tiamat grows tired of her children and plans to kill them, Marduk faces her and shoots his lightning bolts into her throat, splitting her into the dual realms of heaven and earth. In each of Jupiter's origin myths, he conquers his mother. While both Marduk and Zeus kill their fathers successfully, they must settle for subjugating their mothers instead of killing them entirely. Marduk's mother is the material that gives rise to the new world, while Zeus reigns as the supreme god because he alone wields his mother's power of making a new world out of the old.

Jupiter in Rome and Modernity: Married and Tyrannical

Jupiter is very much a Roman god. Julia Hejduk writes that one issue dominated all descriptions of Jupiter: "the tension between Jupiter's functions as tribal god of the Romans and as transcendent God of the universe." She goes on to say, "The Romans saw themselves as the people specially selected by Jupiter to rule the world; their military success was both symbolized and guaranteed by their unique relationship with the most powerful of all gods." Depictions of Jupiter in Rome relate Jupiter to Caesar in battle. Virgil uses lightning imagery to compare Jupiter to Caesar, writing that "great Caesar thundered in war." When the classicist Sarah Nix analyzes this line, she notes that this is the first instance in which the verb *fulmino* (thundered) is used to describe a mortal and not a god. "Virgil was the first to give Jupiter's thunder to Caesar and make the man, not the god, the hurler of lightning bolts." Caesar's army, which wears the *fulmen* or lightning insignia in battle, rages Jupiterlike across his vast empire.

Jupiter, in Rome, has two distinguishing features: he wants both power and fame. As Hejduk continues in her reading of Virgil's *Aeneid,* "First, Jupiter's interest in power is not merely as an end in itself, but also as a means to contain the chaos he fears. Second, in addition to power, Jupiter has one other concern: *honor.* Not the internal quality of moral uprightness, that is, but adulation from others, which for divinities consists of prayers *(vota)* and sacrifices *(honores),* for mortals (and sometimes divinities too) of *nomen* and *fame.* Beyond power and adulation, however, it is accurate to say that Jupiter has no other concerns." The chaos that Jupiter fears, represented sometimes by Juno and other times by Moira, is the chaos of matriarchal rule. Typical readers of *Aeneid* accept that "the basic dynamics of Jupiter (rationality, masculinity, order, good) vs. Juno (irrationality, femininity, chaos, evil)" are fundamentally at odds with one another.

In *Jupiter's Aeneid: Fama and Imperium,* Hejduk writes that in Greco-Roman times, the idea of peace was depicted in a specific way. Peace was depicted through material abundance, overflowing lands filled with milk and honey, grapes spilling out of cornucopias. She contrasts this with the peace that surrounds the Roman Jupiter, which is only defined as the absence of war. Jupiter "conceives of 'peace' in terms of the exercise of power," she notes.

Zeus is rational—a husband who must constantly deal with not only Hera's irrational retributive acts against his love objects but also with Moira's constant terrible changes in temperament that seem to threaten the living world. Zeus/Jupiter is a patriarch who is constantly under attack by the chaotic and matriarchal elements surrounding him. Hejduk writes that "Jupiter cannot refuse the forces of chaos, but can only suppress them forcibly and temporarily." In terms of dealing with Moira, who represents the chaotic mother figure who birthed the world, "Zeus groans that he cannot fight against Moira," and "not once does Virgil's Jupiter . . . express regret or reluctance about bowing to the dictates of Fate." Jupiter, keeper of patriarchal rationality, is never finished with his battle against the chaotic goddesses but must wage storm after storm simply to keep feminine chaos at bay.

The story of Zeus's relationship with Moira is really the story of a war between primordial matriarchy and patriarchy. This story forms patriarchy. The struggle between primordial matriarchal societies and newer patriarchal ones was a modern invention. Writing in 1861, Johan Jakob Bachofen's work *Das Mutterrecht* drew on mythical and poetic sources—not historical cases—to make the case that the ancient world was dominated by matriarchy before being overthrown by patriarchy. Bachofen found evidence within his sources, which include Hesiod, Ovid, Virgil, and Homer, to describe a "gynocracy," that was eventually overthrown by the "divine father principle."

Bachofen's study of the "mother right" was the first work that described primordial matriarchy as a historical reality and not a mythical metaphor. Those influenced by Bachofen's work—including John Ruskin, who wrote that women could easily exercise power "not within their households merely, but over all within their sphere" due to their "perfect, moral condition"—reinforced the theory of prehistoric matriarchal rule using stereotypes of femininity contemporary to their day and not historical evidence. Bachofen's theory that a savage matriarchal sphere was eventually overtaken by patriarchal order comes directly from the mythology of Jupiter. While Bachofen's work styles itself as an anthropological study rather than lyrical poetry, he, in accordance with the Greco-Roman tradition, conflates Zeus and the humanistic gods with civilized patriarchy and the primordial titans with chaotic matriarchy. Although the Greeks and Romans frame mythological events poetically, Bachofen sees mythology as descriptive and historical: "All the myths relating to our subject embody a memory of real events experienced by the human race. They represent not fictions but historical realities. The stories of the Amazons and Bellerophon are real and not poetic." Thus, Bachofen literalized the metaphorical origin story of Zeus and made mythical history.

The conflation of classical mythology and history was common, and Bachofen was highly influential. Supporters of the theory of matriarchy, such as John F. McLennan and Lewis Henry Morgan, debated with theorists who assumed that patriarchal rule was the oldest social order, such as Henry Sumner Maine and Edward Westermarck. There was a paucity of evidence on both sides from the debate, with little evidence that older civilizations resembled the savage societies imagined by European theorists or that modern concepts such as patriarchy existed in ancient society.

Influenced by Bachofen, Friedrich Engels compares the overthrowing of the primordial mother right with the "the world-historic defeat of the female sex," attributing this defeat to the new technologies of agriculture and civilization. Matriarchal societies, for Engels, could only exist in a historically faraway time period, too ancient to be called historic. This prehistoric period, which Engels named Savagery (before the Barbaric period and the Civilized period in his essay "Origins of the Family"), was considered an unevolved society. Engels writes that "the rediscovery of the original mother-right . . . has the same significance for the history of primitive society as Darwin's theory of evolution has for biology." Engels's history is an evolutionary one.

The only description that "Origins of the Family" gives of the primordial matriarchal order—which he claims existed prior to the invention of capital—is not of an older society but of an Iroquois tribe contemporary to his time. He writes that the kinship networks of the "American Indians are essentially identical with the *genea* of the Greeks and the *gentes* of the Romans," creating a parallel between Indigenous societies contemporary to his time and archaic societies depicted in classical poetry. Engels writes that the Iroquois are organized according to mother right, comparing their democracy and common property to the noble Greek and Roman world order that existed before monarchy and capitalism contaminated the community. For Engels, Iroquois societies contemporary to his own period were able to avoid the oppressions of capitalism because they were stuck in antiquity, despite their literal existence in modernity.

Although primordial matriarchy rule was originally a mythological entity found only in the lyrical poetry of Ovid and Virgil, Bachofen assumes that the chaotic and matriarchal state was a historical reality. Engels, accepting this timeline, validates the primordial matriarchal state as a scientific reality through the lens of social Darwinism. Moira's watery world, once a lyrical metaphor, becomes a prehistoric and unevolved period in time that cultural theorists cite as historical reality. This unevolved state was projected onto existing colonial states as Europe declared its realm to be the rational world, and the colonial world to be the chaotic world. Not only did Europeans believe that prehistory was matriarchal; they also saw evidence of this prehistory all around them, especially in the colonies.

The story of how the matriarchy was overthrown by the patriarchy is really the story of marriage. For Bachofen, matriarchs gradually modified marriage until a type of nuclear family was created, although with "matrilineal transmission of property and names." For Engels, family gradually evolved from sexual promiscuity and argued that marriage in Savage times arose from taboos on incest in Barbaric times before eventually becoming the monogamous couple in Civilized times.

Bachofen considers Hera, Zeus's wife, to be a goddess left over from matriarchal rule. Because she originates from the chaotic matriarchal world, she must be conquered by Zeus's patriarchal order. In Greek myth, Zeus seduces Hera by taking the form of a cuckoo—a bird whose name is the origin of the word "cuckold," since the cuckoo likes to lay its eggs in the nests of other birds—and manages to convince Hera to take him inside. Once inside, Zeus rapes Hera. In the final scene of this myth, the problem of Hera's rape is solved by her marriage to Zeus. Once they are married, Zeus breaks their vows over and over again to continue to rape other people. In myth, Hera is characterized as retributive and fearsome due to her reactions to Zeus's behavior.

Both Venus and Jupiter, being benefics, describe power. The mythologies around both planets both also deal with rape. In Inanna's story, Inanna kills Shukaletuda for his violation. In the Greek story about Hera's rape, Hera is not given the right or ability to punish Zeus herself (as Inanna had); rather, she is given the chance to marry him instead of seeking vengeance. By marrying her rapist, Hera legitimized her rape. If Zeus's patriarchal divine right erases matriarchal vengeance and creates justice out of law, then the institution of marriage also legitimizes rape. The problem of rape is solved by the civil institution of marriage.

Engels writes that the overthrow of the matriarchal order resulted in the transmission of property along patriarchal lines. Fathers, not mothers, controlled property. This economic advantage allowed men to defeat the matriarchal world order. Engels writes that marriage "is founded on male supremacy for the pronounced purpose of breeding children of indisputable paternal lineage" and says marriage further alienates the family from other kinship networks. Prior to marriage, the only slaves were prisoners of war; after marriage, "the family itself became a power as against the *gens*," providing for "the first rudiments of hereditary nobility and monarchy" and "preparing the way for the enslavement of fellow members of the tribe."

Kim TallBear writes about the colonizing effects of marriage and the ways in which marriage, family, and monogamy were used to disrupt collective landownership within Indigenous nations: "As part of efforts to eliminate/assimilate Indigenous peoples into the national body, both the church and the state evangelized marriage, nuclear family, and monogamy. These standards were simultaneously lorded over Indigenous peoples as an aspirational model and used to justify curtailing their biological reproduction and steal their children. . . . The breakup of Indigenous peoples' collectively held lands into private-held allotments controlled by men as heads-of-household enabled the transfer of 'surplus' lands to the state and to mostly European or Euro-American settlers." Cree-Métis feminist Kim Anderson writes that "one of the biggest targets of colonialism was the Indigenous family, in which women had occupied positions of authority and controlled property."

While Bachofen theorized about the mythology of the origin of marriage in lyrical terms, referring to myth as history, and Engels wrote on the origin of marriage in speculative terms, finding an image of antiquity within the colonized world, TallBear and Anderson write literally about *the origin of marriage within imperialism*. Marriage, as a historical institution, is not only a rape culture that was enacted by imperialists upon the conquered peoples but also an instrument of land redistribution that imperialists use to begin and maintain an occupation.

The Roman Jupiter, who is only concerned with power and fame, is seen to punish both mortals and gods for one reason only: violating rank. After slaying his father, Jupiter differentiates his own style of rule from that of Kronos by assigning elements of the world to his brothers and sisters. This story, which is really the origin myth of government, sees the governed as righteous because they are ordered and the ungoverned as evil because they are chaotic. This story, also the origin story of the civilized world, was recreated during colonialist Europe to remake the world.

Virgil compared Caesar to Jupiter because Caesar, like Jupiter, was an imperialist. While Jupiter's battle with Moira symbolized the conquering of the earth (raw elements that are unordered) by the world (refined elements that are ordered), Jupiter's marriage to Juno is a metaphor for the civil institution. The civil institution includes marriage, which works as a weapon against Indigenous kinship networks. Jupiter describes power struggles, and the origin story of the power struggle, according to the Greeks, Romans, and modern

Europeans who interpret Greek and Roman texts, lies within the essentially dialectic relationship between man and woman. The struggle between the matriarchal and patriarchal forces that animate entire societies contained battles big enough to break the sky into two because the gendering inherent in such a struggle is not meant to describe individualized bodies but imperialist societies. Neoclassicalists saw the elemental power struggle between patriarchy and matriarchy as the struggle of the imperialist world against the earth and those who were seen to be like the earth. Jupiter's thunder split open not just the junction between heaven and the earth but also the junction between the world and the earth.

Brave New World

Zeus, like Venus, had many epithets, and he was associated with mountains in more ways than one. One of the epithets associated with Zeus was Zeus Lykaios, the wolf god who lived in the mountains. Zeus Lykaios was worshipped through a complex ritual in which a man's entrails were mixed with those of wolves. After mixture, the sacrificed human would become mythologized as a werewolf, roaming the mountains.

In Renaissance depictions of Zeus, he is often painted as an animal, as in Correggio's *Leda and the Swan* or his *Ganymede Abducted by the Eagle*. Correggio's third painting, *Jupiter and Io,* depicts Io kissing a dark, formless mass of smoke. Jupiter, though specifically associated with the werewolf, was also a shape-shifter in general. He often took the form of bulls, swans, eagles, and wolves, especially to capture his sexual prey.

Arthur Bernard Cook writes in *Zeus: A Study in Ancient Religion* that Zeus Lykaios, the wolf Zeus, was the Arcadian Zeus or the prehistorical Zeus. Jupiter's ability to shape-shift is a testament to the longevity of his myth. Like the older gods, who sometimes had eagle heads and turned into dogs or bulls, Zeus had an animalistic side. While the origin story of Zeus shows his removal of the animalistic and primordial titans from power, Zeus also shares with the primordial world a sometimes fantastic and animalistic character. Shape-shifting happens in an animated world in which all life forms have the potential to come to life in humanistic ways. Jupiter, which is exalted in the domain of the Moon (in Cancer), shares with the Moon an ability to take one form after another. While the story of Zeus clearly shows him as a patriarchal conqueror of the golden age in which Saturn and other titans ruled, Zeus's existence as a shape-shifter as well as his ability to comprehend certain aspects of Fate are evidence of his origins in the world that preceded the human world.

The Tempest, one of William Shakespeare's last works, is named after the Jupiter symbol of a storm (tempest meaning a strong storm). In this story, an exiled Duke of Milan, Prospero, lives on an island with his daughter, Miranda, his slave, Caliban, and his spirit, Ariel. Caliban, son of the witch Sycorax, is the original inhabitant of the island and is described as half-human and half-monster. Prospero, who defeated Sycorax upon arrival and stole the island from her, says Caliban is "not honour'd with a human shape." Like Zeus, who is smoke and swans and bulls and wolves, Caliban has no human shape. Characterizations of Caliban, which depict him as inferior to the Italian Prospero, subjugate him. He is introduced as having attempted to rape Miranda and is characterized as being in touch with the natural world of the island. When writing the character of Caliban, Shakespeare drew on Montaigne's "Of Cannibals," an essay that described societies that have never been influenced by Europe as barbaric.

In *The Tempest,* Prospero can be seen as a Jupiterlike figure because he uses his magic to conquer the island, which represents the natural world. Caliban, on the other hand, resembles the chaotic forces that the Jovian forces must seek to contain and civilize. Both of these contrasting elements—barbarism and civilization—constitute what Jupiter means in myth. The duality of Jupiter creates its expansive quality. Jupiter is represented by both colonizers, who create utopias from the tabula rasa of a newly discovered land, as well as the imagined original inhabitants of the colonized world, who are described by their colonizers as animalistic. Descriptions of colonial subjects, such as Caliban, are never static, as humans are described; rather, they shapeshift textually. We imagine the characters of Prospero or Miranda as white people with fixed bodies and identities, but Caliban is harder to visualize. Trinculo, a shipwrecked jester, describes Caliban as "a very shallow monster! . . . A very weak monster! A very weak monster! The man i' the moon! A most poor credulous monster!" and a "puppy-headed monster. A most scurvy monster" whom he cannot find it in his heart to beat.

Humanism was the revival of classical aesthetics. Classical sources provided European philosophers with a path toward the revitalization of their cultures. Humanists believed in a break from religious doctrines and superstition and a move toward rationality and empiricism. Because secular philosophy was so influenced by classicism, humanists relied extensively on ideas about modern Europe's cultural inheritance of Greco-Roman culture to create an enlightened, secular canon.

Colonialism can be described as a humanistic project. Earl Rosebery, the prime minister of England in 1894–95, calls colonial subjects "human but not too human." In 1776, Edward Long writes in his *History of Jamaica* that "Negroes are represented by all authors as the vilest of humankind, to which they have little more pretension of resemblance than what arises from their exterior forms." Like Caliban the half-monster or Jupiter the half-titan, colonial subjects may look human but do not seem to have the humanity that the humanists define as true humanity. Western culture, language, art, and philosophy are studied under the academic discipline of the humanities, while the rest of the world is filtered through anthropology, which combines biology with cultural studies. As McKittrick and Wynter write, the human is a praxis. Humanity is distributed by political institutions.

Like the Roman Jupiter, who defined his realm as an ordered world that keeps the chaotic world at the boundaries, the humanist Jupiter also defines order and chaos. However, Romans described Caesar as terrible. Caesar's empire, as described by the Roman poet Lucan, is tyrannical: "Just as the lightning bolt, pressed out through the clouds by the/wind, with the sound of broken air and the crash of the world,/leaps forth and bursts through the daylight and ter-rifies the/trembling people as it dulls their eyes with its slanted flame:/it rages against its own temples, and with nothing stopping its progress, as it falls and turns back again it causes great destruc-/tion far and wide, and gathers back together its scattered fires" (lines 151–57).

Prospero's imperialism, on the other hand, is described by Shakespeare as natural. In *The Tempest,* the battle between Prospero and Sycorax is not central to the story and is not considered worthy of explicatory detail. The Europe of Shakespeare's time, which was already colonizing the world, assumed that the battle between civilization and chaos had already been fought and won by biology alone. Caliban is inferior to Prospero *by nature* and does not need to be overcome forcibly through the brutal strength for which Virgil and Lucan critique Caesar. The power struggle between Prospero and Caliban is unseen and assumed.

Prospero, having learned his magic from libraries and books, is a scholar. Caliban's mother, Sycorax, is a witch. Caliban's magic is overcome by Prospero's knowledge. For the humanists, there is no need to witness battles between Caliban and Prospero, because the rational world of the Europeans seemed to naturally dominate the irrational rest of the world by simply disillusioning them of their naïvely held superstitions. The human becomes naturalized when power is concealed. While the Roman Jupiter was seen mainly as a conqueror who exercised brutal power through military strength in order to *protect* the rational realm, the humanist Jupiter *obfuscates* the brutality of power and disguises it as education. Power, that which distributes humanity, obfuscates itself.

As Graham Harman states, the humanist and secular intellectualism of Shakespeare's time "insists that human consciousness is nothing special, and should be naturalized just like everything else. On the other hand, it also wants to preserve knowledge as a special kind of relation to the world quite different from the relations that raindrops and lizards have to the world. . . . Raindrops know nothing and lizards know very little, and some humans are more knowledgeable than others. This is only possible because thought is given a unique ability to negate and transcend immediate experience, which inanimate matter is never allowed to do in such theories, of course." Jupiter transcends the earth by remaking the world. The world is the dominion of the earth. The humanistic Jupiter is humanistic because he perceives himself as a secular being who is both part of the natural world and able to transcend the natural world through enlightened philosophy. While the Roman Jupiter separated itself from the titans, the humanistic Jupiter naturalizes dominion. In *The Tempest,* Prospero and Caliban fight over land sovereignty. While Prospero's sovereignty over land depicts the world, Caliban's sovereignty over land depicts the earth.

The origin story of Jupiter is really an origin story of the world. Jupiter's defeat of the titans ended the prehistoric period and began what modernists would come to think of as the humanistic era. At the end of *The Tempest,* Prospero and Miranda sail away from the island where they had spent twelve years in exile and toward Milan. Leaving the island, Miranda exclaims, "How beauteous mankind is! O brave new world,/That has such people in't!" Her exclamation, that the new world is brave, is a direct response to "beauteous mankind." This affirmation of human beauty is directly in opposition to Caliban's perceived monstrosity. Humanism, which sought to create a brave new world with human inhabitants without animalistic or monstrous traits, like Jupiter, could only begin in the collisions between the earth and the world. The difference between the world and the earth is an analogy that obfuscates the struggles from which power emerges and naturalizes colonial power.

War of the Worlds

Shakespeare's Prospero is not only a magician but also a magician who exists as a metaphor for technology. The story of Jupiter is not only a story about a son waging war against matriarchal reign but also the story of a son who defeats his father, Saturn. In this famous story, Jupiter's siblings are swallowed by Saturn, but just as Saturn was about to eat Jupiter, he is tricked into swallowing a rock instead. Jupiter grows strong, kills his father, and creates the new world. This story about a son who conquers his father is the myth of technological progress, development, and innovation. Freud's theory of the Oedipus complex, which theorizes that sons seek to conquer their patriarchal authorities through conflict and their matriarchal authorities through sexuality, was a telling of modernity. During Freud's time, the sons of bourgeois fathers often looked to nationalist ideologies to develop an identity consciousness distinct from that of the social class they inherited from their fathers. In the twentieth century sons saw themselves as burdened with the duty of revitalizing the nation-state. This revival would occur through a technological innovation that represented generational struggle. Both Freud's Oedipus complex and the myth of Jupiter's defeat of Saturn, as stories about generational struggle, are also stories about the myth of progress. If Jupiter stands for technology and Saturn for time, then Jupiter's struggle against Saturn is a story of technology conquering time.

Film, as it turned out, was the perfect medium for conveying Freudian messages. Not only was film literally projected onto the wall, reflecting Freud's projections of the mind; it also had to be cut into pieces for a story to be told. The montage, which came of age in the 1900s, was a technique of cutting film into very short segments to suggest fragmented events and the passing of a large amount of time within a very short space. As James Stolow writes, "Religion is inherently and necessarily technological." However, it is not only religion as an ideology that is necessarily technological; politics is also a consequence of technology. No political ideology could exist separate from the technological hardware that propagates it. Before the montage, it was impossible to depict the entirety of a nation-state within one image. By cutting and piecing together different localities and peoples, the nation as empire emerged as a singular image or narrative from film. Deleuze defines technology as the thing that produces a people. Film, as technology, produces the nation.

The montage is an artificial sequence of time in which fragments are edited together to create the illusion of continuity, often either elongating or condensing the experience of time within a story. The montage forces the viewer to create the story within their own head by bringing shots from different locations and moments together. Because montages look like dreams (or maybe dreams look like montages), filmmakers believed that by using the montage, they were able to speak directly to the subconscious. As Virilio says, "The cinema shows us what our consciousness is. Our consciousness is an effect of montage."

The montage is a film technique that relies on music to create continuity. Without musical narrative, a montage is only a senseless and unfinished collage of images. With music, the montage transforms and becomes a theme. In other words, if the montage is a collage of disparate identities, social classes, languages, and nationalities, then music is the scale of unification. Music, under modernity, was a nationalistic project. The operas of Richard Wagner were so monumental in scope that opera director Anthony Freud called them "the most massive challenge any opera company can undertake." Wagner's operas—which so impressed Hitler that he bought out a theater playing one of them and gave the tickets away, before playing Wagner's compositions on loudspeakers in Dachau—made nationalistic sentimentalism a sensory experience with their giant symphonies, plays that depicted the German *Volk*, and grand narratives that seemed like timeless struggles on stage. Because nationalism required images of geographically distant regions to come together to form a singular voice of the nation, it needed the montage to imagine itself and the technology of the cinema to propagate itself. Nationalism, then, is a consequence of film, and its twentieth-century manifestation would not have been possible without the modern cinema.

Nationalism, like cinema, is a fictional space. The nation-state described by the montage is at once illusory and overwhelming. Soviet filmmakers developed a technique they called creative geography, which created the illusion of a continuous space by using footage shot at different places and times. Before modernity, the concept of nationality was continuously in flux. The official language of the premodern European state was Latin. Only in the 1700s did vernacular languages, such as French, English, or German, become the languages used in the administration of official state affairs. Medieval maps showed general areas for countries and were not fixated upon the precise borders separating them. The *boundaries* of a nation were less important than the *centers*.

Within modernity and through the technology of montage, the totality of a country and all the distinct regions and social classes within it became the voice of a singular nation. This voice of a nation that was heard through the new language of cinema was not the academic Latin that voiced Europe's humanist traditions but the vernacular languages that voiced Europe's bureaucratic affairs. This voice of a nation, cinematic within modernity, has always been fictional. As Michael Billig writes in *Banal Nationalism*, nationalists begin as poets, and nationalism begins as a myth or lyric. Only later, when nationalism is naturalized, do nationalists become politicians and nationalism becomes an ideology: "The nationalist-as-poet is a familiar figure in the early stages of movements to establish new nations. The mystic bond between people and place is a much-repeated theme in their writings. Once nations are established, and nationalism becomes banal, the poets are typically replaced by prosaic politicians, and the epic ballads by government reports. The imagined community ceases to be reproduced by acts of the imagination. In established nations, the imagination becomes inhabited, and, thereby, inhibited. . . . The community and its place are not so much imagined, but their absence becomes unimaginable."

If nationalism emerges as lyrical and reproduces itself as cinematic, then the lyrical quality of nationalism did not become political until close to World War II. As playwright Odeon von Horvath wrote, "If you ask me what is my native country, I answer: I was born in Fiume, grew up in Belgrade, Budapest, Pressburg, Vienna and Munich, and I have a Hungarian passport; but I have no fatherland. I am a very typical mix of old Austria-Hungary: at once Magyar, Croatian, German, and Czech; my country is Hungary, my mother tongue is German."

After the French Revolution, only a small number of those who lived in France actually identified as French. The nation of France described in the Declaration of the Rights of Man and the Citizen was not an entity but a project. Nationalism is a modern phenomenon. National identification did not occur until cinema was invented. As Billig also writes: "Different factions, whether classes, religions, regions, genders, or ethnicities, always struggle for the power to speak for the nation, and to present their particular voice as the voice of the national whole, defining the history of other subsections accordingly. 'The voice of the nation' is a [cinematic] fiction; it tends to overlook the factional struggles and the deaths of unsuccessful nations, which make such a fiction possible." Like the montage that creates a false space using fragments of footage shot at different places and times, the emerging concept of nationality created a sense of identification using fragments of populist, bourgeois, and traditional rhetoric. What the film montage does, as an imaginary space in which the voice of the nation lives, is *erase political struggle*. Nationalism is not only a fiction but one that seeks to erase some political struggles and emphasize others.

This voice of a nation naturalizes and universalizes. Benedict Anderson writes that one of the main paradoxes of nationalism is its "objective modernity of nations to the historian's eye vs. [its] subjective antiquity in the eyes of nationalists." Nationalism, like most forms of technology, recreates the experience of time and history. While nationalism is very much a modern invention and illusion, nationalists themselves see nationalism as a totalizing, universal, and genealogical inheritance. Nationalism is totalizing because it is impossible to imagine identity formation outside of it, universal because the claiming of nationhood positions nations as international, and genealogical because it describes a cultural inheritance that carries the antiquated into the present. As Edelstein writes, "universalism did not precede nationalism but rather depended on it."

Humanism was the revival of Greek and Roman aesthetics and imagery within academia. Paul Oskar Kristeller writes in *Humanism* that "if we go back to the Renaissance, the term 'humanism' is not found. It was coined in the early nineteenth century to designate an ideal of education and of scholarship centred on the classics, and was then applied by historians such as Voigt to the Renaissance movement that embodied a similar ideal." Humanism, then, was *a component of modernity* that was projected backward in time to the Renaissance. Humanists studied Latin texts, Neoplatonism, and Hermeticism in their efforts to resuscitate Europe by going back to the source, which was always Rome, even if they were genealogically unconnected to the Romans (as was the case with the Germans).

Katie Fleming writes that "the confusion of cultural plurality in modern Germany too could be corrected by the unifying power of ancient Greek *paideia*. . . . Both men [Heidegger and Jaeger] shared too the belief in the messianic powers not only of Greece, but also of Germany as mediator of the ancient culture." Nationalism was a totalizing ideology precisely because it lived in a fragmented Europe that was no longer held together by Latin but was scattered into distinct vernacular lineages that all sought their own cultural inheritance. Even though Romans regarded Germania as a foreign and barbaric land, Germans unified their multicultural state by envisioning themselves as the inheritors of Roman and Greek culture. Fleming writes that "Although [national socialists] eschewed traditional elite education, they nonetheless still embraced the exemplary potential of the ancient Greeks." The formerly academic and classical image of a Spartan boy soldier became popularized, through cinema and radio, as a model German youth. Plato's vision of a closed, antidemocratic community ruled by philosopher kings inspired the national socialist vision of a new Germany. Hitler was often compared to Plato. The comparison of Hitler and Plato framed Hitler not as a dictator but as a philosopher and *educator*. Plato writes that the ideal state is an academy. Fleming answers that every modern dictatorship tries to educate its citizens.

National Socialists distributed and popularized classicism, which had formerly resided within the academies and ivory towers of the humanists, through new mediums of technology. Nazis revitalized the anachronisms of Greco-Roman culture and founded a new Germany as a mythic generational struggle between ancients and moderns. Nazis used new instruments—film and radio—to distribute these dialectics and educate their citizens. Education through technology is a nationalist project that revitalizes the nation through generational struggle. Technology replaces the academy as education. If, before modernity, Jupiter stands for academia, then within modernity it stands for technology. As Marshall McLuhan writes, "That Hitler came into political existence at all is directly owing to radio and public address systems. . . . Radio provided the first massive experience of electronic implosion, that reversal of the entire direction and meaning of literate Western civilization."

Nationalism as technology seeks to describe itself as ancient and natural. The "natural consciousness" described by Hegel—a state of mind from which education saved individuals who succeeded at self-cultivation—was the naturalistic state of the titans. For politicians such as Hitler, Germany has to save itself by struggling against the bourgeois father, who represented the sick and weak patriarchy of Saturn, and the cultural influences of non-Aryan races, representing the rest of the titans. While humanists sought to revitalize culture with the inheritance of Greek and Roman forms through academia, nationalists sought to revitalize culture with Greek and Roman forms through technology. Humanists thought the self could be achieved through works by Shakespeare or Goethe, and the National Socialists thought that the nation could be achieved through television and radio. The political struggles of the world— matriarchal/patriarchal, chaotic/orderly, retributive/civil, and animalistic/humanist—are erased by technology. Technological revolution replaces political struggle with technological innovation.

The Roman Jupiter was a tyrant that conquered the world and was often paralleled with Caesar. The humanistic Jupiter assumes that the earth has already been conquered by the naturalistic processes of social evolution. The nationalistic Jupiter attempts to revive both narratives and reunify the world. The world that Jupiter attempts to define and rule is not about the earth as land but as an orientation that positions the world as split between the civil and the uncivil. Jupiter slays the titans and recreates the world, meaning he rids the earth of unevolved elements and redefines civilization. Once, in the humanist world, this refined civilization was found only in the ivory towers of aristocratic institutions. In the nationalist world, technology replaces education as the instrument of cultural refinement. The civilized world is no longer the human race but the technological race.

The world that Jupiter defines and rules is no longer the world but the public. For the nationalistic Jupiter, the public is only defined as those people who exist within the closed communities that Plato once yearned for, ruled over by philosopher kings and educated through the mass communication channels of television and radio. If populist movements, like national socialism, claim that power lies with the people, then it also wields power by defining who is allowed to be human, as Jupiter distinguished the humanistic gods from the titans. If Romans defined humans through empire and humanists defined humans through education, then nationalists define humanity through technology. Technology becomes progress, generational struggle, and power.

Flag

The father of Zionism, Theodor Herzl, once said: "With a flag one can lead men wherever one wants, even into the promised land. [A flag is] about the only thing for which men are prepared to die in masses if one trains them to it." Jupiter often struggles to articulate differences in a world in which the power has already won. Patriarchal Jupiter conquers matriarchy by describing its struggle in mythological times, humanistic Jupiter assumes that Europe has already emerged as the emperor of the new world through biological and social superiority, and postmodern Jupiter assumes that the United States has already conquered the world through economic superiority. If Jupiter's origin story described a power struggle that remade the world, then what is unique about the retellings of this power myth is that they tend to obfuscate power and always assume that the time for struggling against or for power is already over. Jupiter's struggle against the titans happens before history separated from myth. In this telling of the story of power, history loses its political edge when it becomes an apolitical myth. Enlightenment-era and modern Jupiters maintain power by framing time—by pushing the event of their struggle back in the timeline of history.

If Jupiter is the planet that describes ideological rifts that split the world in two, then it would seem that the Cold War–era Jupiter would be the struggle between capitalism and communism. However, as Chomsky describes it, the Cold War was not really the struggle between a capitalist United States against a communist Soviet Union. Rather, it was the collaboration between an imperialist United States and the imperialist Soviet Union against third-world nationalism. In the confrontations of the third world against imperialist technology, masses upon masses of foot soldiers from China, Korea, and Vietnam would die facing American tanks, bombs, and artillery. The wars between imperialists and third-world nations were wars between bodies and machines. While the side of the bodies (third-world nations) are depicted as nationalistic and reactionary, the imperialist power of the United States is often seen as fighting against authoritarian nationalism and as a benefactor that grants technological innovation as a resource.

Carolyn Christov-Bakargiev says a study of images of the US war against Vietnam shows that the real loser of the war is the grassland, the foliage, and the ecological balance of the land the war is fought upon. Within the emerging industrial third world, communities were called upon to sacrifice ancestral lands and traditions in order to support national industrialism. Since fascists represented the public through technology, former colonies had to industrialize in order to nationalize the land and humanize the people. Up to World War II, Jupiter's ideological battles tended to stand for great, big, grand narratives that sought to describe the world (ideological and political) against the earth (raw and secular). The totalizing concepts—forces that guard the world from itself, which are founded upon the primordial splits between matriarchy/patriarchy, humanistic/animalistic, and civil/uncivil—of Jupiter are about ideological splits. Jupiter describes the struggles between the ordered/chaotic, the rational/irrational, the human/not human, the secular/religious, and the first world/third world. These struggles are always played out through mediated representations—first through myth, then through theater and cinema, and finally through the private screen.

Nationalism is a media phenomenon. Postmodern nationalism is no longer only a banal and bureaucratic rendering of national identity through the apparatus of the state but also a vibrant, tasteful, and commercial rendering of national identity through the technologies of film, social media, and pop music. Even if we do not conduct our international affairs in a democratic way, we do represent them in a commercial way. Koichi Iwabuchi calls the commercial representation of nationalism "brand nationalism." Brand nationalism does not truly recognize differences among cultures according to their own contexts and perspectives; instead, it articulates consumable differences in terms of brand image (differences in food, fashion, pop culture) using ready-made formats. The genres and formats available for this type of brand articulation follow conventions that originate from the United States. To use an anthropological framework, different national identities can coexist, but only if they are understood and explored through their differences to the cultural monopoly of United States. Differences in food and fashion, visible in what sociologist John Urry calls the global screen of international spectacle, can only achieve visibility when seen by the American tourist. Here, the use of the word "screen" is important. Nationalism is only a symptom of technology. Within the mediated world, the tourist's gaze doesn't see other national identities as truly different or even threatening. Instead, it views nationality as ready-made. Cultural sights are ready for viewing, ethnic foods for tasting, and kitschy souvenirs for buying. For the tourist, nationalities only differ from one another in terms of taste.

When it is assumed that power has already been won, the national identities of the third world no longer pose any threat to the existing power dynamic and can be enjoyed through the free market. Jupiter is imperialism that disguises itself as tourism. As Herman Hesse writes in *Autobiographical Writings,* describing his own Sagittarius (and Jupiter-ruled) ascendant, "Long before I could read and write they [statues of Asian deities found in his grandfather's glass cabinet] so filled me with age-old Eastern images and ideas that later, whenever I met a Hindu or Chinese sage, it was like a reunion, a homecoming. And yet I am an European, was in fact, born with the sign of the Archer on the ascendant, and all my life have zealously practiced the Western virtues of impetuosity, greed and unquenchable curiosity." As a Sagittarius rising whose ruling planet is Jupiter, Hesse is allowed to fully enjoy colonial encounters with "Eastern images and ideas" because, like Jupiter enjoying the encounters with titans he has already conquered, the national identities of the Hindu and Chinese sages are no political threat to Western capitalism and can be freely consumed. If Saturn was the father who swallowed his children, then Jupiter seeks to swallow the entirety of the world through the staging of an anthropological banquet. This anthropological banquet is experienced through its ability to be seen, heard, tasted, and felt—in other words, the anthropological banquet of the postcolonial world is appetizing because it is hypervisible. The place where the hypervisibility of this anthropological banquet exists is the screen of brand nationalism.

If modern nationalism is a sense of identification cultivated through mass public education and technology, then postmodern nationalism is an exotic feeling of ethnicity without political struggle. The nationalist colonies of the nineteenth century understood representation to be surveillance. Anderson writes that "the colonial state did not merely aspire to create, under its control, a human landscape of perfect visibility; the condition of this 'visibility' was that everyone, everything, had (as it were) a serial number. This style of imagining did not come out of thin air. It was the product of the technologies of navigation, astronomy, horology, surveying, photography, and print, to say nothing of the deep, driving power of capitalism." Visibility under commercialism is a style. Style, because it is made for the tourist's gaze, is a feeling mediated by the American eye.

Postcolonial theorists are concerned with questions surrounding representation and identification within the entertainment industries because nationalism resides within the mediated world of film, television, music, and social media rather than within any geographical place. Postmodern, and even leftist, critical theory overwhelmingly focuses on popular representations of racial, national, or gender identities rather than on tensions between international and national Marxism. In the mediated world, politics is no longer about struggle but about visibility. To be clear, this visibility has both a democratic basis and a capitalist basis: democratic because visibility relates to the ideal of elected, democratic representation, and capitalist because visibilities in entertainment mediums are commercial enterprises. In postmodernism, technology becomes representation. If Jupiter originally sought to civilize the natural world, then the postmodern Jupiter seeks to represent the invisible world.

The politics of gender representation, queer representation, representation of racial minorities, and representation of marginal colonies cannot be considered separately from the politics of surveillance. Jupiter is a diurnal planet and works for the Sun. As Rey Chow writes, "Becoming visible is no longer simply a matter of becoming visible in the visual sense (as an image or object) but also a matter of participating in a discursive politics of (re) configuring the relation between center and margins, a politics in which what is visible may be a key but not the exclusive determinant." In other words, visibility is not just the ability to be seen, heard, smelled, tasted, or felt. Visibility is a power structure.

Chow continues: "There is, in other words, a visibility of visibility—a visibility that is the condition of possibility for what becomes visible, that may derive a certain intelligibility from the latter but cannot be simply reduced to it." Or, as Deleuze writes: "Visibilities are neither the acts of a seeing subject nor the data of a visual meaning. . . . Visibilities are not defined by sight but are complexes of actions and passions, actions and reactions, multi-sensorial complexes, which emerge into the light of day." This is what Christov-Bakargiev meant when she said that the true loser of the Vietnam war was the land; visibility is not just about what comes to the foreground but what retreats to the background. The background is the land, environment, and historical backdrop that visibilities are staged upon.

Nimbus/Cloud

If national representation relies on technology, if technology is the contemporary representation of Jupiter, then it is possible to conduct a material analysis of nationalism by analyzing the artifacts of technology. Technology, nationalism, and the origin of the world— that original power struggle between matriarchy and patriarchy— these are all hyperobjects. Timothy Morton defines hyperobjects as objects that are so big they cannot be seen but can be experienced through their effects on surrounding objects. Morton compares hyperobjects with storms: "You can't perceive the actual raindrop in itself. You only ever perceive your particular, anthropomorphic translation of the raindrops. . . . Isn't this similar to the rift between weather, which I can feel falling on my head, and global climate, not the older idea of local patterns of weather, but the entire system?"

Jupiter is a *storm* god. Jupiter's weapon is a lightning bolt, and he is rarely seen, in Roman and Greek imagery, without a nimbus or small blue cloud. If Jupiter, that son of Saturn who kills his father, represents generational struggle, then Jupiter's storm clouds represent progress. Walter Benjamin, writing about a Paul Klee painting, says:

A Klee painting named Angelus Novus shows an angel looking as though he is about to move away from something he is fixedly contemplating. His eyes are staring, his mouth is open, his wings are spread. This is how one pictures the angel of history. His face is turned toward the past. Where we perceive a chain of events, he sees one single catastrophe which keeps piling wreckage upon wreckage and hurls it in front of his feet. The angel would like to stay, awaken the dead, and make whole what has been smashed. But a storm is blowing from Paradise; it has got caught in his wings with such violence that the angel can no longer close them. The storm irresistibly propels him into the future to which his back is turned, while the pile of debris before him grows skyward. This storm is what we call progress.

In his essay "The Storm Cloud of the Nineteenth Century," John Ruskin quotes his own recording of the weather and describes a new storm cloud, which he calls a plague-cloud and compares it with the clouds "compelled by Jove." This plague-cloud, which darkens the sky, blanches the sun, and manufactures mist, is pollution: "By the plague-wind every breath of air you draw is polluted, half round the world; in a London fog the air itself is pure, though you choose to mix up dirt with it, and choke yourself with your own nastiness."

Bryan J. Day, interpreting the essay, describes Ruskin's plague-cloud as a metaphor not only for environmental pollution but also for moral decay. The cloud, as storm, has an almost mythological significance for Ruskin. He writes that the scientific technicians of his time are unable to see the plague-cloud because the cloud is not a scientific problem but a moral one. "For Ruskin, as oracular Christian and ocular seer, nature intuitively perceived by the human viewer acts as a moral index—a mirror or register of human moral activity—with environmental (or external) pollution and degeneracy signifying moral (or internal) pollution and degeneracy."

Ruskin describes his plague-cloud in three ways: "Blanched Sun,—blighted grass,—blinded man." Day writes that within

Ruskin's moral ecology, "What we do to the atmosphere ('blanched Sun') affects the earth ('blighted grass'), which, in turn, affects humankind ('blinded man'). As Ruskin witnessed the depletion of his home country of England and the social costs of technological progress, he urged his countrymen to 'found colonies as fast and as far as she is able . . . seizing every piece of fruitful waste ground she can set her foot on' and to 'advance the power of England by land and sea.'" Ruskin writes that: "The England who is to be mistress of half the earth, cannot remain herself a heap of cinders, trampled by contending and miserable crowds; she must yet again become the England she was once, and in all beautiful ways,—more: so happy, so secluded, and so pure, that in her sky—polluted by no unholy clouds—she may be able to spell rightly of every star that heaven doth show."

Progress is a storm—one that leaves Europe a "heap of cinders."

The early colonists often represented the Americas as a storm. William Strachey writes in 1609 that he reached the New World in "a dreadfull storme and hideous . . . which swelling, and roaring as it were by fits . . . at length did beate all light from heaven; which like an hell of darkness turned blacke upon us." America the storm represented a raw wildness that needed cultivation if it were to ever become the "enchanted garden, a sacred Circe" that Ruskin yearned for. Like Prospero, who sent a storm out to sea, colonists spread their storms and sent them out to sea.

In *The Machine in the Garden,* Leo Marx writes that, while the industrial machine that represented the manufacturing cities was often compared with the pastoral countryside in early American literature, both were actually instruments in describing American national identity. He writes that "man's primary relation to nature is technological."

The cloud is a hyperobject. Today, there are several types of clouds. There are public clouds, private clouds, polyclouds, community clouds, and multiclouds. The cloud is the place where we put our files that we want to make accessible to others in our cyber-communities or simply where we put files that we are not currently using when we run out of local storage. Our machines automatically upload our files to the cloud. We imagine the cloud as an invisible thing that hovers above each computer or up in the sky. The cloud is lighter than air, despite its ability to hold all of the world's contents and discontents. All of our visibilities, our representations of gender, of queerness, of nationalisms, and of ethnicities live in the cloud. Our politics live in the cloud.

The cloud is an actual place. It exists on the floor of the Atlantic Ocean, along with sunken ships and corpses. Bridle writes that "the cloud is not some magical place, made of water vapor and radio waves, where everything just works. It is a physical infrastructure consisting of phone lines, fibre optics, satellites, cables on the ocean floor, and vast warehouses filled with computers, which consume huge amounts of water and energy and reside within national and legal jurisdictions." If our representational politics live inside the cloud, then these politics also live under the Atlantic Ocean and consume huge amounts of water and energy, living within national and legal jurisdictions.

Since the beginning of modernity, we have developed political consciousness over political struggle and a politics that relies on technology. If politics is the struggle for *power* (the kind that politicians and activists talk about), then technology is the material basis for that *power* (the kind measured in watts). Jupiter is the diurnal benefic, and the Sun is visibility. If visibility is a power relation, and if, as Spivak argues, we should be asking questions not only about who is being represented but who is doing the representing, then we should also be asking questions about what kind of machinery is doing the representing and how many kilowatts of power it requires in order to create political power. The material reading of the ideology of representation can only be conducted through a reading of the cloud. The cloud seeks to hide its materiality just as Jupiter seeks to mythologize its inherent struggle for power. As Bridle writes, "The cloud shapes itself to geographies of power and influence, and it serves to reinforce them. The cloud is a power relationship, and most people are not on top of it."

In Chen Qiufan's science fiction novel *Waste Tide,* the American corporation TerraGreen tries to consolidate the nuclear waste processing industry on Silicon Island, a fictional island near Guangzhou, China. The businesses in this industry are controlled by the local mafia, who exploit workers known as waste people. Silicon Island is described as a literal hell on earth, where women wash their clothing in black water contaminated with nuclear waste, and where fish riddled with strange tumors swim; where children play with pieces of trash that release radiation; and where every family has at least one member who is dying of cancer. This hellscape is the result of the actions of the developed Western nations, who ship their trash to Silicon Island since there are no Westerners willing to take the environmental and biological risks that result from nuclear waste processing. Luo, the head of a local clan that controls some of the waste processing on Silicon Island, thinks back to when he studied in Australia and realizes that the initial praise he heard from Australians about China "disguised terror and disgust. . . . They compared the Chinese to locusts who robbed the Australians of their resources and accumulated unbelievable wealth without giving anything back to public welfare and disadvantaged groups." These same Australians continue to deposit their nuclear waste in China.

Both Luo and an American executive named Scott who represents TerraGreen understand why TerraGreen proposes to build a new industrial park on Silicon Island: TerraGreen, positioning itself as an environmentally friendly company that helps the third world clean up the disastrous consequences of being a trash receptacle for the West, wants Silicon Island's renewable resources. In the colonial past, these resources were available for the Western powers to buy cheaply. Then the clans took over, and the prices became higher than what companies like TerraGreen were used to paying. Under their new proposal, TerraGreen would have "the right to purchase Silicon Island's recycled renewable resources at a favorable price." As Luo sees it: "They had long coveted the wealth accumulated by these industrious outsiders [the clans], and now, they had a chance to carry out their robbery and brutality under the guise of 'law' and 'environmental protection' without restraint."

Though *Waste Tide* is a science fiction story, the story of trash, the third world, local governments that behave like gangs, and corporations that buy governments and destroy any emerging industry or power, is a mundane one. Silicon Island is a fictional world, the antithesis to the real-world Silicon Valley; but the hellscapes it represents—which include the regions near the Ganges River, where almost every child is born with a deformity due to industrial pollution, or the regions near Apple factories in central China where residents drink contaminated water—are real.

At the end of *Waste Tide,* a huge typhoon engulfs Silicon Island. The scene that this tropical storm washes through is this: Scott, the American executive, has been killed by a waste girl who developed mutant superpowers due to her proximity to nuclear waste, while the rest of the waste people reluctantly but collectively help the clan members survive the flooding. Chen writes about the typhoon: "Typhoon Wutip, by now only a tropical storm, headed for Shantou, leaving a serene sea behind around Silicon Island, as though nothing had happened."

"This is the storm that we call progress," writes Benjamin.

However, remember that the world is an illusion conjured up by mythological reimaginings. Jupiter defeated Saturn and created the world out of the earth. After the storm hits Silicon Island, it is as if nothing has happened. What's left? Not the world.

10

LABOR:
MERCURY AND JUPITER

the underworld/the world

the subaltern/nationalism

inhuman objects/humanism

magic/power

book/flag

sexuality paranoia/patriarchal and matriarchal struggle

conductivity/lightning bolt

assimilation/representation

idea/ideology

cyberspace/cloud

On Representation

Representation collides with both democracy and capitalism. In democracy, representation is the idea that public servants in government—legislators, senators, presidents, judges, city council representatives, police, bureaucratic agents, advocates—should represent the interests of the public. It means we stand a better chance of being represented when our public servants come from similar economic conditions as us, experience the same types of discrimination we do, and live with us in our communities. In the commercial sense, representational politics has come to mean the idea that the images we see and consume in the mediated world should contain actors who represent our racial and gender identities. It is the idea that the mediated world affects the everyday decisions of those who are subject to its presence enough that we should advocate for a sort of democracy of representation within a commercial world.

Representation is a technology. It always produces a people.

The representational politics within commercialism is summed up in the following statement: we should be able to turn on the TV and see people who look like us. If children see people who look like them (people who are gendered like them, sexualized like them, raced like them) doing the heroic things they want to do, they will be able to visualize themselves doing these heroic things. Representational politics has a touch of manifestation logic. You will be able to do what you are able to visualize yourself doing. Media, which turned so many stereotypes of the popular imagination— everything from immigrants to working class whites to women— into character types, is the instrument of the manifestation ritual of representational politics. Representational politics looks toward the television, which reproduced the prevalence of stereotypes, to subvert its own historical work. Conversations around identity and representation center around the United States, around immigrant identities and working-class sensibilities and ethnic so-called "minorities."

The phenomenon of what Sun Jung calls "Asianphiliac pop cosmopolitan"—which includes J-pop, J-dramas, K-pop, K-dramas, anime, and Taiwanese pop—is a commercial representation and rendering of identity. Asian pop is a multidimensional type of nationalism that brands itself differently according to its context. In his book *Recentering Globalization,* Iwabuchi describes Japanese popular culture made for Western consumption through the concept of *mukokuseki,* or cultural odorlessness. Animators such as Osamu Tezuka created racially ambiguous characters and environments that seemed to transcend the boundaries and borders associated with specific nationality. This ambiguous racial character and nationality, in addition to providing a neutral environment onto which Westerners can read themselves in Japanese stories, solves the problem of, as Stefan Tanaka puts it, "how to become modern while simultaneously shedding the objectivist category of Oriental and yet not lose an identity."

The cultural odorlessness of Japan's internationally consumed representations bring two sides of Japanese nationality into conversation: the Japan that "described itself as multiethnic, with a good mix of North Asians, South Asians, Chinese, and Korean populations coexisting in their culture" and in a position "to assimilate all of Asia to compete with the West," as Japanese nationality represented itself as during World War II; and the "American ethnic essentialism" and "monolithic victimhood" they adopted after World War II. The cultural odorlessness of modern Japanese pop culture is a strategy of self-Orientalism that responds to Western hegemony. Hiroki Azuma writes that "*otaku* culture in reality originated as a subculture imported from the United States" and that "between the *otaku* and Japan lies the United States." Later, in his book *Otaku: Japan's Database Animals,* Azuma goes on to write that "the 'Japanese' themes and modes of expression created by *otaku* are in fact all imitations and distortions of US-made material" and that the only nationality identity left for Japan is "a pseudo-Japan manufactured from US-produced materials."

While anime was intended from its beginning to read as accessible to a Western audience, K-pop began as a specifically Asian pop culture phenomenon with hopes of entering a global market. Jung describes Korean pop culture as *mugukjeok,* which "does not mean complete odorlessness or *non*-nationality" but rather "the transcultural hybridity of popular culture, which is not only influenced by odorless global elements, but also traditional (national) elements." Jung describes Korean soft masculinity as a cultural hybrid of *seonbi* or Confucian—and Chinese-influenced—masculinity, *bishounen* or pretty boy—and Japanese-influenced—masculinity, and global— and Western-influenced—metrosexual masculinity.

When Korean idols represent themselves, they strategically employ usage of the words "global" and "Asian." JYP Entertainment represents the K-pop idol Rain not as Korea's star but as "Asia's star." JYP founder Park Jin-Young insists that "I believe that now is the time for Asia's star to enter into the US market and that it is my job to make it possible." When the Wachowskis cast Rain with a role in the film *Speed Racer,* Rain asked to change his character's name from a specifically Japanese name to the ambiguously Asian name Taejo Togokahn. Kim Junsu of the K-pop idol group Dong Bang Shin Ki, which has a dual presence in Japan as Tohoshinki, named himself Xiah after the second syllable of "Asia" to appeal to a panasian audience.

Rather than representing a specifically Korean identity, K-pop idols represent themselves as generally Asian, not for the benefit of non-Asian consumers but for consumers in Asian countries who read their cultural ambiguity as the defining aesthetic of a modern Asian identity. In order to project modern brand nationalism, K-pop idols present themselves as cultural hybrids rather than specifically Korean. Dredge Byung'chu Kan-Nguyen finds that this culturally hybridized aesthetic, which they call "white Asian aesthetic," is copied by both queer and straight K-pop fans across Asia. In their essay "The Softening of Butches," they connect the queer Thai *tom* identity to its Korean and Japanese influences, and they interview Em, who works at a *tom* fashion store. "Given that

[Em] was a purveyor of K-style at the shop," Kan-Nguyen writes, "looking 'Korean' was her job." While the aesthetics within K-pop are made for an Asian audience, these aesthetics, like the culturally odorless Japanese aesthetics of anime, must undergo cultural ambiguity through hybridity before they are legibly *modern* and *useful* to their Asian audience. If the United States lies between the *otaku* and Japan, then the United States also lies between Korea and the rest of Asia or Asia and its representations of itself to itself.

K-pop also distinguishes itself from Japanese pop culture or Western pop culture not only because it assumes that its audience is an Asian one that wants to read itself through modernity rather than a Western one that looks for its own images on screen, but also because it is a media industry that does not derive income from its fan base but from the advertisers that seek access to its fan base. In other words, while Western and Japanese media companies function like the mass media technologies of television, magazines, and radio, requiring consumers to pay the subscription or hardware fees that sustains the industry, K-pop functions more like social media, providing its products for free online and making most of its income from the corporations that idols endorse.

Like social media companies such as Facebook, what K-pop sells is not music or content but attention. The real object of K-pop's brand nationalism is not the idols who perform on stage or screen but the fan bases themselves, who are organized carefully on televised performances, named, and color coded to increase their attractiveness to the real consumers of K-pop: corporations looking to advertise to the fan bases. If K-pop were a store, then the spectacular mass mobilizations of ARMY, Cassiopeia, ELF, or SONE at airports and in arenas where their idols appear would be the commodities placed on its shelves. These fan bases as commodities are branded as "Asian" or "global" by K-pop companies as selling points to corporate consumers who desire particular ethnic markets. In the context of race relations, when fans of K-pop believe they are consuming the global hybrid Asian aesthetic of the idols, they are actually consuming the global hybrid Asianness of themselves, resembling what Émile Durkheim described in his studies of religious experience: a group that gathers to worship a totem is actually worshipping themselves. Because the real product of K-pop is not music but consumer attention, K-pop places an emphasis on creating hype around their idol-actors, engineering scandals and controversies, so that the fan base potentially becomes marketable even before an idol officially debuts. In a similar way, social media is also a hype- or viral-based industry since its product is not any kind of content but pure attention.

In the United States, where ethnic essentialism is the ideological doctrine of race representation, formerly colonized or developing countries are often framed as more culturally pure and free from the intoxication of modernization or Westernization. People who identify as belonging to a diaspora, or the movement away from a homeland into the West, frame their identification outside of a more ethnically authentic place or origin. Diaspora is imagined as a tree that grows from the cultural roots of the homeland. Those concerned about representational politics in the United States are often concerned about the ethnic authenticity of characters on screen since ethnic characters are often performed by white actors, written by white writers, and created with a white audience in mind. The authenticity of representation that US representational politics is concerned with, which only exists in a commercial representational framework, is a manufactured authenticity. Sometimes this authenticity is wrapped up with ethnic or cultural purity, and other times with proximity to the imagined homeland where the root of cultural heritage is thought to lie.

The anxiety around a loss of authenticity through on-screen mediation within American representational politics often directs itself at both the visible parts of pop culture—its actors and pop stars—and at the invisible parts of the industry: the writers, producers, and studio heads. As Amy Aniobi, writer for *Insecure,* states: "If the heads of studio were of color, that's really what's going to change the industry." Aniobi critiques the lack of diversity in all stages and roles of production. Is the goal of representational politics to create a self-contained virtual world in which ethnic identities represent themselves for themselves and away from white viewers? As the commercial representation of race moves away from mass-media technologies, in which the roles of studio head, writer, director, and actor are all separate people, and toward social media, in which the consumers, producers, and actors of media representations are often the same person, can issues of authenticity within representation be solved by capitalism? If social media allows us to become not just the alienated consumers of media images but also the active producers and fetishized commodities, then is technology saving us from becoming alienated from the production of our own race identity? If we view representation not as an ideology, as it is in democracy, but as a technology, then are we able to overcome the religious ramifications of representatives as totem?

Representation, in a strictly democratic sense, is less spectacular and more insular. As Billig writes in *Banal Nationalism,* "previously, politicians were remote figures, seen by only a tiny fraction of the population." Only in democratic capitalist society does the politician become what Neil Postman calls the "politician-as-celebrity." When politicians speak publicly, as most politicians are expected to do in a democratic capitalist society, it is understood that the supporters who gather around them are part of the spectacle. They speak as if they are addressing not just the local audience in the room but a universal audience transcending the boundaries of the room and, sometimes, of the nation itself. Billig describes the experience: "Politicians still talk from platforms to audiences gathered to hear them, but they aim to be overheard by a wider audience, whom they simultaneously address. The politicians, speaking to an audience of supporters, seek applause, so that their rhetorical successes can be broadcast nationally." These "rhetorical successes" are often broadcast not only nationally but also globally. Referring to the televised appearance of George W. Bush immediately after 9/11, Billig writes that Bush addresses "us," as in not only the American audience to which his speech is being broadcast but also "the universal audience," which implied that "any reasonable person—whether listening or not, whether American or belonging to a less than greatest nation—should recognize this majesty, 'our' democratic majesty." The ambiguity of Bush's audience assumes that any reasonable audience would be able to understand American interests and that American interests are universal.

In a mediated world in which big data measures not just national but also global spectacle, politicians are operating more and more like pop idols or cartoons. Both politicians and idols perform identities that they believe will make them more intimate with their audience. Both politicians and idols use technology to produce a people. For both politicians and idols, the audience is the spectacle. This spectacular audience is attractive to corporations that wish to capitalize on the audience as a market. Politicians, like idols, derive most of their income not from their constituents but from corporate donors. As representation within democracy aligns itself more closely with representation within commercialism, the image becomes more accessible and relatable. Those of us who have not been able to see ourselves reflected on screen are given more and more opportunities to do so. However, the closer the audience identifies with the image, the more the audience actually becomes part of the image and spectacle—the de facto product of the spectacle. Rather than voting directly for politicians who represent local interests in a strictly democratic society, voters living in a democratic capitalist society can only support their politicians indirectly by participating in their media spectacles in the hope that an increase in attention can make their candidate more attractive to the real buyers of democracy: the corporate donors who fund public discourse.

Representation is a technology. Technology, however, is always a mask for ideology. Commercialism masks the ideology of representation. Technology doesn't solve the problem of alienation that capital produces; rather, it reproduces the problem. As politics and performance coalesce and collide, is there any political expression that cannot be categorized as performative, especially when our political identities (at least in terms of race and gender) are also performances?

The Unimaginable World

Several Nazi philosophers, including Heidegger, Schmitt, and Gadamer, expressed the fear that a loosening of European control over the world would result in the loss of humanity. These German thinkers would go on to influence those in the Frankfurt school, including Karl Jaspers and Theodore Adorno. Both Jaspers and Adorno reacted to globalization with a very specific type of fear. Like the Nazi philosophers, they feared that a postmodern world would also be a world where technology replaces culture. In this imagined world, where technology is the only thing that can create collective identity, the world could be infected with a cultural sameness and uniformity that would ultimately alienate people from the world. As Adorno writes in 1944, "culture today is infecting everything with sameness." Jaspers speculates that "with the unification of our planet there had begun a process of leveling-down which people contemplate with horror" and fears that this "leveling-down" will result in "the same dances, the same types of thought, and the same catchwords . . . making their way all over the world." Both the Frankfurt School and Nazis feared what Dipesh Chakrabarty calls "the mass man." As Chakrabarty writes, "the Uniform figure of the 'mass-man' haunts many German thinkers, from Heidegger to Adorno, as a nightmare of modernity."

As we saw in previous chapters, it is a symptom of whiteness to project into race theater certain horrors that white people do not want to define as being associated with whiteness. For example, in chapter 2 we discussed that, while white people often labeled brown and Black people as cannibals, white cannibalism of brown and Black people was more common historically. The mass-man is often used to describe people in the colonies, where the culture is perceived to be more conformist, the governments more authoritarian, and the people more brainwashed. These cultures, governments, and peoples are not thought to be syncretistic but monolithic.

Mercury and Jupiter are both about technology. Technology shows up in Mercury because we tend to think of technology as a mimetic plane that floats above reality, as a plane that mimics parts of reality and dialogues it back. Technology shows up in Jupiter when Jupiter, as the human god, struggles against the natural world. Technology is the machine that struggles against nature. The word "technology" is related to the Greek word *techne,* which means to uncover or disclose nature. Because Mercury and Jupiter are both about technology, they are also about the human. "The human is a praxis." For Mercury, the human is elusive, while Mercury remains extractive. Mercury extracts living material out of inhuman things in the same way that Hermes extracts living music out of a turtle that was turned into a lyre. People who are perceived as inhuman may sometimes mimic human behaviors, but their performance of humanity, like Martellus's automata or Bhabha's mimic men, grows closer and closer to a lie as it becomes more convincing. Jupiter, on the other hand, frames the human as that which must be extended into an inhuman world. The human is never environmental but always an actor. Jupiter's humans become human when they conquer the natural environments they exist in.

For the religio-cultural man, what Wynter calls ManI, those who were considered to be outside humanity are pieces of a natural world that the Western philosopher must struggle against and extract from spiritually in order to transcend his own natural existence. For the rational-enlightened man, what Wynter calls Man2, those who are considered to be outside humanity are parts of a natural world that must be classified and converted into energy so the Western scientist can again transcend natural existence.

Western climate change scientists and theorists use the word "anthropocene" to describe the current geological epoch. *Anthropos-* means "human," and the anthropocene is an epoch in which human actions define the Earth. Chakrabarty asks, "Why blame all humans or humans in general when the addiction to fossil fuel is shared by only a minority of humans, the global rich, the consuming classes of the world, and, of course, by interested groups such as the producers and marketers of fossil fuels and their advocates?" Chakrabarty points out that "the word *anthropos,* when used thus, ends up falsely and unfairly implicating the poor and their 'survival emissions' of greenhouse gases in the crime of those whose 'luxury emissions' are actually responsible for the current crisis of global warming." In fact, Will Stephens finds that carbon emission trends closely follow financial trends. Chakrabarty argues that the anthropocene should really be renamed as the "capitalocene," which he defines as the period when "the capitalist mode of production that made our greenhouse gas emission and technologies have an impact on the climate of the planet."

Climate change is often described as a natural phenomenon that all of humanity must unify against in order to defeat it. The "we" of humanity are united under a common interest against both the natural world and the machine world. This common interest becomes a global political will that stages a collective future for humanity. However, historically speaking, not everyone has always been included in the category of the human. Colonized subjects have historically been categorized as belonging to both the natural world and as components of technology that the human is contrasted against. When Western propagandists write about climate change, they often frame international cooperation as something that comes from the West, which former colonies must become integrated into. By doing so, propagandists ignore the reality that the majority of pollution actually comes from Western corporations and that toxic waste and risk are imported from the West into the former colonies and Indigenous governed lands.

Likewise, fears about artificial intelligence and automatic labor in the West often align with fears around immigrants who come to take "our" jobs. Whether job security is threatened by robots or by immigrants is not important; what is important is that good, American jobs meant to sustain white lives and white families are seen to be constantly under threat. Technology seems to threaten both resources and labor. The Western chauvinist wants us all to unify and fight climate change together but draws a clear line between "us" and "them" when it comes to distributing resources. Western chauvinists ignore the role that finance plays in the economy. As early as 1857, Marx observed that technology was beginning to usurp the worker as the main productive force behind an economy. He writes, "The entire production process appears as not subsumed under the direct skillfulness of the worker, but rather as the technological application of science. *It is hence a tendency of capital to give production a scientific character.*"

When theorists—from both the left and the right—characterize technology's role in the economy and the world, they often characterize it as being *too* efficient and *too* productive. While the Frankfurt school theorists feared technology's influences on culture, they feared it because they saw it as working too well. To them, uninhibited technology had the ability to make us all into machines. They feared that people would begin to "dress alike" (Jaspers) and that technology would never fail to "deliver the goods" (Marcuse), but they were resigned to the fact that technology was part of man's inevitable progression into the future (Bell). However, as Stanley Aronowitz and William DiFazio write in *The Jobless Future,* none of the Western Marxists, who came primarily from bourgeois families, ever looked at technology's influences on the third world. Rather, Bridle says, they began to treat technology as if it were a powerful god-figure that no human could ever wish to affect. Aronowitz and DiFrazio call this image of technology as being all powerful and invincible "the postmodern equivalent of deus ex machina" and "the universal problem solver." Western leftists tend to fear the consequences of overreliance on technology to solve all of the world's problems. They do not doubt that technology could solve these problems because they see technology as a powerful, albeit terrible, god.

The hyperlinked, technologically seamless world that characterizes the West's dreams of the future is only seamless because the problems and risks associated with developing technology have been exported to the third world. To the West, technology acts as a problem solver. We use technology to order food when we are hungry, to conduct our research, to archive our memories, and to build community when we feel alienated. We encourage those who have been historically disadvantaged to build online businesses and rely on technology to level the playing ground of capitalism.

The last time I went back to Henan, China, I found out that Apple had built several factories in my hometown. Everywhere in the city there were calls posted for workers to join the factories. At my *da yi*'s house, which is a little outside the city center but in a region that was quickly becoming urbanized, we began to see numerous small, white particles in the water. Without knowing what these particles were and whether boiling the water would help the situation, my *da yi* began the practice of setting jugs of water out to sit so that the mysterious particles could fall to the bottom before she poured water off from the top to use for cooking, drinking, and washing dishes. However, because we don't know what these particles are, it is also impossible to know whether separating the bigger and more visible pieces out of the water actually removes toxins effectively.

It is not just that technology displaces problems from one region of the world to another and that, sometimes, we are able to witness these displacements of problems within one family; it's also that in the third world, technology is not a problem solver but a presence of capital that often creates problems. Only when we are able to move to a certain side of a power relation does technology begin to solve problems. On the other side of that power relation, technology is not monstrously efficient but is actually *an imperfect thing that often malfunctions.* It does not produce people but is produced by people. Technology is not an overwhelmingly powerful god. Rather, like capitalism, it often fucks up.

The Imaginable World

In her book *Are Prisons Obsolete?* Angela Davis talks about how too few of the slavery abolitionists tried to imagine and describe a world without slavery, just as prison abolitionists often do not do the work of imagining a world without prisons. This leads abolitionists to reform, which reinforces the history of the prison. She quotes Foucault, who finds that histories of reform or improvement, histories of prisons, and histories of commodities developed together. Mark Fisher defines the term "capitalist realism" as the "exhaustion" and "cultural and political sterility" that results from there being no political alternatives to capitalism: "It is easier to imagine the end of the world than the end of capitalism." It is even easier to imagine a constant and endless rebellion against capitalism than a world without it. This is why "'alternative' or 'independent' cultural zones . . . endlessly repeat older gestures of rebellion and contestation as if for the first time."

Prisons have not been around for that long. The prison-industrial complex has not been around for that long. The neoliberalism that our paychecks and rent payments and lives seem to depend on haven't been around for that long. Race is not an ancient, primordial drive but a modern invention. Race was invented relatively recently, and racism is not something that should be relegated to the dustbins of history but something that is happening in current time. White patriarchal capitalism is not something that is an intrinsic part of human nature but something that was invented, implemented, and maintained.

In my book *Astrology and Storytelling,* I talk about how the three basic dichotomies within Western astrology point to three different dichotomies in terms of narrative building in the West. The luminaries opposing Saturn is about the hero's journey, the opposition between Venus and Mars is about the love story, and the dichotomy between Mercury and Jupiter is the gap between the real and the fictional. Mercury's and Jupiter's boundaries lie between what is often imagined to be real and what can be imagined as real. Capitalist realism is a pessimism that sees only the flows of capital as real. Capitalist realism is both a symptom and a cause of capitalism. It is a gaslighting. Gaslighting works like a virus. Those who have been gaslit continue to gaslight themselves and others.

Capitalism likes to make itself look very seamless. Algorithms are *branded* as artificial intelligence in the same way that fascists *brand* themselves as machines of efficiency. However, fascists were not really efficient. Their economies have historically been poorly planned and unsustainable. Algorithms are not actually intelligent. AI is a marketing keyword with sci-fi cultural cache that some developers use to brand their skill sets. AI is just a set of algorithms that someone wrote. When we believe that artificial intelligence exists and that fascists are efficient, we are erasing the labor that creates the digital world and the fascist state. The ones who labor to create these worlds know that technologies are not seamless or gods but are manufactured and inherently flawed.

Technology and labor are hard to define. There are cultural technologies, industrial technologies, and digital technologies. There is emotional labor, mental labor, and hard labor. Both technology and labor seem to produce each other. Technology extracts labor, while labor builds technology. Technology and labor are both really just power relations. They are power relations that divide and align geographies and bodies to one another and to the future. Mercury and Jupiter work to make these boundaries and alignments. Mercury likes to make boundaries between the human and the inhuman, while Jupiter likes to orchestrate struggles between the human and the inhuman. The lines drawn by Mercury and Jupiter work horizontally, vertically, and temporally.

The thing I've avoided in my discussion of Mercury so far is language. Colloquially, Mercury is strongly associated with language. I avoided language in the etymology I provided of Mercury because I wanted to avoid a meta-reframing of capitalism. I wanted to avoid writing about simulations, metafiction, and hyperreality. Instead, I wanted to ground language to the power relations that it becomes comprehensible through. Language that works within capitalism is language that extracts labor and builds technology. Languages demarcate certain boundaries between the known and the unknown. Certain languages are deemed to be more understandable than others. Languages are also not always words. Sometimes they are actions or emotions. By writing about Mercury as labor instead of language, I begin at Hermes's treatment of the turtle and hope to expand what can be articulated by Mercury working. Mercury may be about sitting, reading, and writing but it is also about doing, loving, and caring.

When doing work with yourself or a client around Mercury and Jupiter, it is important to register the dynamics of power that the supposed horizontal boundaries between languages and geographies seek to conceal. It is important to reveal the boundaries between vertical dynamics of power.

When doing work with yourself or a client around Mercury, it can be useful to ask the following questions: What does your labor go toward? From whom do you extract labor? Who does your labor imitate, and whose reality does it make real? Who does your labor extract from, and whose reality does it make unreal?

When doing work with yourself or a client around Jupiter, it can be useful to ask the following questions: Who is made real by your knowledge? Who is made unreal by your knowledge? What knowledge do you simplify and thus institutionalize? What knowledge do you make more complex and thus destabilize? Whose world do you live in, and where are the boundaries of that world? What is pushed out and genocided to make place for your world? To where do you export the storms that arise from your progress?

Neither Mercury or Jupiter work by themselves. They both derive power from the Sun, which is the capital that controls death. Mercury follows the Sun around, and Jupiter is the daytime benefic. Capital orchestrates power by distributing death. The extraction of labor and the building of technology is animated by the control of death. Thus, both Mercury and Jupiter have to do with the Sun. Not everyone will experience labor and capital the same way. Some people will experience it in the alienation of feeling fragile in an unforgiving workplace, others will find it when ex-lovers shut them out, and still others will find it in the impossibility of making friends. All of these issues benefit from being contextualized into the larger flows of labor and social capital.

Mars is the out-of-sect malefic to Jupiter. Mars is the unassimilable outsider that acts as a symbolic threat to the human. Mars is sometimes friendly with Mercury and sometimes not. Mars is integrated into society through the prison. The prison is where labor is extracted. Angela Davis finds that the invention of the prison coincided with the invention of the commodity. As prisons multiply and the number of those incarcerated grows, the number of commodities also grows. Corporations that rent labor power from prisons do not need to worry about unions or living wages. While Marx thought that money alienated consumers from the origins of their commodities since it prevents you from knowing where that commodity came from, Davis finds that many of these commodities are produced in prisons. It isn't just that money alienates—racism and prisons also alienate.

Saturn is the in-sect malefic to Jupiter. Institutions of knowledge that invent the human often refer to ancestry and genealogy. Institutions gain power when they present themselves as tradition. Venus is the out-of-sect benefic to Jupiter. Venus is the femininity that is symbolically protected by patriarchy. Jupiter has often framed femininity as a rival that must be killed before it can be controlled. Jupiter is about foreignness because Jupiter exalts in the Moon's domain. Foreignness does not live "out there" but at the border. The Moon rules borders. Jupiter is a world-building agent that expands and glorifies the Moon's foreignness. The boundary between the foreign and the human loses its specificity and encompasses the globe. Jupiter accelerates the Moon's subjects.

No astrological body functions on its own. Every planet derives meaning in relation to other planets. When we talk about Jupiter and institutions, we are also talking about the six other planets that symbolize capital, the market, exodus, power, war, and extraction.

Astrology is traditionally ruled by Mercury. This means astrology is a language or technology created by labor. Astrology is care work. The meanings of the planets that arise within astrology are not spontaneous but are created by astrologers. As a technology, astrology is also a power relation. Cosmology is the making of orientations. These orientations are mapped onto the world and the sky. Western astrology has been created by certain power relations between East, West, North, and South. Eastern symbols are often hypervisible and appropriated within Western astrology. Southern labor is exploited and made invisible.

Astrology is not a technology of representation. It is a storytelling tool. The difference between representation and storytelling is imagination.

Representation is about inclusion. It is the advocacy for othered identities to join the apparatus of power. Representation tells the same stories over and over again. It is the single story repeated and heightened until the single story is the only story. Representation seeks to remake non-Western people into bourgeois subjects. It does not destabilize our understanding of the human but tries to equalize the accessibility of the human. Representation flattens experience and removes the edges of the stories that it tells. It removes, erases, and marginalizes the stories that it doesn't tell.

Storytelling is not about inclusion but about survival. Storytelling is a multiplicity—a cacophony, to borrow Jodi Byrd's word—of stories that intersect, contradict, and overlap. New stories emerge from the intersections of this cacophony of stories. Storytelling does not seek to rescue the other with the human but destabilizes the human through encounters with nonhuman kin. Storytelling is an erotic activity—not a literary one. Stories always leave something to the imagination. Storytelling comes alive when we remix and fictionalize our experiences and fantasies. Stories contain cathybrids, monsters, and the undead. Representation is the politics of what stories you want told to you. Storytelling is about taking things into your own hands.

The point of *Postcolonial Astrology* is not to make a case for the inclusion of non-Western identities or cultures in Western astrology. That would be a pointless exercise. Contextualizing Western astrology within the history of the West is not about *improving* upon Western astrology so that the current power hierarchies can remain intact. Astrology is not about representation. It's not a language that can tell you any story that you have not already told to yourself. Astrology is about storytelling. The struggle for astrology is a struggle for the imagination. What does technology separated from capitalist realism look like? What does labor separated from capitalist realism look like? What about power and capital? And what about you? What would you look like if you were able to do the naïve act of imagining yourself in a world without capitalism?

Conclusion

ASTROLOGY IS TIME MAGIC. All astrologies are tools that deal with change. Chinese divination comes from the *Book of Changes,* which maps change to synchronicity. The West calls change evolution. The word "evolution" has often been defined in terms of hierarchy. Eugenicists see Darwin's survival of the fittest in terms of population control and social design. Social Darwinism is the liberal application of evolutionary theory. It sees some people as inferior. Social Darwinism designs the elevation of those born into superiority and calls this progress. While eugenics is often associated with overt forms of murder—concentration camps and genocide—it has operated for far longer and more often in covert forms: prisons, sterilization, denial of resources.

I'm not a fan of evolutionary astrology. Evolutionary astrology sees certain expressions of signs or planets as less or more evolved. Expressions of astrological placements that operate on so-called "higher levels" are seen to be superior to expressions operating at so-called "lower levels."

To understand the word "evolution," it is important to contextualize Darwin. Darwin was a Whig, which was the ruling party of England during his time. As a Whig, Darwin came from a cultural environment that aimed to protect its privilege. Whigs were often liberals who wanted to free the market from regulations that prevented its expansion. Whigs linked Darwin's survival of the fittest to the deregulation of the market, and they used evolution to frame their oppression of the working class. When evolution is thought of as hierarchical, it always supports neoliberalism. Because of its history, the word "evolution" always implies hierarchy. It is a word that originated with Darwin in the white institution.

Astrology does change because people change. Evolution is really just change. It's not progress and it's not social decay. It's just change. Change doesn't care about our values. It just happens. There's no such thing as a higher level or lower level because there's no such thing as good or bad change.

Octavia Butler wrote about shaping change:

> *All that you touch*
> *You Change.*
> *All that you Change*
> *Changes you.*
> *The only lasting truth*
> *Is Change.*
> *God*
> *Is Change.*

In Chinese divination, broken lines are used to signify material, and unbroken lines are used to signify spirit. In the *I Ching*'s cosmology, broken lines sink to the bottom naturally, while unbroken lines rise to the top. The best hexagram is 11 or T'ai, and the worst is 12 or P'i. Hexagram 11 shows three broken lines on top and three unbroken lines on the bottom. Hexagram 12 shows three broken lines on the bottom and three unbroken lines on top. Hexagram 11 is considered lucky because it shows yin and yang in their most unnatural dynamic—with yin on top and yang on the bottom. Hexagram 12 shows yin and yang in their most natural position, with yin on the bottom and yang on top. These hexagrams are not just ideograms but images of motion and change. Hexagram 11 is lucky because by putting yin on top of yang, it shows a situation that is about to change. Hexagram 12, on the other hand, with yin below yang, shows stasis. Stasis is impossible to hold on to and is unlucky. Change is the only constant and is lucky.

Astrology is time magic because it frames and reframes temporality. We use astrology to talk about emotions because, as Sara Ahmed put it, "Emotions tell us a lot about time; emotions are the very 'flesh' of time." Ahmed elaborates on this statement when she writes that emotions are often framed as being behind or under the present, as a recurrence of something that once happened but no longer does. She writes that "evolutionary thinking has been crucial to how emotions are understood: emotions get narrated as a sign of 'our' prehistory, and as a sign of how the primitive persists in the present," and she quotes Darwin: "With mankind some expressions, such as the bristling of the hair under the influence of extreme terror, or the uncovering of the teeth under that of furious rage, can hardly be understood, except on the belief that man once existed in a much lower and animal-like condition." Ahmed writes that "the Darwinian model of emotions suggests that emotions are not only 'beneath' but 'behind' the man/human, as a sign of an earlier and more primitive time." Emotions are associated with a past that the aesthetics of the future pull us away from. Emotions are thought to emerge from the primitive, the primal, and the primordial.

Antiracism and feminism are not about social progress. They are not about evolution. They are about change.

Astrology changes because the histories of emotions change. The ways we see the present changes not only how we anticipate the future but also how we imagine the past. History is a power struggle. This power struggle decides whose memories are allowed to be remembered. Just as memories are not static but are added to and revised after the first remembering, histories are also dynamic and are revised after the first recording. Often the first recordings of an event are written after the second recording. Origin myths are often decided in post, after the narrative is already framed. The origins of emotions are also decided after the emotion is felt. These emotions are not only whimsical and personal but also ancestral and intergenerational. It takes seven generations to heal trauma. When change is our only constant, healing is an alignment.

It's often said that Western astrology, which is the system that uses Greek names for the signs and Roman names for the planets, is not really Western. Origin stories for astrology locate its beginnings in Mesopotamia, Ethiopia, India, and Persia. Among contemporary astrologers, there are also traditional and modern astrologers. For those who follow the traditional school, the essential dignity scheme from the *thema mundi* is prioritized. Those in the modern school use modern planets—that is, objects either too small or too far away to be seen by the naked eye, and therefore unavailable for astrologers who lived before the telescope's invention. Those who work in the traditional school see the modern planets as too new and experimental. They believe that astrology accumulates meaning over time and that newer planets have not been around long enough to stand for anything essential. Those who work in the modern school see traditions as too limiting. The essential dignity scheme is also a scheme that describes citizenship and gender. Traditions around citizenship and gender have historically been violent.

Both tradition and modernity have been instrumental in shaping the West. The West is an anachronistic entity. The West invented itself as traditional and progressive. Western institutions are neo-classical institutions. They like to blend archaic aesthetics with modern ones. The West sees itself as a multicultural entity, or as an entity that seeks to control what multiculturalism means. This multiculturalism has often been weaponized against the Indigenous nations of settler colonial states. Non-Western cultures are often anachronistically fetishized as the archaic ancestors of the West. Alan Leo, for example, collages his book *Esoteric Astrology* with a variety of textures. He begins the volumes by writing:

It was not until I had made a second visit to India that I was able to obtain the clue to the central idea that could unify all of my numerous thoughts upon the subject of Esoteric Astrology. . . . In ancient civilizations the relics of which remain to-day in India, the Chieftain of the race, the MANU, or Divine King, arranged groups of men into what is known as Caste or as we would say in the West into grades of society. . . . A Hindu can explain this confusion much more adequately than a Western Astrologer. . . . It is the hope of the genuine Hindu astrologer that his Western brother will restore the ancient knowledge of the zodiac and its divisions by means of a more accurate and precise method of calculation.

By citing India, then a British colony, as his source, Leo draws upon Orientalist imagery that assumes that Asian cultures are older and mystical. However, Leo also draws upon other aesthetics, both modern and classical. He compares the influence of "heavenly bodies" to "wireless telepathy" and the "blending" of planetary influences to "chemical compounds." Leo's text can be thought of as a collage piece that fully encompasses Orientalist motifs, neoclassical terminology, and rational scientism. This collage piece is one of the fundamental texts of Western astrology.

Western astrology must be contextualized within the history and invention of the West in order to be understood. This history is not linear but anachronistic. It is more useful to think about Western history as an archive or a collage rather than a timeline since, so often, events are often added to it and claimed by the West retrospectively. The archive of the West is not racially singular but multicultural. It relied upon the invention of and control over images of people and places outside of the West to make itself up. It has relied upon the invention of and control over the past and future to make itself up. The West makes itself up. This making up of the West works through its origin myths, the memories of those who witness, and its historical recountings. These origin myths, memories, and recountings are never archived or preserved perfectly but are added to, rethought, and replaced after the fact. Histories are always anachronistic.

The West into which Western astrology must be contextualized is a present. It does not matter whether the techniques and symbols within what we now experience as Western astrology come from Persia or Egypt or India or Africa or Iraq. What we experience as Western astrology, with its horoscope columns and white self-styled gurus and pseudoscientific aura, has power and popularity because of the institutions of the West. Horoscope columns rely on the hegemony of the Western publishing industry. White wellness culture relies on food industries that send diverse forms of life matter to the capitals while distributing death elsewhere. Pseudoscience is attractive only in cultural contexts where the legitimacy of scientific institutions supersedes all other legitimacies. While the West imagines itself to be multicultural or syncretistic, it is actually hegemonic. It is a hegemony that controls and distributes positive images of multiculturalism while enacting genocides.

When we contextualize Western astrology within the West, we should not rob anyone of their cultural history. It is true that what we know now to be Western astrology encompasses techniques and symbols that originate in histories that precede the invention of the West. It is true that Lucian attributed astrology to Ethiopia, writing that "the Ethiopians were the first who invented the science of stars, and gave names to the planets, not at random and without meaning, but descriptive of the qualities which they conceived them to possess; and it was from them that this art passed, still in an imperfect state, to the Egyptians." It is true that Volney describes the origin place of astrology in North Africa: "It was, then, on the borders of the upper Nile, among a black race of men, that was organized the complicated system of the worship of the stars, considered in relation to the productions of the earth and the labors of agriculture." It is important to understand that the signs which we call by Greek and Roman names today were not invented by white people, despite the white claims to Rome. It is also important to recognize that Western astrology, because it lives within Western institutions that have power, whether that be publishing or wellness culture, is, like the mythological figures of Plato or Valens, something that became Western *retrospectively*. Western astrology, Plato, and Valens are all things that preceded the invention of the West but become Western in the present.

For example, the opposition between body and spirit is fundamental to Western astrology. Not only does this opposition describe the opposing sects; the concept of the dichotomy also describes the positions of the signs. Dichotomies animate the zodiac wheel. Planets that are in rulership in one sign are in exile in its opposite sign. Dichotomies in Western academic thought are frequently attributed to Hegel. However, the idea of the dichotomy has lived in Western thought long before Hegel and can be traced back to Plato. What becomes harder to trace are the places from which Plato drew. This dichotomy between body and spirit—between concrete reality and abstract thought—is the origin of magic and art. When we credit Plato with the invention of the dichotomy, we are also erasing the origin lines of magic and art. When Fanon extended Hegel's dichotomy between the master and slave to discuss race and the power dynamics within binaries, Fanon did not just incorporate an understanding of race into a Western concept but took something back for himself that the West had stolen. The dichotomy is a magical technology that does not originate in the white world. Fanon used this dichotomy, as a magical technology, to create new theories. By doing so, he was, in some sense, reclaiming Rome.

Throughout the course of his life, Freud recorded four dreams that he dreamed about Rome. He dreams of Catholic Rome as "the promised land seen from afar," of Rome as a center of pleasure through which the earth can recreate and resurrect itself, of Rome as an ancient and pagan place, and of Rome as papal castle and imperial tomb. When writing about these dreams, Freud describes three distinct Romes. The modern Rome is "hopeful and likable." The Catholic Rome, which Freud conflates with the Jewish promised land, is "disturbing" and a "lie of salvation." The third Rome, the Rome of antiquity, is Freud's favorite. He writes, when imagining the ancient Rome, that "I could have worshipped the humble and mutilated remnant of the Temple of Minerva."

In many ways, Freud's relationship to Rome mirrored the West's relationship to Rome. Through images of Rome, Europe sought to resurrect and recreate itself not only in the nineteenth and twentieth centuries but also during the Renaissance, during the revolutions of the seventeenth century, and throughout the era after the world wars that is often described as postmodernity. Like Freud, the West imagines hope in the cultural fragments and remnants of ancient Rome.

Freud's first dream, his deeply disturbing dream of Rome as the Jewish promised land, is interesting. In this dream, and in Freud's writings around the period when he had the dream, Freud describes Rome as a false Jerusalem and a place in which the Jewish minority held out against a vast majority through sheer tenacity. "To my youthful mind Hannibal and Rome symbolized the conflict between the tenacity of Jewry and the organization of the Catholic church," Freud writes in 1900. "And the increasing importance of the effects of the anti-Semitic movement upon our emotional life helped to fix the thoughts and feelings of those early days." Freud understood Rome as the place where the independence of Jewish peoples was destroyed and where Jewish peoples also, in an act of defiance, celebrated Passover in Rome. He saw his reinterpretation of Roman fantasies and myths through his own work, which deals with Oedipus and Electra and Roman complexes, as a double transgression—one that transgresses by conquering Rome as a Jew and one that transgresses by disrupting Hebraism, as Freud exchanges Jerusalem for Rome. Freud saw himself, within his dreams, as the

Roman general Hannibal, whose father made him swear in boy-hood to take vengeance upon Rome.

Rome, for Freud, represented the foundation of Western civili-zation and culture. By twisting and warping images of Rome, Freud celebrates Passover.

This book, *Postcolonial Astrology,* has often begun almost each etymology in Rome. It does not seek to resist colonialism by begin-ning in the colonies but looks for colonization in the mythic origin of whiteness: Rome. If there is antiracial work to be done, we must accept that race does not exist in the colonies but that race is some-thing which whiteness implements upon the colonies. Thus, anti-racist work can only and must be done inside of whiteness. The problem with race is whiteness.

However, whiteness does not exist in a vacuum, as white suprem-acists would prefer to believe. Whiteness is not a pure expression of the regions that we have come to call the West. Rather, it is rela-tional. It is a twisting and warping of all of the regions that the West has exploited. Whiteness is not invisible. Whiteness is precisely those images and fantasies that the West circulates about non-Westerners: whiteness is primitive, it is Orientalist decadence, it is authoritarian and despotic, it is martial law and rape culture, and it seeks to exoticize itself by reproducing images of cultural Others. The images we have come to accept about cultural Others—that we are too primitive, too authoritarian, too sexually deviant, and too power hungry—do not describe nonwhite people. They are stories, and stories only describe their authors. These stories are imag-ined by white people. Thus, stories that perpetuate racial fantasies describe whiteness.

As Walter Mignolo writes in the foreword of Hamid Dabashi's book *Can Non-Europeans Think?,* "Similarly, Western intellectu-als are convinced that their minds and cultures are open, self-critical—in contrast to ossified Asian minds and cultures—have no 'sacred cows.' The most shocking discovery of my adult life was the realization that 'sacred cows' also exist in the Western mind." The "sacred cows" within the Western imagination that Mignolo writes about are the archaic, primitive, and despotic images that Western-ers imagine when they imagine people of color. The Western imagi-nation is ossified precisely because it reproduces ossification within how it conceives of and perceives its images of people of color. Race is a social construct that originates in the West. Thus, racial images describe white people.

Astrology is a story that connects modernity to Rome—a story about whiteness. When has there ever been a whiteness that is not built by, supported by, and reproduced by people of color?

Suketu Mehta writes:

> These days, a great many people in the rich countries complain loudly about migration from the poor ones. But as the migrants see it, the game was rigged: First, the rich countries colonized us and stole our treasure and prevented us from building our industries. After plundering us for centuries, they left, having drawn up maps in ways that ensured perma-nent strife between our communities. Then they brought us to their coun-tries as "guest workers"—as if they knew what the word "guest" meant in our cultures—but discouraged us from bringing our families.
>
> Having built up their economies with our raw materials and our labor, they asked us to go back and were surprised when we did not. They stole our minerals and corrupted our governments so that their cor-porations could continue stealing our resources; they fouled the air above us and the waters around us, making our farms barren, our oceans life-less; and they were aghast when the poorest among us arrived at their borders, not to steal but to work, to clean their shit, and to fuck their men.

Western astrology, like most Western symbols, is not truly West-ern in material but only Western in affect. In *The Intimacies of Four Continents*, Lisa Lowe discovers the material history of the English tea ceremony: "The colonial relations on which the 'English' ritual depended [on], sugar from the West Indies, tea and china services imported from China, tables made of hardwoods from the West Indies, splendid dresses made of Indian cottons—these are subordinated as drinking tea becomes the quintessentially 'English' custom." The materials extracted from the colonies are subordinated as they are consumed by the English tea ceremony. Like the English custom of drinking afternoon tea, Western astrology is also full of symbols and materials that are subordinated when they are consumed and reproduced in the making of those symbols.

Modernity is often conflated with the West, and countries that modernize are also countries that Westernize. However, neither modernity nor the West are things that are inflicted upon people of color from the outside or from the top. Rather, both modernity and the West are things that people of color are forced to *build*. Technology that is often owned by whiteness is designed and built by people of color. Circuit boards are *owned* by IBM, Apple, and Microsoft but were originally designed by Dine women who had weaving experience. New York City operates as the financial center of the white world, but its buildings were made by Africans with carpentry expertise gained in Africa and on stolen Leni-Lenape land.

The cast of characters that play out the dramas within astrology—the Sun, the Moon, Saturn, Venus, Mars, Mercury, and Jupiter—begin with Rome when we perpetuate the myth that the West originates and ends in Rome and when we assume that Rome resurrects the West. This is not true. The West is resurrected when it consumes and reproduces, when it cannibalizes, people of color. Within the images of the Sun, the Moon, Saturn, Venus, Mars, Mercury, and Jupiter are also images of people of color. These images are reproduced and used by whiteness as it tries to establish itself through myth and metaphor. We live in Saturn's associations of noble savagery; Venus's erotic complexes; Mars's threats, perils, and imagined enemies; Mercury's cults of the subaltern; and within Jupiter's power struggles between the technological and natural worlds. Within the Sun's spectacular societies, we are robbed so abundance can exist elsewhere. Within the Moon's stories about foreigners and money so fertile that all it has to do to beget itself is sit in a bank, our bodies produce and reproduce value over and over again so capital can continue to exist.

Every story about Jupiter's technology conquering the natural world, about Jupiter and abundance, about Jupiter and luck is also a story about Western theft and the environmental pollution that primarily targets the third world. Every story about Mercury's occult tendencies is also a story about non-Western magic swallowed by modern science. Every story about Mars and warriors is also a story about the martial state built to appropriate public resources and anticipate terrorism from every brown body. Every story about Venus and sexual desire is also a story about the illusions of civilization and sexual fetishism.

Astrology has meaning because it gathers meaning historically. It does not only have meaning for white, bourgeois people who might put on costumes that signal transgression or whoredom or magic or primitivism when they play among themselves, when they need a bit of invincibility, or when they want to feel something deviant. Astrology's archetypes are not apolitical. They are not blank slates that assume neutrality through whiteness. The martial power, the sexual power, the magical power, and the technological power that live within images circulated by astrology have gathered meaning through histories of colonization. Talking about capital without considering colonization as foundational to capitalism would be like talking about sexual desire without addressing rape culture. It would be a game of pretend, whimsical fantasy, and empty significance. It would be a game that speaks to and helps no one.

For astrology to be a healing practice, it cannot be empty of significance. It must talk about sexual desire by addressing rape culture and explore capital means in the context of colonization. It must consider Jupiter's progress and technology while understanding that pollution wrecks the poor countries so rich countries can continue to be rich. It has to understand that Venus's and Mars's sexual power was extracted from the bodies of people of color through a rape culture that consisted mostly of white men raping brown and Black people but that framed things to make it seem as if the problem was that brown and Black men posed a sexual threat to white women. For astrology to be healing, it can't frame lightness as some abstract form of life but understand that lightness has a racial context and that the capitals associated with radiating light are also distributors of death. For astrology to be healing, it must address capital, power, and labor.

Western astrology is not a universal truth. It is not something from which you will gain an understanding of your authentic self. It is a cosmology that has accumulated meaning through the histories of the West. Western astrology is a language that can be used to discuss the issues of the West and how these issues affect your life. It is a language that can only be used to discuss how the issues of the West affect your life. Using astrology to resist colonialism is not the work of improving upon Western astrology so that those who have been historically excluded and exploited by the West can be integrated into its cosmology. When those who have been defined as foreign are absorbed into white institutions, white institutions expand and continue to commit genocide and erase. Stealing astrology back is about making the white institution smaller and more specific so there is more room around it for Indigenous and migrant cosmologies to live. For decolonization to happen, the West and its cosmological claims to land must shrink.

Western astrology is a set of symbols that refer to things built on stolen land by people forced to do it. It's a pile of stuff. We look at this stuff and ask ourselves, "What do we want to do with it?"

When practicing astrology, don't let technical stuff intimidate you. Treasure your own experiences and your own capacities as a spin artist. There's nothing wrong with Sun sign astrology as long as you unpack the Sun as a symbol of capital, centers, and sovereignty.

Bad astrology reproduces capital, power, and labor even when it is technically precise. You can track every midpoint, declination, or zodiacal release period and still do bad astrology when you do not challenge the conditions of capital, power, and labor that capitalist racial patriarchy accepts to be true, real, or inevitable. Good astrologers are storytellers. Good astrology acknowledges and resists capital, power, and labor. Good astrology shrinks the West. There is no one way to practice good astrology.

The West is a story. It is a dream within a dream—an anachronistic archive. Our job as astrologers is not to tell the story of the West better or to tell more stories using the West's vocabulary but to acknowledge that the story of the West was built by real histories of pain. The West may be a story, but your trauma is real.

Shrink the West in your healing practice. Use Western astrology to only acknowledge the influence of the West and to talk about capital, power, and labor. Don't use it for your stuff. Make some room for your stuff. Make up your own stuff. Don't rely on Western astrology to heal you. Heal yourself despite of and in resistance to the West. Understand that, when you heal, the healing comes from your survival and not from astrology. Western astrology is like race—it is an archetypal and magical imagination that classifies and limits. Any counseling session that does not acknowledge race, patriarchy, and capitalism will not be a counseling session that heals. Use Jupiter to talk about your institutional complicity and resistance. Use Saturn to talk about the settler state.

Don't use Western astrology to talk about your own stuff. Don't use it to try to talk to your ancestors. It's not made for that and you don't need anything Western to do that.

There's an old adage in astrology. The first part of the adage is often quoted to talk about how the stars influence our behaviors: "As above, so below." However, this isn't the complete adage. The second part of the adage tells us: "As below, so above." The meaning of the sky comes directly from us. You are the thing that animates heaven.

Works Cited

Agamben, Giorgio. *State of Exception*. Chicago: University of Chicago Press, 2003.

Ahmed, Sara. "A Phenomenology of Whiteness." *Feminist Theory* 8, no. 2 (2007): 149–68. doi:10.1177/1464700107078139.

———. *The Cultural Politics of Emotion*. Edinburgh, Scotland: Edinburgh University Press Ltd, 2014.

———. *Living a Feminist Life*. Durham, NC: Duke University Press, 2017.

Ahuja, Neel. *Bioinsecurities: Disease Interventions, Empire, and the Government of Species*. Durham, NC: Duke University Press, 2016.

Allen, Theodore, and Jeffrey Babcock Perry. *The Invention of the White Race*. New York: Verso, 2012.

Alves, Maria Thereza. "Cannibalism in Brazil since 1500." November 7, 2013, www.mariatherezaalves.org/assets/files/2013alvesengcannibalism-in-brazil-since-1500-kopie.pdf.

Anderson, Benedict R. *Imagined Communities: Reflections on the Origin and Spread of Nationalism*. New York: Verso, 2016.

Arendt, Hannah. *Between Past and Future: Eight Exercises in Political Thought*. New York: Penguin Books, 2006.

Arroyo, Stephen. *Exploring Jupiter: The Astrological Key to Progress, Prosperity & Potential*. Petaluma, CA: CRCS Publications, 1996.

Assandri, Frederike. *Supermarket of the Dead: Burnt Offerings in China and the Cult of Globalised Consumption*. Edited by Wolfgang Scheppe. Köln, Germany: Verlag Der Buchhandlung Walther König, 2015.

Atanasoski, Neda, and Kalindi Vora. *Surrogate Humanity: Race, Robots, and the Politics of Technological Futures*. Durham, NC: Duke University Press, 2019.

Aveni, Anthony F. *Conversing with the Planets: How Science and Myth Invented the Cosmos*. Boulder: University Press of Colorado, 2003.

Bamberger, Joan. "The Myth of Matriarchy: Why Men Rule in Primitive Society." In *Woman, Culture, and Society,* edited by Michelle Zimbalist Rosaldo and Louise Lamphere, 263–80. Stanford, CA: Stanford University Press, 1974.

Beik, William, and John J. Hurt. "The Absolutism of Louis XIV as Social Collaboration." *Past & Present* 188 (2005): 195–224.

Benjamin, Walter. *Illuminations: Essays and Reflections.* Edited by Hannah Arendt. Translated by Henry Zohn. Boston: Mariner Books, 2019.

———. *Walter Benjamin: Selected Writings.* Edited by Michael W. Jennings, Howard Eiland, and Gary Smith. Cambridge, MA: Harvard University Press, 2005.

Bhabha, Homi K. *The Location of Culture.* New York: Routledge, 2004.

———. "Of Mimicry and Man: The Ambivalence of Colonial Discourse." October 28 (1984): 125–33.

Billig, Michael. *Banal Nationalism.* London, UK: Sage, 2018.

Bishop, Kyle William. "The Idle Proletariat: Dawn of the Dead, Consumer Ideology, and the Loss of Productive Labor." *Journal of Popular Culture* 43, no. 2 (2010): 234–48.

Blackburn, Mary Walling. "From the Gnome's Genome to Trash DNA: Technologies of Ancestor Phantasy for a Final Generation." *e-flux* no. 106 (February 2020). www.e-flux.com/journal/106/314856/from-the-gnome-s -genome-to-trash-dna-technologies-of-ancestor-phantasy-for-a-final -generation/.

Borisonik, Hernán. *$Oporte: El uso del dinero como material en las artes visuales. $Upport: Money as Material in Visual Arts.* Buenos Aires, Argentina: Miño y Dávila Editores, 2017.

Bramble, John C. *Modernism and the Occult.* London, UK: Palgrave Macmillan, 2015.

Brennan, Chris. *Hellenistic Astrology: The Study of Fate and Fortune.* Denver, CO: Amor Fati Publications, 2017.

Brewer, John. *The Pleasures of the Imagination: English Culture in the Eighteenth Century.* New York: Routledge, 1997.

Bridle, James. *New Dark Age: Technology and the End of the Future.* New York: Verso, 2019.

Byrd, Jodi A. *The Transit of Empire: Indigenous Critiques of Colonialism.* Minneapolis: University of Minnesota Press, 2011.

Campion, Nicholas, Patrick Curry, and Michael York, eds. *Astrology and the Academy: Papers from the Inaugural Conference of the Sophia Centre, at Bath*

Spa University College Held on 13–14 June 2003. Bristol, UK: Cinnabar Books, 2004.

Chakrabarty, Dipesh. "The Human Condition in the Anthropocene." Lecture presented for the Tanner Lectures in Human Values, Yale University, New Haven, CT, February 18, 2015. https://tannerlectures.utah.edu/Chakrabarty%20manuscript.pdf.

Chen, Kuan-Hsing. *Asia as Method: Towards De-Imperialization*. Durham, NC: Duke University Press, 2010.

Chen, Qiufan, and Ken Liu. *Waste Tide*. New York: Tor, 2020.

Cheng, Anne Anlin. *Ornamentalism*. New York: Oxford University Press, 2019.

———. *The Melancholy of Race: Psychoanalysis, Assimilation and Hidden Grief*. New York: Oxford University Press, 2001.

———. "Shine: On Race, Glamour, and the Modern." *PMLA* 126, no. 4 (2011): 1022–41.

Chomsky, Noam. *Power and Terror: Post-9/11 Talks and Interviews*. New York: Seven Stories Press, 2010.

Chow, Rey, and Paul Bowman. *The Rey Chow Reader*. New York: Columbia University Press, 2010.

Chu, Seo-Young. *Do Metaphors Dream of Literal Sleep? A Science-Fictional Theory of Representation*. Cambridge, MA: Harvard University Press, 2010.

Chun, Wendy Hui Kyong. *Control and Freedom: Power and Paranoia in the Age of Fiber Optics*. Cambridge, MA: MIT Press, 2006.

Ciavolella, Massimo, and Amilcare A. Iannucci, eds. *Saturn from Antiquity to the Renaissance*. Ottawa, Canada: Dovehouse Editions, 1992.

Coleman, Gabriella. *Hacker, Hoaxer, Whistleblower, Spy: The Many Faces of Anonymous*. New York: Verso, 2015.

Colomina, Beatriz. "Domesticity at War." *Discourse* 14, no. 1 (1991): 3–22.

Connell, Raewyn. *Masculinities*. Vancouver, Canada: Langara College, 2018.

Cook, Arthur Bernard. *Zeus: A Study in Ancient Religion*. Cambridge: Cambridge University Press, 2010.

Davis, Angela Y. *Are Prisons Obsolete?* New York: Seven Stories Press, 2010.

———. *Women, Race and Class*. New York: Random House, 1983.

Day, Brian J. "The Moral Intuition of Ruskin's 'Storm-Cloud.'" *Studies in English Literature, 1500–1900* 45, no. 4 (2005): 917–33.

Day, Iyko. *Alien Capital: Asian Racialization and the Logic of Settler Colonial Capitalism*. Durham, NC: Duke University Press, 2016.

Debord, Guy. *Society of the Spectacle*. Detroit, MI: Black & Red, 2016.

deepad. "I Didn't Dream of Dragons." Dreamwidth. 2009. https://deepad
.dreamwidth.org/29371.html.

Deloria, Philip Joseph. *Playing Indian.* New Haven, New Haven, CT: Yale
University Press, 2007.

Eco, Umberto, and Alistair McEwen. *On Beauty.* London, UK: Secker & War-
burg, 2004.

Edelstein, Dan. *The Enlightenment: A Genealogy.* Chicago: University of Chicago Press, 2010.

Edensor, Tim. "Rethinking the Relationship between Light and Dark."
Urban Studies 52, no. 3 (2015): 422–38.

Elliott, Robert C. "The Shape of Utopia." *Elh* 30, no. 4 (1963): 317–34.

Fanon, Frantz. *Black Skin, White Masks.* New York: Grove Atlantic, 2008.

Fantazzi, Charles. "Golden Age in Arcadia." *Latomus* 33, no. 2 (1974):
280–305.

Federici, Silvia. *Caliban and the Witch.* New York: Autonomedia, 2004.

Fisher, Mark. *Capitalist Realism: Is There No Alternative?* Hants, UK: Zero
Books, 2010.

Fleming, Katie. "Heidegger, Jaeger, Plato: The Politics of Humanism."
International Journal of the Classical Tradition 19, no. 2 (2012): 82–106.

Foucault, Michel. *The Birth of Biopolitics: Lectures at the Collège de France,
1978–1979.* Edited by Michel Senellart. London: Picador, 2010.

———. *Security, Territory, Population: Lectures at the Collège de France,
1977–1978.* London: Picador, 2009.

———. *"Society Must Be Defended": Lectures at the Collège de France, 1975–1976.*
London, UK: Penguin Books, 2020.

Fowles, John B. "From Arcadia to Elysium in *The Magic Flute* and Weimar
Classicism: The Plan of Salvation and Eighteenth-Century Views of
Moral Progression." *BYU Studies Quarterly* 43, no. 3 (2004): 85–103.

Freedman, Lawrence. *Strategy: A History.* New York: Oxford University
Press, 2015.

Friedman, Milton. "Franklin D. Roosevelt, Silver, and China." *Journal of
Political Economy* 100, no. 1 (1992): 62–83.

Goffman, Erving. *The Presentation of Self in Everyday Life.* New York: Anchor
Books, 1959.

Goldner, Loren. "Race and the Enlightenment." *The Charnel-House* (blog).
Previously published in *Race Traitor* no. 7 (spring 1997). https://
thecharnelhouse.org/2017/03/19/race-and-the-enlightenment/.

Goldstein, Rebecca. *Incompleteness: The Proof and Paradox of Kurt Gödel.* New
York: W. W. Norton, 2006.

Graeber, David. *Debt: The First 5,000 Years.* New York: Melville House, 2014.

———. *The Utopia of Rules on Technology, Stupidity, and the Secret Joys of Bureaucracy.* New York: Melville House, 2016.

Graves, Robert, and Grevel Lindop. *The White Goddess: A Historical Grammar of Poetic Myth.* New York: Farrar, Straus and Giroux, 2013.

Graw, Isabelle. *High Price: Art between the Market and Celebrity Culture.* Berlin: Sternberg Press, 2010.

Greene, Liz, and Howard Sasportas. *The Luminaries.* New York: Samuel Weiser, 1992.

Guttman, Arielle. *Venus Star Rising: A New Cosmology for the 21st Century.* Santa Fe: Sophia Venus Productions, 2010.

Haiven, Max. *Cultures of Financialization: Fictitious Capital in Popular Culture and Everyday Life.* London: Palgrave Macmillan, 2014.

Halter, Ed. *From Sun Tzu to Xbox: War and Video Games.* New York: PublicAffairs, 2006.

Han, Byung-Chul, and Amanda DeMarco. *Topology of Violence.* Cambridge, MA: MIT Press, 2018.

———, and Erik Butler. *Psychopolitics: Neoliberalism and New Technologies of Power.* New York: Verso, 2017.

Hand, Robert. *Horoscope Symbols.* Atglen, PA: Bushwood Books, 1981.

Haraway, Donna J., and Adele Clarke, eds. *Make Kin Not Population.* Chicago, IL: Prickly Paradigm Press, 2018.

Hejduk, Julia. "Jupiter's Aeneid: Fama and Imperium." *Classical Antiquity* 28, no. 2 (2009): 279–327.

Hodgson, Godfrey. *The Myth of American Exceptionalism.* New Haven, CT: Yale University Press, 2010.

Hover, W. "A World of Corpses: From Hiroshima and Nagasaki to AIDS." *Positions: East Asia Cultures Critique* 2, no. 1 (1994): 1–14.

Hyde, Lewis. *Trickster Makes This World: Mischief, Myth, and Art.* New York: Farrar, Straus and Giroux, 2010.

Israel, Jonathan. "Enlightenment! Which Enlightenment?" *Journal of the History of Ideas* 67, no. 3 (2006): 523–45.

Iwabuchi, Koichi. "Against Banal Inter-nationalism." *Asian Journal of Social Science* 41, no. 5 (2014): 437–52.

James, E. L. *Fifty Shades of Grey.* New York: Vintage Books, 2015.

Jones, Graham M. *Magic's Reason: An Anthropology of Analogy.* Chicago: University of Chicago Press, 2017.

Kapoor, Nisha. *Deport, Deprive, Extradite: 21st Century State Extremism.* New York: Verso, 2018.

Katznelson, Ira. *When Affirmative Action Was White: An Untold History of Racial Inequality in Twentieth-Century America.* New York: W. W. Norton, 2006.

Keen, David. *Complex Emergencies.* Cambridge, UK: Polity, 2008.

Klein, Naomi. *The Shock Doctrine: The Rise of Disaster Capitalism.* New York: Penguin, 2014.

Klibansky, Raymond. *Saturn and Melancholy Studies in the History of Natural Philosophy, Religion, and Art.* Montreal, Canada: McGill-Queen's University Press, 2019.

Lazzarato, Maurizio. *Governing by Debt.* Los Angeles, CA: Semiotext(e), 2015.

Le Guin, Ursula K. "A Non-Euclidean View of California as a Cold Place to Be." *Yale Review* 72, no. 2 (1983): 161–80.

Lears, Jackson. *Fables of Abundance: A Cultural History of Advertising in America.* New York: Basic Books, 1996.

Leo, Alan. *Esoteric Astrology: A Study in Human Nature.* Rochester, VT: Destiny Books, 1978.

Levy, Jonathan. *Freaks of Fortune: The Emerging World of Capitalism and Risk in America.* Cambridge, MA: Harvard University Press, 2014.

Lewis, James R. *The Astrology Book: The Encyclopedia of Heavenly Influences.* Canton, MI: Visible Ink Press, 2003.

Liu, Ken. *Broken Stars: Contemporary Chinese Science Fiction in Translation.* New York: Tor, 2020.

Lofton, Kathryn. *Consuming Religion.* Chicago, IL: University of Chicago Press, 2017.

Lorde, Audre. *Sister Outsider: Essays and Speeches.* Crossing Press, 2007.

Lowe, Lisa. *The Intimacies of Four Continents.* Durham, NC: Duke University Press, 2015.

Mahbubani, Kishore. *Can Asians Think?* Singapore: Marshall Cavendish Editions, 2009.

Marx, Leo. *The Machine in the Garden.* New York: Oxford University Press, 2000.

Marx, Karl. *Das Kapital.* New York: Penguin Classics, 1993.

Mazower, Mark. *Dark Continent: Europe's Twentieth Century.* New York: Vintage Books, 2000.

Mbembe, Achille, and Steve Corcoran. *Necropolitics.* Durham, NC: Duke University Press, 2019.

McCann, David. "Skyscript: Mars in Myth & Occult Philosophy." Skyscript.co.uk. Previously published in *The Traditional Astrologer* no. 16 (March 1998). www.skyscript.co.uk/marsmyth.html.

McKittrick, Katherine. "On Plantations, Prisons, and a Black Sense of Place." *Social & Cultural Geography* 12, no. 8 (2011): 947–63.

———. *Sylvia Wynter: On Being Human as Praxis*. Durham, NC: Duke University Press, 2015.

Mead, Corey. *War Play: Video Games and the Future of Armed Conflict*. New York: Eamon Dolan/Houghton Mifflin Harcourt, 2013.

Mehta, Suketu. *This Land Is Our Land: An Immigrant's Manifesto*. New York: Farrar, Straus and Giroux, 2019.

Meyer, Stephenie. *Twilight*. New York: Atom, 2015.

Morin, Jean Baptiste. *Astrologia Gallica Book Twenty-Two: Directions*. Tempe, AZ: American Federation of Astrologers, 1994.

Morton, Timothy. *Hyperobjects: Philosophy and Ecology after the End of the World*. Minneapolis, MN: University of Minnesota Press, 2014.

Neimneh, Shadi. "The Anti-Hero in Modernist Fiction: From Irony to Cultural Renewal." *Mosaic: An Interdisciplinary Critical Journal* 46, no. 4 (2013): 75–90.

Nix, Sarah A. "Caesar as Jupiter in Lucan's 'Bellum Civile.'" *The Classical Journal* 103, no. 3 (2008): 281–94.

Ortiz, Paul. *An African American and Latinx History of the United States*. Boston, MA: Beacon Press, 2018.

Otter, Chris. *The Victorian Eye: A Political History of Light and Vision in Britain, 1800–1910*. Chicago: University of Chicago Press, 2008.

Painter, Nell Irvin. *The History of White People*. New York: W. W. Norton & Company, 2011.

Pappas, Nickolas. "Nietzsche's Apollo." *Journal of Nietzsche Studies* 45, no. 1 (2014): 43–53.

Pennachio, John. "Gnostic Inner Illumination and Carl Jung's Individuation." *Journal of Religion and Health* 31, no. 3 (1992): 237–45.

Pettifor, Ann. *The Production of Money: How to Break the Power of Bankers*. New York: Verso, 2018.

Plotinus. *The Six Enneads*. Translated by Stephen McKenna and B. S. Page. Whitefish, MT: Kessinger Publishing, 2004.

Prado-Richardson, Tabitha. "Who Needs Astrology?" *Literary Hub,* March 6, 2019, https://lithub.com/who-needs-astrology/.

Prettyman, Gib. "Gilded Age Utopias of Incorporation." *Utopian Studies* 12, no. 1 (2001): 19–40.

Ptolemy and Manetho. *Tetrabiblos*. Translated by J. M. Ashmand. London, UK: Heinemann, 1948.

Rabkin, Eric S., and George S. Slusser, eds. *Aliens: The Anthropology of Science Fiction.* Carbondale: Southern Illinois University Press, 1987.

Rangasami, Amrita. "The Study of Starvation and Famine: Some Problems." In *Les Spectres Des Malthus,* edited by Francis Gendreau, Claude Meillassoux, Bernard Schlemmer, and Martin Verlet, 41–60. Paris: Editions de l'Atelier, 1991.

Razack, Sherene H. "The Camp: A Place Where Law Has Declared That the Rule of Law Does Not Operate." *Public* (fall 2007): 109–23.

Riggs, Don. "Utopia's Timing: Saturn, Jupiter and Michelangelo's 'David.'" *Journal of the Fantastic in the Arts* 14, no. 3 (2003): 342–49.

Roberts, Dorothy. *Fatal Invention: How Science, Politics, and Big Business Recreate Race in the Twenty-First Century.* New York: The New Press, 2012.

Rushoff, Douglas. "Survival of the Richest" *OneZero,* July 5, 2018, https://onezero.medium.com/survival-of-the-richest-9ef6cdddocci.

Ruskin, John. *The Storm Cloud of the Nineteenth Century.* Crows Nest, Australia: Allen, 1884.

Sakai, J. *Settlers: The Mythology of the White Proletariat from Mayflower to Modern.* Oakland, CA: PM Press, 2014.

Savage, Jon. *Teenage: The Creation of Youth Culture.* New York: Viking, 2007.

Schmidt, James. "Inventing the Enlightenment: Anti-Jacobins, British Hegelians, and the 'Oxford English Dictionary.'" *Journal of the History of Ideas* 64, no. 3 (2003): 421–43.

Schoenberger, Erica. "Why Is Gold Valuable? Nature, Social Power and the Value of Things." *Cultural Geographies* 18, no. 1 (2011): 3–24.

Schorske, Carl E. *Fin-de-Siècle Vienna: Politics and Culture.* Milan, Italy: Bompiani, 2004.

Schuller, Kyla. *The Biopolitics of Feeling: Race, Sex, and Science in the Nineteenth Century.* Durham, NC: Duke University Press, 2018.

Shlain, Leonard. *The Alphabet Versus the Goddess: The Conflict between Word and Image.* New York: Penguin/Compass, 1999.

Silber, William L. *The Story of Silver: How the White Metal Shaped America and the Modern World.* Princeton, NJ: Princeton University Press, 2020.

Simmel, Georg. *The Philosophy of Money.* Translated by Tom Bottomore and David Frisby. New York: Routledge, 2011.

Spivak, Gayatri Chakravorty. "Can the Subaltern Speak?" In *Marxism and the Interpretation of Culture,* edited by Cary Nelson and Lawrence Grossberg, 271–313. London: Macmillan, 1988.

Sylla, Richard, and David J. Cowen. "Hamilton and the U.S. Financial Revolution." *Journal of Applied Corporate Finance* 31, no. 4 (2019): 10–15.

Tarn, W. W. "Alexander Helios and the Golden Age." *The Journal of Roman Studies* 22, no. 2 (1932): 135–60.

Toufic, Jalal. *Vampires: An Uneasy Essay on the Undead in Films*. Barrytown, NY: Station Hill, 2003.

Trilling, Lionel. *The Liberal Imagination: Essays on Literature and Society*. New York: Doubleday, 1953.

Turner, Fred. *From Counterculture to Cyberculture: Stewart Brand, the Whole Earth Network, and the Rise of Digital Utopianism*. Chicago: University of Chicago Press, 2008.

Virilio, Paul, and Lotringer Sylvère. *Pure War*. Los Angeles, CA: Semiotext(e), 1983.

Vizenor, Gerald Robert. *Manifest Manners: Postindian Warriors and Survivance*. Middletown, CT: Wesleyan University Press, 1993.

Volpp, Sophie. "The Discourse on Male Marriage: Li Yu's 'A Male Mencius's Mother.'" *Positions: East Asia Cultures Critique* 2, no. 1 (1994): 113–32.

Wang, Hui. *Carceral Capitalism*. Los Angeles, CA: Semiotext(e), 2018.

Wang, Jackie. "Against Innocence: Race, Gender, and the Politics of Safety." *LIES* 1, 2012, www.liesjournal.net/volume1-10-againstinnocence.html.

Westenholz, Joan Goodnick. "Tamar, Qědēšā, Qadištu, and Sacred Prostitution in Mesopotamia." *The Harvard Theological Review* 82, no. 3 (1989): 245–65.

Woodard, Vincent. *The Delectable Negro: Human Consumption and Homoeroticism within U.S. Slave Culture*. Edited by Justin A. Joyce and Dwight A. McBride. New York: New York University Press, 2014.

Wooden, Warren W. "Utopia and Arcadia: An Approach to More's 'Utopia.'" *College Literature* 6, no. 1 (1979): 30–40.

Worden, Nigel. *The Making of Modern South Africa*. Hoboken, NJ: Blackwell, 2000.

Wulff, Wilhelm. *Zodiac and Swastika*. London, UK: Arthur Barker Limited, 1968.

Wynter, Sylvia. "Unsettling the Coloniality of Being/Power/Truth/Freedom: Towards the Human, after Man, Its Overrepresentation—An Argument." *CR: The New Centennial Review* 3, no. 3 (2003): 257–337.

Xun, Lu. *Lu Xun Selected Works*. Translated by Yang Xianyi and Gladys Yang. Beijing, China: Foreign Languages Press, 2003.

Young, Kevin. *Bunk: The Rise of Hoaxes, Humbug, Plagiarists, Phonies, Post-Facts, and Fake News.* Minneapolis, MN: Graywolf Press, 2018.

Yusoff, Kathryn. *A Billion Black Anthropocenes or None.* Minneapolis, MN: University of Minnesota Press, 2018.

Zuboff, Shoshana. *The Age of Surveillance Capitalism: The Fight for a Human Future at the New Frontier of Power.* New York: PublicAffairs, 2020.

Index

About the Author

ALICE SPARKLY KAT is a qpoc astrologer. They use astrology as a speculative language that has the capacity to heal through storytelling. Their astrological work has inhabited MoMA, Philadelphia Museum of Art, and Hauser and Wirth. Their books include *Astrology and Storytelling, Planetary Alignment for Mental Bliss,* and *Cancer: Zodiac Series.* They're available for readings in person or by phone at www.alicesparklykat.com! Follow them on Instagram or Twitter @alicesparklykat for astrology content.

About North Atlantic Books

North Atlantic Books (NAB) is a 501(c)(3) nonprofit publisher committed to a bold exploration of the relationships between mind, body, spirit, culture, and nature. Founded in 1974, NAB aims to nurture a holistic view of the arts, sciences, humanities, and healing. To make a donation or to learn more about our books, authors, events, and newsletter, please visit www.northatlanticbooks.com.